DISCOVERING QATAR

Frances Gillespie

Discovering Qatar

Published by
Medina Publishing Ltd
310 Ewell Road
Surbiton
Surrey KT6 7AL
medinapublishing.com

with the kind support of

ISBN: 978-1-909339-62-0 hardback
ISBN: 978-1-909339-61-3 paperback

Designed by Richard Wood

Printed and bound by Emirates Printing Press llc, Dubai

Pictured right: Desert Hyacinth (Cistanche phelypaea).

DISCOVERING
QATAR

Frances Gillespie

Dedication

Discovering Qatar is dedicated with affection and respect to the memory of Geoffrey Bibby (1917-2001), a pioneer of Arabian archaeology, and the ethnographer Klaus Ferdinand (1926-2005), both of whom contributed so much to the knowledge of the prehistory and cultural traditions of Qatar.

Klaus Ferdinand

Geoffrey Bibby

Five percent of the profit from sales of this book will be donated to the

Friends of the Environment Centre

to support environmental activities in Qatar.

Contents

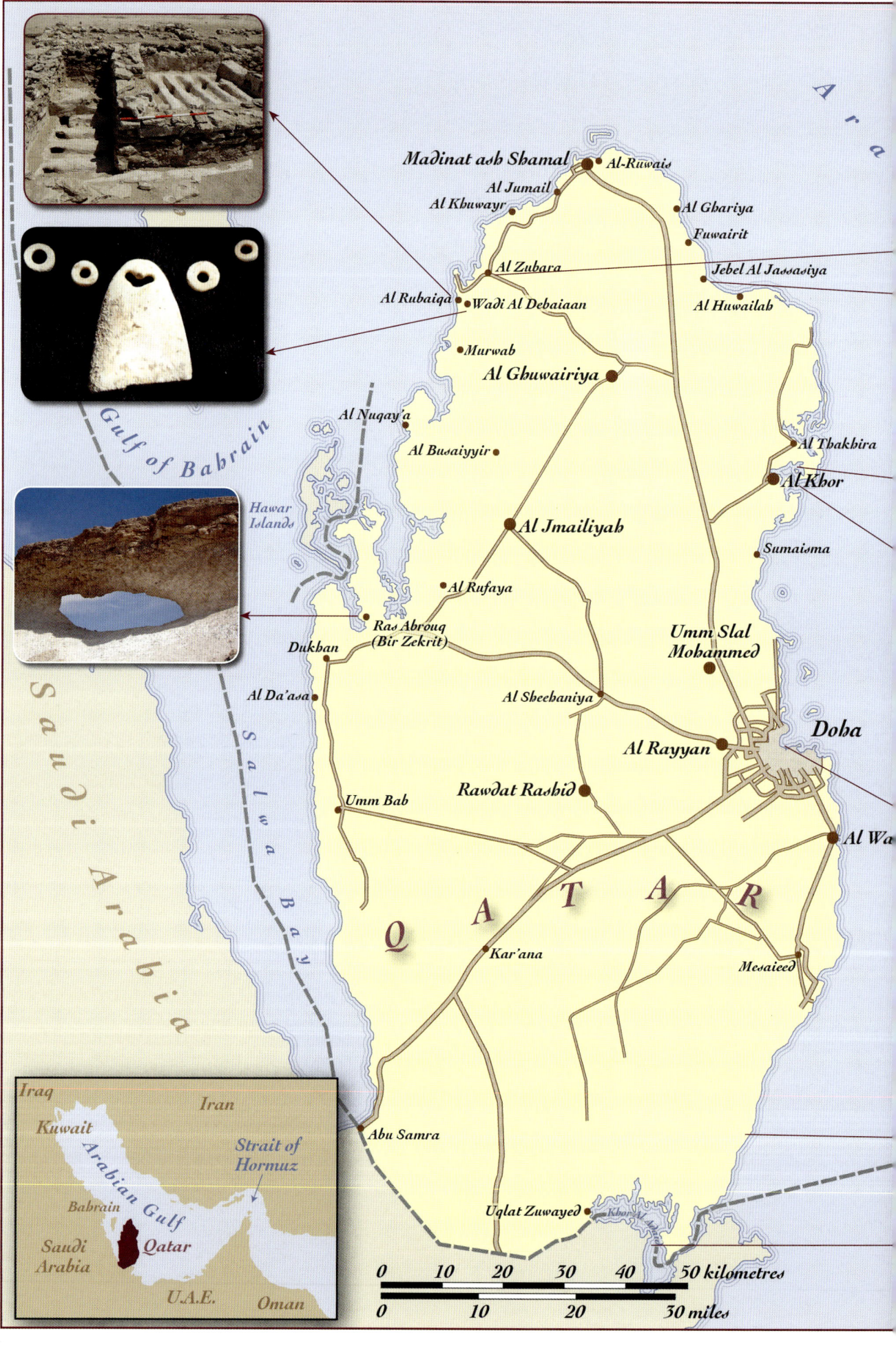

Madinat ash Shamal • Al-Ruwais

Al Jumail

Al Khuwayr

Al Ghariya

Fuwairit

Al Zubara

Jebel Al Jassasiya

Al Rubaiqa • Wadi Al Debaiaan

Al Huwailah

• Murwab

Al Ghuwairiya

Al Nuqay'a

Al Thakhira

Al Busaiyyir •

Al Khor

Al Jmailiyah

Sumaisma

• Al Rufaya

Ras Abrouq
(Bir Zekrit)

Umm Slal
Mohammed

Dukhan

Al Da'asa •

Al Sheehaniya

Al Rayyan

Doha

Umm Bab •

Rawdat Rashid

Al Wa

Q   A   T   A   R

Kar'ana

Mesaieed

Gulf of Bahrain

Hawar
Islands

Saudi Arabia

Salwa Bay

Ara

Abu Samra

Uqlat Zuwayed • Khor Al

Iraq

Iran

Kuwait

Arabian Gulf

Strait of
Hormuz

Bahrain

Saudi
Arabia

Qatar

U.A.E.   Oman

0   10   20   30   40   50 kilometres

0   10   20   30 miles

Foreword

by Dr Saif Al-Hajiri

Although two of the natural resources of Qatar – liquefied natural gas and oil – attract the spotlight of attention, the natural environment surrounding us is immensely rich and varied. However, the hectic pace of our daily lives means we seldom experience at first hand this richness of our geological heritage and the abundance and diversity of our flora and fauna. As fast as the human population increases, so too do the thousands of living organisms in our country.

This book *Discovering Qatar* (now in its third edition) by Frances Gillespie, provides an up-close look at nature in Qatar. Thanks go out to her for enriching the culture and for her interest in the wildlife in Qatar.

Over the past quarter of a century, and since its initiation in the early 1990s, Friends of the Environment Centre (FEC) has worked to increase people's understanding and appreciation of nature in Qatar through community awareness campaigns and different events. Through its numerous programmes, FEC aims to instil a love of nature in the hearts of Qatar's population from an early age. In the framework of Qatar's National Vision 2030, we continue to work to achieve a balance between economic development for the continued well-being of the present inhabitants and the concepts of sustainability, in order to protect nature now and in the future.

It is worth mentioning that this edition of the book would not be possible without the support provided by both Sasol (an international integrated energy and chemical company), and ExxonMobil Qatar (an international oil and gas company). In the context of social responsibility they are committed to support the local community on a continuous basis.

We hope that this book encourages you and guides you to explore the diversity of nature in the State of Qatar.

Dr Saif Al-Hajiri
Chairman
Friends of the Environment Centre

Introduction

In this book I have attempted to outline the prehistory and history of Qatar, give a brief introduction to its topography, and aspects of its natural fauna which have interested me over the years. My aim is to enable others to share some of these interests, and to enjoy to the full their stay in hospitable, friendly Qatar, however long or short it may be.

When I arrived in Qatar with my family in August 1985, I knew almost nothing about the desert landscape of Arabia and its inhabitants, human or otherwise. As soon as the temperature dropped enough to allow exploration, we set out on what has proved to be a 30-year expedition, and one that has still to be completed. Small though the peninsula of Qatar is, there are still far-off corners that remain to be fully explored.

We had previously lived for some years in the steaming, tropical rainforest region of West Africa, and I quickly grew to love the wide open spaces of Qatar, the way the immense sky met the far horizon, the ever-changing colours of the shadows on the great dunes of the south, the golden landscape studded with shining white limestone *mesas* along the western coast. We liked, too, exploring the little coastal villages with their friendly people, and watching the fleets of fishing *dhow*s which set off at sunset from Al Wakra, Al Khor and Al Ruwais. Doha in those days was a quiet city with comparatively little traffic, a shadow of the bustling 21st century metropolis it has now become.

Everywhere on the floor of the sandy desert I could see patterns left by myriads of small feet, like writing in a foreign language waiting to be interpreted. I knew so little about Arabian animals that the first time I saw a hedgehog I took it for a juvenile, not realising that Arabian mammals are smaller than their European cousins. Small, thin fragments of what looked a little like Chinese ceramics, but clearly were not, which we found on old settlement sites, puzzled me mightily until one day I learned that within the last century a species of ostrich unique to Arabia had roamed the plains of Qatar.

There was a lot of learning to do, and finding sources of information about all the wildlife was at first not easy. We joined the Qatar Natural History Group and there followed many years of Friday expeditions, guided by amateur ornithologists and botanists and sometimes by geologists from the oil companies, who were ever ready to share their knowledge with others.

A study of the ecology and flora of Qatar had been published by the University of Qatar in 1981, and soon after we arrived the Ministry of Information issued a useful guide, *Qatar and the Sea*, written by a marine biologist at the National Museum, which included colour photographs of fish, cetaceans and sea snakes. But it seemed that little was available on the terrestrial mammals and reptiles of Arabia for the general reader.

Then in 1987, Marijcke Jongbloed, a Dutch doctor based in the UAE, published *The Living Desert*, a fascinating month-by-month guide to the plants, insects, reptiles, birds and mammals she had encountered on her peregrinations. These had first appeared as weekly articles in the *Khaleej Times*. For years, this book accompanied us everywhere on our weekend excursions.

Dr Jongbloed was appointed Director of the state-of-the-art Sharjah Natural History Museum and I invited her to lecture to our Natural History Group. We became friends, and over the years I relied on her for information. Most encouraging of all was the fact that she, beginning as an amateur, became in time renowned as an authority on the natural history of the region.

For 20 years I contributed features to the *Gulf Times* daily newspaper on all aspects of natural history and the environment, as well as on the archaeology and history of Qatar. Following the example set by Dr Jongbloed, this book has grown out of these articles. My study of the country's archaeology was assisted by the staff of the original National Museum, who allowed me access to all excavation reports, both published and unpublished, and more recently by staff and directors from expeditions working with the Qatar Museums Authority, who have provided many of the photographs. Over the years I met most of the archaeologists who had worked in Qatar, including the pioneers Geoffrey Bibby and Beatrice de Cardi, and the great ethnographer Klaus Ferdinand, whose work on recording the traditional way of life of the bedouin will always be remembered with gratitude by the people of Qatar.

There are still comparatively few publications available for the visitor or expatriate resident who wishes to know more of this country. This is the book I would have liked to have had when I first came to Qatar. First published in 2006, reprinted in 2008 and again in 2014, it is now issued in a completely revised and updated edition, with many new photographs and six new chapters.

Frances Gillespie
2015

The History of Qatar

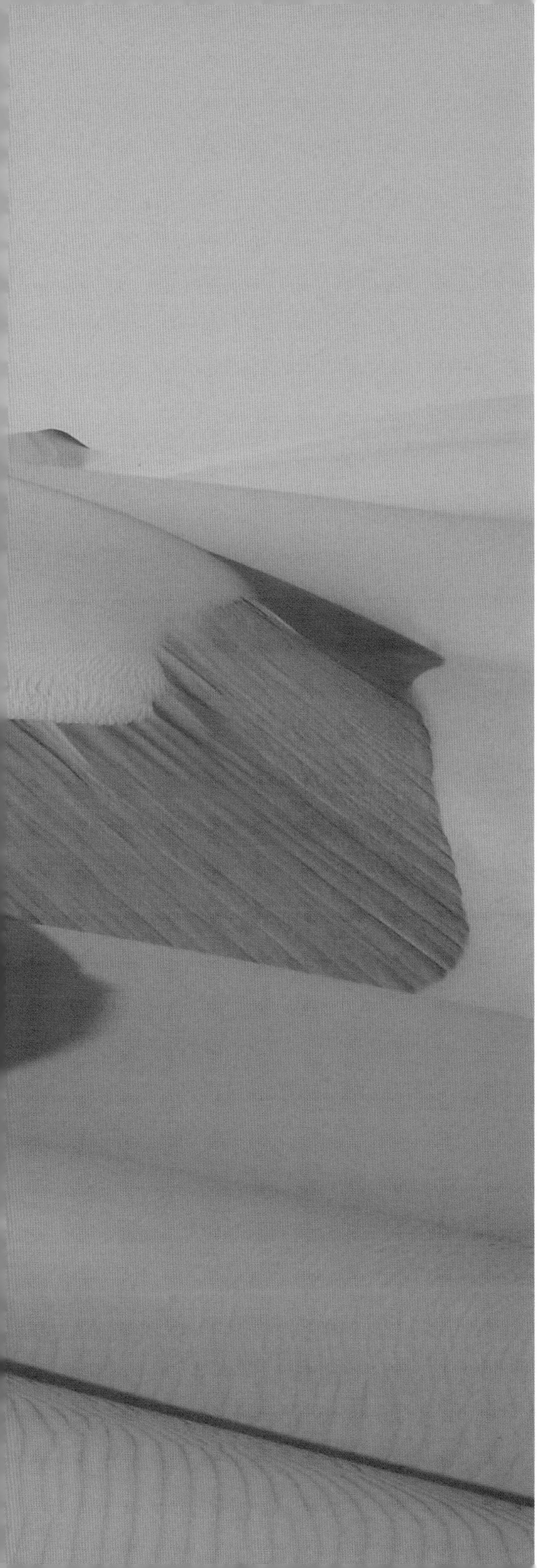

The Land

Halfway along the western coast of the Arabian Gulf lies the small peninsula of Qatar, extending almost 180 kilometres northwards into the warm, shallow seas of the Arabian Gulf. Appropriately, as Qatar is one of the world's leading producers of oil and gas, its 11,437 square kilometres resemble an oil-flare in shape.

From the air the impression is of a predominantly flat terrain, with colours ranging from the golden-brown of the arid desert to the pale cream of the coastal salt-flats (*sabkha*), patched here and there with the vivid green of farms and date palm plantations. On three sides it is surrounded by the sea, which runs through a spectrum of colours from a brilliant blue-green to a deep indigo blue, with yellow shoals and sand banks dotted around the coast. To the south, Qatar shares a border with Saudi Arabia. So narrow is the base of the peninsula that it used to be said that three men strategically placed could watch the whole border from coast to coast. Qatar has less than five inches of rain per year and summer temperatures are searingly hot, but in the winter months the north wind blows almost continuously and despite the almost constant sunshine the temperature is pleasantly cool.

Selenite (calcium sulphate) crystals in a radiating formation near Salwa Bay.

13

Once on the ground, the visitor's first impression of uniform flatness is quickly modified as, given its modest size, the landscape of Qatar is surprisingly varied. With no rivers and low rainfall, it has been shaped only by the forces of wind and sea.

There are several distinct regions. The highest point is a hill of 103 metres in the south-west. Bordering the western coastline at Ras Abrouq are lofty plateaux of gleaming white Miocene limestone, topped with a harder greyish layer of the same rock. Over aeons of time, windblown sand has scoured and honed the edges of the platforms into strange, fanciful shapes: spindly pinnacles and free-standing giant mushrooms. Green forests of mangroves fringe the north-eastern and the far north-western coasts, while sparse patches of natural vegetation growing in depressions known as *rodats* are found on the rolling central gravel and sandy plains.

Mangrove forests of north-east Qatar.

In the south the coastal salt-flats give way to one of the most spectacular landscapes in the entire Gulf region: majestic dunes of fine golden sand, varying from crescent-shaped barchans, 50 metres in height, to the long, undulating ridges known as *seif* dunes. Driven by the prevailing north-westerly wind, the *shamal*, the dunes drift steadily down to Khor Al Adaid, a tidal lagoon which marks the southern border of Qatar. In time, as the dunes continue their slow march southwards ahead of the wind, this stretch of water will disappear beneath the sands.

The Geology

Deep within the earth lie the massive deposits of hydrocarbons which have transformed Qatar in less than a century from a sparsely-populated country, whose principal income came from pearl-fishing, to one of the world's largest suppliers of energy and the richest nation, per capita, on earth. However, there is little evidence at the surface for the source of this vast wealth, other than the elongated

Dukhan dome. This is the surface expression of the structure that trapped the oil-yielding marine sediments in the Jurassic and Cretaceous strata some 250 million years ago.

With the exception of the islands of Halul and Shraouh, east of the mainland of Qatar, which expose rocks of Cambrian age (500,000,000 years), the oldest surface rocks of Qatar are the comparatively youthful limestones of the Middle Eocene period of 48 to 45 million years ago. Salts within the limestone have precipitated, through evaporation, to become gypsum, providing material for the finely-carved decorative facings on traditional buildings. Caves and depressions were formed in the 'karst' limestone by the dissolution of the evaporites by rainwater, the most spectacular being the large cave known as Dahl Al Misfir, the 'Cave of Brightness', south-west of Doha. Present-day oases are found in some of the depressions.

The spectacular Dahl Al Misfir cave.

Also from the Middle Eocene period are the Midra shales containing sharks' teeth and other marine fossils, for at this time the land that was to become Qatar lay under water and all kinds of sea creatures swam over what is now sun-baked desert. The sea level was to rise and fall many times over the millennia. Many inland *sabkhas* were shallow marine entrapments as recently as 8,000 years ago, and today sea-shells lie scattered on the desert floor, far from the sea.

Gastropod fossil, south-west Qatar.

In the hills bordering the Bay of Salwa in the far south-west are to be found the spectacular gypsum pavements of the following Miocene period, composed of radiating rings of glittering crystalline slabs. During this period a gradual lifting of the land raised parts of it above sea-level.

Five million years ago a great river flowing from Eastern Arabia deposited a blanket of river gravel over much of central and eastern Qatar. Some of these many-coloured, smooth pebbles were rolled and shaped by the wind to form the curious three-faceted stones known to geologists as 'ventifacts' or 'dreikanters'.

During the Pleistocene period of approximately two million years ago successive ice ages, confining much of the earth's water in the polar ice caps, caused a global drop in sea levels. The basin which forms the Arabian Gulf became dry between about 70,000 and 44,000 years ago. Repeatedly re-flooding between the ice ages, it became comparatively dry, enough to support human settlement. Then, from around 15,000 years ago it gradually flooded over thousands of years and left Qatar the shape it has now. Winds blew sand from the bed of the Gulf onto the land to form tall dunes, along with the thin layer of powdery reddish topsoil which supports the desert vegetation of today.

Limestone eroded by wind-blown sand.

The First Signs of Man

The dates for humans first moving out of Africa are constantly being revised, but the most recent discoveries by archaeologists point to the first migration of anatomically modern humans into Arabia around 106,000 years ago. At that time the basin of the Arabian Gulf was flat land, marshy in places, with a slow-moving river, the Shatt Al Arab, running along its length from what is now Iraq, towards the Strait of Hormuz. Among its tributaries were the present-day Tigris and Euphrates rivers in Iraq.

In addition to the river there were two large lakes and a mosaic of springs, mangrove swamps and estuaries with thick beds of tall reeds. Because the land was flat the slow-moving river deposited silt which created fertile soil for growing crops. No one yet knows how long ago humans first settled in this wet and marshy region, but underwater surveying and research by archaeologists may one day provide the answer. The people living beside the river and lakes may have built their houses of reeds, and they probably cultivated date palms. It is possible that their lifestyle was not unlike that led until recently by the Marsh Arabs of Iraq.

The climate was wetter than now, and the landmass of what is now the Qatar peninsula had plentiful fresh water welling up from springs along the coast and even from beneath the sea.

When the last Ice Age drew to a close around 15,000 years ago, melting ice at the poles caused sea levels to rise. Gradually, the Gulf basin began to be inundated with saline water from the Indian Ocean through the Strait of Hormuz. What had been fertile land slowly disappeared beneath the sea water, and people would have been forced to move their camps onto higher ground. The inundation of the Gulf reached its height about 7,500 years ago and many settlements along the present shores of the Gulf date to this time. The remains of early settlements have been found at Al Shagra in the south-east, Al Da'asa on the south-west coast and, most recently, Wadi Al Debaiaan in the

A small glass vessel from an Iron Age burial site at Al Mazrouah.

north-west. Some are more than a kilometre inland from the present coastline.

The hunters and fishermen who lived in these camps, which were probably occupied seasonally, trapped birds and preyed on animals such as gazelle, onager (a species of wild ass), oryx and hares. There were also Arabian ostriches, now extinct. Besides fish, the sea yielded shellfish, dugongs and turtles. Higher rainfall 7,000 years ago resulted in shallow freshwater stands forming on the west coast near what is now Umm Bab. There is evidence that fish were caught and dried, perhaps for trading. Few traces of the hunter-gatherers' shelters remain, but many of their stone tools still lie upon the desert surface where they were abandoned so long ago. Among them are some of the most beautiful ever produced by any Stone Age peoples.

Besides hunting and fishing, Qataris in the New Stone Age (Neolithic) period gathered wild cereals and ground them into meal in stone querns. The discovery of spindlewhorls – circular discs of stone used to weight spindles – indicate that thread was being spun and presumably woven into cloth. The presence on half-a-dozen sites, including Wadi Al Debaiaan, of shards of thin pottery with painted decoration in red and brown known as *Ubaid* (after the modern settlement near the site of its manufacture in Iraq), provides evidence that people in Qatar were trading with other lands. Rich deposits of first-grade flint in Qatar enabled the export of 'blanks' – roughly-shaped tools which could be precision-finished later – down the coast to what is now the UAE.

Clay tablets with written records discovered in Mesopotamia, in what is now modern Iraq, refer to long trading voyages taking place along the Arabian peninsula as early as the fourth millennium BCE. The Sumerians of Mesopotamia had established the world's earliest city-states in the fertile plain between the Tigris and Euphrates rivers. Inscriptions refer to trade with the land of Dilmun which included the whole eastern coast of Arabia. The Sumerian states traded textiles, silver jewellery and oil in exchange for copper, timber and hard stone for building.

Channelled through the Gulf, the trade resulted in Bronze Age civilisations springing up and flourishing along both coasts. From 2450 to 1700 BCE the trading civilisation known as Dilmun was centred in Bahrain. That Qatar played a part in the trading network is evident from the presence of fine red Barbar pottery with a ridged decoration, which was manufactured in Bahrain. It is named after a site where large quantities of it have been found, a temple near the modern village of Barbar in the north of Bahrain. This pottery has been found in a depression on the Ras Abrouq peninsula on the west coast of Qatar and on a small island in the eastern bay of Khor Shaqiq.

By around 1700 BCE the power-base in the region shifted, as southern Mesopotamia, which had previously imported materials mainly from the east and south-east, reoriented towards the north and west. The Kassites, a northern people from the Zagros mountains, had assumed power in the middle of the second millennium, and Dilmun gradually became part of Kassite Babylonia.

There is little evidence of human occupation of Qatar at this period, but a unique site dating to around 1400 BCE exists on a small island in the bay of Al Khor. Here, middens contain the crushed remains of millions of shells of a sea-snail, *Thais savigni*. This shellfish yields a scarlet dye and the island is the first, and so far the only, dye-producing site to have been found in the Arabian Gulf. Scarlet- and purple-dyed cloth was much in demand for clothes worn by the elite in Kassite Babylonia. Besides producing the valuable dye, people living on the peninsula of Qatar participated in the pearl trade since very ancient times.

Camels had been domesticated as far back as the third millennium BCE, probably first as milk animals and later as beasts of burden. By the Iron Age some of the inhabitants of Qatar may have become

A selection of beautifully-made, pressure-flaked arrowheads found in Qatar

Objects found at Murwab: a bronze lamp, a small bronze lion and a copper-glazed water jar.

nomadic pastoralists, the ancestors of the bedouin, herding goats and sheep besides camels. The climate was now drier than in the Neolithic period.

More Recent History

By the 6th century BCE settlers and nomads had become interdependent, exchanging commodities and using camels for overland trade, augmenting the traditional sea-routes. Herodotus, a Greek historian writing in the 5th century BCE, said that the inhabitants of this region were excellent sailors and good tradesmen. In the 1st century BCE the Roman writer Pliny the Elder refers to the nomadic people of the region as 'Catharrei', and in the 2nd century CE the writer Ptolemy recorded 'Catarra' on a map of Arabia.

In 326 BCE Alexander the Great conquered Persia. Invading the Indian sub-continent, he had a large fleet of ships constructed near present-day Karachi. He then sent his admiral, Nearchos the Cretan, to explore the coast of Arabia. Nearchos entered the Arabian Gulf at Ras Musandam, but Alexander's untimely death, three days before the planned campaign to conquer Arabia, ended the attempt. The vast empire of Alexander was divided among his generals. The eastern region was taken by Seleukos Nictator, who established his capital at Seleucia on the west bank of the Tigris. The city of Gerrha, on the coast of Arabia north of Qatar, became a centre for trade between India and Arabia by both land and sea. Pottery fragments from this period, known as Seleucid ware, have been found at Ras Uwainat Ali on Qatar's west coast. A nearby scattering of burial mounds on the west coast peninsula of Ras Abrouq has been provisionally dated to this period, as well as a fish-processing complex on the same peninsula.

The Parthians, a Persian people, rose to power around 140 BCE and began to interrupt the Graeco-Roman trading routes between Europe and Asia via the Arabian Gulf, so that the routes shifted to the Red Sea. In 225 CE the Parthians were overthrown and the Sassanid dynasty was established. Their capital was established at Ctesiphon in Iraq, and trade routes reverted to the Gulf and the Indian Ocean. These routes over land and sea were not only arteries of trade, but also enabled the dissemination of knowledge and the spreading of cultural influence.

It is likely that pearls and the red dye obtained from shellfish continued to be exported from Qatar during the Sassanid period. At Al Mazrouah, north-west of Doha, a group of burial mounds contained two skeletons, one of a tall male with an iron arrow-head still embedded in a bone of his forearm and another beside his waist. Another mound covered the remains of a warrior with an iron sword and a bundle of iron arrowheads beside him. A third grave had been robbed long ago, and all that remained was a small Sassanian glass flask. Around the grave were the remains of sacrificed camels. Near Umm Al Ma, on the north-west coast, a small settlement has been excavated from this period: it contained fragments of glass and pottery, including Sassanian-Islamic glazed ware. Finds like these indicate that the standard of living of the villagers was well above subsistence level.

In the early centuries CE it seems likely that small settlements of Nestorian Christians existed in Qatar, as there is a reference to a synod of bishops meeting in the country. Ancient churches have been excavated on Failaka Island off Kuwait, at Jumail in Saudi Arabia, and on the island of Sir Bani Yas in Abu Dhabi. The Christian communities appear to have existed alongside their pagan neighbours.

These fragments of Ubaid pottery were excavated on a site near Al Khor in the 1980s.

The call to embrace Islam came in 627-9 CE. The new faith was adopted by the Christian governor of Hasa Oasis in the Eastern Province of Saudi Arabia. Others followed and the new ideology, which taught the equality and brotherhood of all Muslims, introduced an era of exploration and expansion. The earliest stone-built house in Qatar dates from this period. Situated south of Al Wakra between natural stone ridges about a kilometre from the present coastline, it has three large rooms, and radiocarbon dates suggest it was built some time between 600 and 630 CE.

By the end of the 7th century Islam had spread throughout the whole of the Arabian peninsula. The Abbasids, who were descended from the uncle of the Prophet, overthrew the Ummayid dynasty, centred in Damascus, in 750. This ushered in a golden age of trade in the Arabian Gulf that spanned two centuries. The Abbasids set up their capital in Baghdad and constructed the port of Basra at the mouth of the Euphrates and Tigris to handle the vast range of goods pouring into the region. Tang dynasty ceramics found at widespread Gulf sites indicate well-established trade with China. China exported spices, musk, camphor and silk to the Abbasids, who sent garments of cotton and wool and a variety of metal goods. Besides the exchange of commodities with China, trade with India and East Africa increased, and Suhar in Oman became an important port.

Little is known about Qatar in this period, but undoubtedly the local pearling industry benefited from the demand for pearls in Abbasid Baghdad. Two Arab geographers of the 10th century mention Qatar, and there is a reference by the geographer Yaqut al Hamawi, who died in 1229, to the export of red woollen cloaks from Qatar. He also mentions the renowned markets for horses and camels. One such market may well have existed at Murwab, a town south of Al Zubara, which dates from the 9th to 11th centuries CE. It is the only sizeable ancient settlement in Qatar not located on the coast. Some 250 houses, a fort and two mosques have been excavated. The fort, rebuilt on the site of an even earlier fort which had been destroyed by fire, is the oldest yet discovered in Qatar and is of a style similar to forts in Iraq of the 8th to 11th centuries. Remains of fine quality ceramics and glassware are an indication of the affluence of the inhabitants.

The island of Hormuz at the mouth of the Gulf became important as a maritime power, and gained increasing control over trade in the region. But, in 1515, Hormuz was taken by the Portuguese admiral Albuquerque. Bahrain fell to the Portuguese shortly afterwards, followed by other Gulf ports. Maritime traffic in the Gulf remained under Portuguese control for almost a century. Meanwhile, north of the Gulf the Ottoman Turks occupied Basra and made several attempts to oust the Portuguese from their strongholds. This was finally achieved by Shah Abbas of Persia, who allied with the English and took Hormuz from the Portuguese in 1622. In 1650 they were finally expelled from Muscat. The English East India Company was formed in 1600 and its Dutch counterpart two years later, and for most of the 17th century Gulf trade was dominated by 'merchant adventurers' from England, Holland and later, France.

Qatar played little part in these struggles for domination, having too few natural resources to attract the cupidity of conquerors. The central plains were the domain of the bedouin (*badu*) tribes with their herds of camels and flocks of sheep and goats, constantly moving in search of fresh pastures. The settled people of the coast (*hadar*) continued with the immemorial activities of pearling, trading and fishing. Al Huwaila on the north-east coast developed as the principal pearling port in the early 18th century, to be superseded in the later part of the century by Al Zubara in the north-west. Other settlements of the time were at Al Wakra, Al Ghuwairiyah and Al Bida'a, the village which was one day to become Al Doha, the capital.

Al Zubara developed around 1760 when members of the Bani Utub migrated there from Kuwait, and it quickly became an important centre for trade and pearling. In 1766 Basra fell to the Persians and many of its inhabitants moved to Al Zubara. Al Murair fort was built in 1768 to protect Al Zubara from land attack, and the following year a two-kilometre-long canal was constructed between the sea and the fort. A wall was constructed around the settlement, and enlarged when the population expanded in the 19th century.

A colourful figure from this period is Rahmah bin Jabir. A member of the Jalahaimah branch of the Utub, he became a lifelong enemy of the Al Khalifah, another branch which had settled in Bahrain. He established his base in Khor Hassan, a few miles north of Al Zubara. For the next half century the

Above: Aerial view of Doha, 1947.   *A view of the waterfront of Al Khor in 1958.*

Doha clock tower with Arabic numerals, 1956.

history of Qatar was dominated by his vendetta against the Al Khalifah. He attacked the ships of the Ottoman empire, Kuwait, Bahrain and Persia, on one occasion capturing a fleet of 20 *battil*s en route from Kuwait to Muscat. He was careful, however, not to incur the enmity of the British. By 1800 Rahmah had become the most powerful tribal leader in Qatar. Over the next few years he captured 18 cargo vessels belonging to the Bani Utub. Omani attacks on Bahrain and Qatar then forced him to remove to Dammam in Al Hasa, from where he renewed his seafaring activities against the Al Khalifah. When his stronghold in Dammam was blown up by Saudi forces, Rahmah, together with 500 families of his followers, removed to Bushire. Returning to Dammam in 1818, he continued his attacks on the ships of those he regarded as his enemies, finally agreeing, reluctantly, to a declaration of peace in 1824. The peace proved short-lived. In 1826, in battle with an Utub fleet, he blew up his own ship with himself and his eight-year-old son on board, rather than face defeat. A British official of the time left a description of the formidable appearance of the old man in his last days, his arms, legs and head covered with the scars of battle.

The British were concerned that fighting among the Gulf tribal rulers could disrupt their trade with India, and in 1820 they persuaded the ruling sheikhs to agree to a General Treaty of Peace. A Maritime Truce, formulated by the British, took effect from 1832, outlawing warfare during the pearling season from May to November.

By the middle of the 19th century, Sheikh Mohammed bin Thani Al Thani had become the most influential leader in Qatar. The family stemmed from the Bani Tamim and the Al Maadhid of central Arabia. It was with Sheikh Mohammed that the British political agent, Col. Pelly, negotiated a new treaty in 1868. As a result of this pact Sheikh Mohammed agreed not to make war at sea and to allow the British to act as negotiators in settling any quarrels that might arise between Bahrain and Qatar. Through skilful leadership the whole peninsula of Qatar gradually came under the control of the Al Thani family.

The influence of the Ottoman Turks expanded in the second half of the 19th century and in 1872 a hundred Ottoman troops landed at Al Bida'a and established themselves in a fort. It was alleged that the troops had been sent in response to the harassment of the town-dwellers by bedouin tribesmen. The Ottoman presence continued in Qatar for around 40 years, reluctantly tolerated by the population. In 1893, on the occasion of the visit to Al Bida'a by Nafiz Pasha, the Wali of Basra, matters came to a head. After an attempted surprise attack on Sheikh Jassim bin Mohammed Al Thani at night in his fort at Al Wajba, west of Al Bida'a, he successfully routed the Ottoman forces in battle. This victory marked a watershed in the history of Qatar, not only in the reinforcement of Al Thani rule but in strengthening the concept held by Qataris of themselves as citizens of an independent state. Ottoman influence waned, and during the First World War the last remaining Ottoman troops withdrew from Qatar.

In 1916 the Ruler of Qatar, Sheikh Jassim's son Sheikh Abdullah who had succeeded him in 1913, signed the Anglo-Qatar Treaty. Sheikh Abdullah agreed not to have relations with any foreign power without British consent, to admit British subjects to Qatar, and to allow the establishment of postal and telegraph services. In return, Britain promised to protect Qatar in the event of attack by land or sea.

The 1930s were years of severe economic hardship for Qatar. The recession affecting the Western world caused the demand for pearls to fall. In 1933 the development of the cultured pearl by the Japanese was among the factors that dealt a crippling blow to the Gulf pearling industry, from which it never recovered. Many families emigrated, and those that remained struggled to survive.

The Oil Era

At this bleak time, new hope appeared. The possibility of the existence of oil in the Gulf region had been recognised as early as 1908, but for many years little effort had been made to prospect for oil in the southern Gulf. Then, in 1932, the American oil company Socal struck oil in Bahrain. Socal offered the ruler of Saudi Arabia very attractive terms, but in Qatar the British managed to convince Sheikh Abdullah that he should accept the more modest offer made by the British-controlled Iraq Petroleum Company.

Oil was discovered in Qatar in 1939, but World War II brought a halt to the planned production. It was not until 1949 that exploitation of the country's enormous oil reserves began. No one at that time could have imagined their extent or the extent of the wealth that would transform Qatar and its people.

In 1944 Sheikh Abdullah retired from active government and handed over to his son Sheikh Hamad. Sheikh Hamad, who suffered from ill-health, died in 1948 and his brother Sheikh Ali became the Ruler in 1949 when old Sheikh Abdullah formally abdicated. On Sheikh Ali's abdication in 1960 his son Sheikh Ahmed came to power. In 1971 Qatar became independent of Britain's protectorate role, and the following year Sheikh Khalifa bin Hamad assumed power from his cousin. In 1995 HH Sheikh Hamad bin Khalifa Al Thani took over the rule of the country from his father, and in June 2013 he abdicated and handed over power to his son HH Sheikh Tamim bin Hamad bin Khalifa Al Thani. Within two decades of the first production of oil the country developed rapidly. Education was a priority and in 1956 the state education system was set up. The University of Qatar opened in 1973. Women began to play an ever-increasing part in decision-making at a national level and in the workplace.

Heading the educational revolution is the Qatar Foundation for Education, Science and Community Development, set up in 1995 and chaired by HH Sheikha Mozah bint Nasser Al Misned, the consort of HH the Emir and mother of HH Sheikh Tamim bin Hamad bin Khalifa Al Thani. The Foundation aims to provide the highest standards of education. Education City has been established on the historic site where Sheikh Jassim bin Mohammed Al Thani defeated the Ottoman forces in 1893. It houses Qatar and Awsaj Academies, a Learning Centre for children with special needs, and branch campuses of some of the world's leading universities. Several hospitals were built during the 1960s, with the state-of-the-art Hamad General Hospital opening in Doha in 1982.

In the 1970s the discovery of the North Dome Gas Field began the switch from an oil-based to a gas-based economy. Still, many years of development were needed before the shipments of liquefied natural gas began to be exported from Ras Laffan in the north to the Far East.

In the last two decades, Qatar has seen more rapid development than at any previous period in its history. In 1996 the world's best-known Arabic news channel, Al Jazeera, was founded. With millions of viewers world-wide and rapidly expanding, Al Jazeera has helped to make the name of Qatar famous. In 2006 Al Jazeera International began broadcasting in English.

The capital of Qatar, Doha, has expanded to become a structured city around the shores of the bay of Doha. Its skyline changes month by month, as more and more high-rise buildings are constructed. North of the bay, a vast offshore holiday, retail and residential development, The Pearl, is under construction, with large areas already completed and occupied, and marinas full of opulent-looking pleasure craft.

In December 2006 Qatar hosted the Asian Games, which necessitated the upgrading of road networks and the construction of purpose-built sports venues, plus accommodation for thousands of athletes. Now the nation is proudly gearing up to host the World Cup in 2022. With a per capita income among the highest in the world, Qatari citizens have every reason to look forward to the future with confidence.

An aerial view of Doha, with the Fanar Islamic Cultural Centre and Mosque in centre foreground.

The Diplomatic Club, Doha, designed by Qatari architect Ibrahim Jaidah, opened in 2004.

(This page) The Museum of Islamic Art, Doha, designed by IM Pei, opened in 2008.

Opposite (top) The iconic pyramid of the Sheraton Doha Resort and Convention Hotel, opened in 1979.

(middle) A view of The Pearl-Qatar, an extensive man-made island in Doha's West Lagoon area.

(bottom) Ras Laffan Industrial City.

The Colour Purple

A little island, with fine golden sand and low limestone cliffs, lies in a wide bay, close within the curving embrace of the nearby mainland. The sparkling water is jade green in the shallows and merges into a soft aquamarine where the natural channels lie. Surrounding the island is a forest of green, salt-encrusted mangroves, the home of countless birds. Jewelled kingfishers flash by, and purple herons, pink flamingoes and glossy ibis wade in the shallows. Their strange, haunting calls echo over the island. Over all, arches the deep and infinite blue of the sky.

A peaceful scene, rich in natural hues. But no colour is so intense as that over which a huddle of brown-skinned men are toiling on the sandy shores of the island. In front of a group of small stone-walled hovels, roofs roughly thatched with palm fronds, are large vats made of coarse, thick, green-coloured clay. Within each a hellish brew made of the flesh of shellfish mixed with potash and water is gently heating over deep pits of glowing charcoal. The stench of rotten fish is nauseating. More than once a worker turns away to retch. The viscous red liquid steams. The men's hands are red to the wrists, their garments splashed with scarlet. Their brows seem to be smeared with blood as they pause, now and again, to wipe away the sweat with the back of a hand…

Scenes very like this actually happened in Qatar more than three thousand years ago. On a small island in the bay of Khor Shaqiq, known as Jazirat bin Ghannam or Al Khor Island, an industry was set up to supply one of the most valuable of ancient commodities – one that was more precious than gold. The rich, purple-red dye produced from a species of sea snail was used only for the robes of kings and the élite few whom they chose to honour. Red, the colour of blood, of fire, of the sun and therefore of life itself, was seen in many ancient societies as a symbol of power and strength. It is not difficult to understand how a man wearing garments of purple or red became a symbol of power, particularly if the use of the colour was confined to the ruler and his immediate associates. Even today we associate purple and red with authority, in expressions such as 'born to wear the purple', and 'purple airway' – air traffic controllers' jargon for a route reserved for an aircraft carrying royalty!

The dyes produced from sea snails ranged from a deep bluish-purple to the most brilliant scarlet, depending on the species used and the method of preparation. In the languages of the ancient peoples who made the dyes, there is no clear distinction between purple and red; they are interchangeable. The earliest manufacturers of shellfish dyes were almost certainly the Phoenicians, a Mediterranean people originating in Lebanon. They are sometimes referred to as Canaanites, but the Greeks called them *phoinikes* – the red people — because of the red cloth they exported, or possibly because of their dye-stained skin! From the 9th to the 6th centuries BCE they dominated trade in the Mediterranean, establishing colonies in Cyprus, Greece, Italy, Spain and North Africa. One of the great Phoenician cities in Lebanon, Tyre, was the home of the dye industry, which began around 1600 BCE. But dye was produced all over the Phoenician empire. At Tarentum in Italy there is a small hill composed entirely of the remains of murex shells.

A Phoenician legend recounts the discovery of the purple dye. The god Melkarth was strolling along the beach with his sheepdog one day when the animal crunched on a shellfish. Noticing the dog's jaws stained with red, the god realised its significance. He had a gown made from wool dyed in the new colour and presented it to his girlfriend, the nymph Tyros, thus starting a fashion trend which has lasted more than three thousand years.

The most commonly used sea snails were *Murex trunculus*, which yields a bluish-purple colour, and *Murex brandaris* which gives a red-purple. The dye is released when the hyperbranchial gland in the animal is crushed and reacts with a naturally present enzyme. In the case of *Murex trunculus* the presence of light is also necessary for the colour to develop, but not in the case of *Murex brandaris*. Many other species of sea snails yield the dye, among them *Murex tribulus*, still widely eaten in Spain today, as well as *Thais purpura haemastoma* and, on the little island off the coast of Qatar, *Thais savignyi*.

The Roman writer Pliny, writing in 70 CE, has left us a detailed description of the dye-extraction process. The shellfish were harvested in the winter months. Murex are carnivores, living at depths of 5 to 15 metres and feeding on other shellfish by boring holes in their shells. According to Pliny, the shell-fishers used to lower baskets of shellfish bait, wait for murex to gather on them, and then quickly draw them up. The murex were then kept alive in tanks until a sufficient quantity had been gathered and dye production could begin. Ancient writers state that the dyers' hands were permanently stained red, and that the stench from centres of the trade, such as Tyre, was formidable!

Pliny says that the smaller shellfish (*Murex trunculus*) were crushed, shell and all, whereas the larger ones (*Murex brandaris*) were pierced and the hyperbranchial gland extracted. The crushed mass was macerated in heavily salted water for three days. This may have been to suppress the bacterial content of the vats, as the bacteria produced by rotten fish (*Clostridium carnis*) are highly dangerous. The rotting shellfish were then rinsed thoroughly and gently heated for ten days until reduced to a sixteenth of the original amount. Testing by dipping wool then began and reduction continued until the dye had reached the desired degree of brilliance.

Wool was always dyed in the strand, never in the cloth. So valuable and expensive was the genuine dye, which retained its brilliant hues without fading, that in classical antiquity a whole industry sprang up, forging purple dyes using cheaper materials. Among them were flowers such as mulberry blossoms and amaranth, and the roots of plants, and the dyes had to be fixed using additions of ferro-acetate, laurel, cantharidae or haematite. A lustre could be imparted to the thread by adding gall-nuts or iris roots to the mixture. A document in demotic Greek known as the Stockholm Papyrus, found in a grave in Egypt of the 3rd century CE, actually lists as many as 70 recipes for these dyes, and its author claimed, with evident satisfaction, that it was impossible to distinguish the counterfeit from the original purple. The headquarters of the counterfeit dye production business was in Egypt.

There are countless references to the wearing of purple in ancient literature. Only the Roman emperors and senior imperial officials could have a purple border on their togas. The Achaemenian kings of Persia wore purple: Darius the Mede advanced in state to meet Alexander the Great wearing a robe of purple and white. And when Alexander conquered the Persian capital, Susa, in 331 BCE he found 200-year-old purple robes in the royal treasury that glowed as brightly as the day they were woven. Alexander himself adopted the Persian custom of wearing purple and his generals also sported purple cloaks.

In Babylonia, a region in what is now Iraq, a mountain people called the Kassites invaded and took control of the country soon after 1595 BCE, and the next three centuries saw a period of great economic prosperity in the region. Production of purple dye on Jazirat bin Ghannam (Al Khor Island) in Qatar occurred as part of the take-over of the Dilmun trading civilisation by the Kassites between 1425 and 1225 BCE. The Dilmun trading empire included the islands and mainland between Kuwait and Bahrain.

In the early 1980s an American archaeologist, Christopher Edens, working with the Mission Française Archeologique à Qatar, excavated a site on the island. The remains of pottery enabled it to be dated to around 1400 BCE. It consisted of about

Different species of shellfish yield colours ranging from pale violet to deep purple.

five rectangular structures, several hearths and stone kists. One pit contained the remains of around 38,000 shellfish, a species called *Thais savignyi*. There was also a huge shell midden measuring 10 by 15 metres. The top layer consisted of food remains – shells and fish bones and debris from hearths – but as the archaeologists dug down they came upon a deep, solid layer of shells of *Thais savignyi*. The archaeologists calculated, to their astonishment, that the mound they had excavated contained the remains of almost three million shellfish! There were other mounds that appeared to contain similar quantities. *Thais savignyi*, which still lives under rocks in the intertidal zone, produces a bright red dye. It requires light plus an enzyme to release the dye from the hyperbranchial gland.

The archaeologists conducted experiments collecting the shellfish. They concluded that collecting three million snails would have taken 42,000 man-hours of labour: 20 people working one month a year for seven years. There was only one possible conclusion: the site had been used for dye production. It was unique – the first site of its kind in the entire Arabian Gulf and the only one found outside the Mediterranean. The pottery found on the site, which included the remains of huge, thick-walled vats, was identified as Kassite. Evidently the dye was being produced for use in Babylonia. The Kassites were a literate people. Their records mention that their kings wore red-purple garments and gave gifts of the same to political supporters and senior officials. The red cloth was often presented in combination with linen and gold.

So who were the shell-gatherers, the men who toiled in wretched conditions to produce this rare commodity? Were they local tribesmen, or slaves of the Kassites, or even Kassites themselves? We will never know. They left no graves, no trace of themselves save the few remains that provide clues as to the nature of their activities. No source of fresh water has been found on the island, so they probably had to bring supplies across from the nearby mainland. Pearl fishing was undoubtedly being carried out in Qatar at this time, possibly even from the same island. It is indeed ironic that the men who laboured to supply two of the most beautiful and expensive luxuries of ancient times themselves lived the simplest and harshest of lives.

The excavated remains of buildings on the Kassite dye production site at Jazirat bin Ghannam.

The Cup-Marked Rocks at Jebel Al Jassasiya

Around the coasts of Qatar, and at two sites on Jazirat Al Huwar located to the north-west of the peninsula, are low limestone hills (*jebel*) bearing numbers of cup-marks cut into the rock. Some of these small, circular depressions are single; others are massed together in a wide variety of formations: one, two, three or four lines of cups, sometimes straight and sometimes curved, or clustered together in 'rosettes' with anything from six to sixteen cups surrounding a central depression. The southernmost of these hills is Jebel Al Wakra (now enclosed by a security fence and inaccessible to visitors) to the south of Doha. At Jebel Al Jassasiya, an hour's drive to the north, can be seen the greatest number of carvings anywhere in the country. A short distance northwards lies Jebel Fuwairit, also with numerous cup-marks, and isolated carvings occur on small, scattered limestone mounds around the northern coast leading down to the second major petroglyph site, a line of limestone jebel outcrops between Fraiha Al Gharbiya and Al Zubara in the north-west.

The Danish archaeologist Holger Kapel and his son Hans surveyed and drew the carvings at Jebel Al Jassasiya in 1974, and in 1984 a consultant working at Hamad Hospital, Professor D F Hawkins, carried out a similar careful study at Jebel Al Fraiha. At Jebel Al Jassasiya, of the 874 carvings recorded by the Kapels in 1974, 333 consist of cupmarks in rows. Both Kapel and Hawkins considered that the parallel rows of cup-marks were used for playing the ancient board game known to archaeologists as the 'mancala game', because that happened to be the African name under which it was first recorded by Europeans. Before going on to consider the drawbacks to this theory, it is worth taking a look at the game itself. It is easy to make a cup-mark on a horizontal limestone surface using basic tools. A lump of flint placed on the rock and hit with a hammer soon leaves a depression in the soft stone. When a sufficiently deep indentation has been made, the inside can be scoured and smoothed with the sharp edge of a piece of flint.

The mancala game is of immense antiquity. Several boards have been found carved into the stone surfaces of the Khurna temple at Thebes in Egypt, which dates to 1400 BCE. It occurs all over the Arabian Gulf from Kuwait to Oman and also in Iran, although Qatar is unique in the sheer quantities of its carvings. In some parts of Arabia it went by the name of *Al Huwais*, and in Qatar it was known as *Al Haloosa* or *Al Huwaila*.

The game is found in almost every African country, where it appears under countless names. It may well have been introduced into Africa by the Arabs. From Africa the slave trade took the game to Cuba. In India and Malaya two of its names are *Narani*

Parallel rows of cup marks, possibly used for the ancient mancala game.

Circular petroglyph known as a 'rosette'.

and *Chanka*. The number of holes and rows of holes and the number of counters used vary considerably from country to country, but the basic principle of the game is the same throughout.

In a version recorded in Kuwait two players sit, one each side of the board, and place their counters into the row of holes on their side, dividing them equally between the holes. Small pebbles or seeds are usually used as counters. Each player in turn removes the counters from a hole in his own row, selected at random, and drops them consecutively one by one into other holes, starting to the immediate right of the emptied hole. On reaching the last hole in the row, he continues to deposit the counters into his opponent's holes. The second player then does the same. Often a large number of counters may accumulate in one cup: a player may check on the number of counters in one of his own holes but not in his opponent's.

As the game proceeds, if the hole in which a player places his last counter is on his opponent's side and contains, after the addition, either two or

three counters he may 'capture' and remove them, and may also do the same with counters from the consecutively preceding cups on his opponent's side if they contain either two or three counters. The skill of the game lies in the player rapidly calculating from which of his holes to move the counters in order to capture as many as possible of his opponent's. The game continues until one opponent cannot move or until there is no possibility of further capture. The player with the greatest number of captured counters is the winner. (To play the game online, visit http://medinapublishing.com/hidden-in-the-sands/mancala-game/index.html.)

In addition to the game boards on the jebel are the 'rosettes', with numbers of shallow holes arranged in a circle around a central hole. This is said to be a game known as *Al Aila* in Qatar and *Um Al Judaira* in Kuwait, Bahrain and Oman. At Jebel Al Jassasiya, Holger Kapel recorded a total of 333 game boards, of which 193 had two rows each of even holes. Seventy-one rosettes were recorded, of which 49 have nine holes in the circle. At Jebel Al Fraiha Professor Hawkins counted 24 game boards and 62 rosettes.

If we accept that the parallel rows of cup-marks at these sites and others are, in fact, variations of the mancala game, then a number of problems occur. Foremost is the sheer number of boards. Why would anyone go to the trouble of carving out a new board each time he wanted to play? The game can be played just as easily on the sand, in instantly-created scoops, as on a solid surface. Then there is the apparently random number of holes, ranging from as few as two rows of three holes to two rows of 14, and even three and four rows of holes. It seems inconceivable that the game people of Al Jassasiya played such a wide number of variations.

At Al Jassasiya and Fraiha some of the so-called game boards are carved on the sloping surfaces of the rock, where the cups could not possibly have retained any seeds, shells or pebbles used as counters. Some are so close to each other that there would not have been room for players to gather round them at the same time. And in some of the parallel rows of holes, particularly those with three and four rows, the individual holes are too small to hold any counters larger than a grain of rice.

So if the rows of cup-marks are not games, what are they? It has been suggested that the cup formations were used for the sorting and storage of pearls. But it seems highly unlikely that such small, precious, easily lost objects would have been exposed to a rough, windswept rock surface. Although in Qatar the cup-marks always occur in areas associated with pearl fishing, in other parts of the world similar carvings are to be found which can have no connection with pearls.

Another suggestion is that they were used in some way for divination. Yet another theory is that the series of rows of holes were systems for computing time and tides. Of the 333 sets of holes in rows, 193 consist of two rows of seven. When doubled their sum is 28, the approximate number of days in the lunar month. Twenty-eight is also, in ancient Arabian astronomy, the number of the moon's 'mansions': the groups of stars through which it passes as it progresses east.

Some of the bas-relief ship designs which are such a prominent feature at Jebel Al Jassasiya are simple representations of sailing vessels, but others incorporate lines and cup marks superimposed upon the outline of the ship. One, of a many-oared boat, with a rope and anchor at one end and trailing what may be a fishing net at the other, has been compared with the constellation of Orion, and the suggestion is that the cup marks represent stars. Another appears to resemble the constellations of Canis Venitici and Ursa Major.

To begin to comprehend the purpose of the cup-marks it may be helpful to compare them to other similar carvings worldwide. Professor Hawkins notes the similarity of the sites in Qatar to those of southern Scotland, where petroglyphs always occur on low horizontal rock outcrops with an open view of the sea. In both places many of the carvings have connecting lines running downhill. Many rosettes in Scotland closely resemble those in Qatar, except that they always have a circumferential ring. As in Qatar, they are associated with large 'basins' cut deep into the rock.

No date has yet been suggested for the Qatar cup-marks. Comparable carvings in Scotland are believed to date as far back as 3000 BCE, but that does not mean that the Jebel Al Jassasiya petroglyphs are as ancient. Some are more weathered than others, as the sand carried by the wind gradually scours the surface smooth. The unequal degree of erosion does not necessarily indicate the relative age of the carvings, simply the exposure of that particular site to the prevailing wind.

The most recent research on the petroglyphs seems to indicate that they were made between 400 and 250 years ago. Archaeologists working in Qatar today say that because limestone is a soft rock, constant wind erosion makes it unlikely that any carvings date back to ancient times.

Large circular pits cut into the jebel at Al Jassasiya and Fraiha have been compared with fire-pits found throughout the Gulf region. In Iran they are associated with the fire cults of pre-Islamic times. At both sites foot marks are carved into the rock, sometimes a simple narrow oval or pair of oval shapes but, in one example at Jebel Al Jassasiya, complete with toes. The making of foot and hand marks on rock and the painting of hand prints in caves is of extreme antiquity. Experts have dated hand prints discovered a few years ago in a cave near Cassis in southern France to 25,000 BCE.

More research still needs to be done on the rock carvings of Qatar. Meanwhile, anyone who visits these lonely, windswept rocks is free to speculate as to the meaning and age of these enigmatic carvings.

The Boat Carvings at Jebel Al Jassasiya

Many people who explore the landscape of Qatar are intrigued by the range of carvings on the low, wind-etched rocks, known as *jebel* in Arabic, at Al Jassasiya on the eastern coast, north of the old pearling port of Al Huwaila. Here, a long line of scattered limestone outcrops stand near a lonely shore, surrounded by barren desert. However, the range of potsherds and other objects found near the rocks, including a blue-glazed bowl fragment of the 13th-14th centuries CE, water jars of the 14th-16th centuries AD and a Persian coin dated c.1700 CE, together with the remains of a stone-built settlement to the south-east, indicate that Al Jassasiya was not always so isolated a site as it is today.

Al Jassasiya is one of about a dozen major rock-carvings sites in Qatar, and all but one are coastal. There are also numerous examples of petroglyphs on isolated rocks along the coast, but Al Jassasiya and Jebel Fuwairit, a little to the north, are among the few sites with carvings of boats. On Jazirat Al Huwar off the north-west coast of Qatar there are two *jebel* outcrops with petroglyphs of simple canoe-shaped vessels, some of them over two metres in length, but these differ in style from the carvings on the Qatar mainland and may represent reed rafts rather than boats.

Unlike rock paintings, carvings are often very difficult to date, and no definite dates have been found for the oldest of the carvings in Qatar, although some similar designs in Oman have been tentatively dated to the 3rd millennium BCE. As in Oman, where outlines of Land Rovers are depicted next to designs which are obviously more ancient, the carvings at Al Jassasiya have been added to at different periods up to and including the last century. They range from a series of configurations of cup marks, some with a surrounding ring, to two very different styles of petroglyphs depicting boats. It is possible that the earliest may belong to the Neolithic period, others could be a mere couple of hundred years old.

One type of ship carving is made in bas-relief, where the boats are shown in plan. The others are depicted in linear profile and the lines appear to have been 'pricked' onto the soft rock surface with a metal tool.

Outline sketch of a dhow *imposed onto a photo of the original plaster carving found during recent excavations at Al Zubara.*

The carvings were first photographed in 1962 by a Danish archaeological expedition led by P V Glob and the British archaeologist Geoffrey Bibby. A more

thorough investigation of the site was carried out in 1974 by the Danish pre-historian Holger Kapel, whose son, Hans, meticulously planned and drew all the petroglyphs. They recorded a total of 124 of the bas-relief designs. Many of the boats are fish-shaped with sharply pointed sterns, and cross-seats, thwarts and the stepping for the mast are clearly depicted. Some boats trail large anchors, either the metal European anchor (*bawara*) or the ancient Arabian form (*sinn*): a round or triangular stone attached to a rope, with a hole in the centre through which a beam of wood or bar of metal was fixed. These stone and wood anchors were in use well into the 20th century. In his guide to the pearl-oyster beds of the Gulf, published in Bahrain in 1920, the famous pearling captain Rashid bin Fadhl Al Binali recommends them for certain anchorages, including Halul Island.

The design of boats and ships in use in the Arabian Gulf barely changed over many centuries until the coming of the oil era. The *boums* in which the merchant adventurer Sindbad the Sailor made his voyages over 1,000 years ago, in the Abbasid period, did not differ greatly in overall design from the *dhows* which can be seen today in the harbours of Al Ruwais, Al Khor, Doha and Al Wakra. The ancient method of steering a boat was with a single or pair of steering oars, and some of the boats have these at the stern; others have details which could be interpreted as a rudder. Some have a roughly-carved appendage which could represent a fishing net. Many have oars, depicted as straight lines at right angles to the hull. There are mostly six, eight or ten pairs of oars to each boat, although some have a seemingly random arrangement, with more oars on one side than the other. Some authorities believe that these petroglyphs represent boats on the pearl banks, where oars were used to manoeuvre about the banks and were left unshipped as support for the divers. It has also been suggested that they might be oared fishing boats for inshore use. The nearest thing to such a vessel today is probably the *badan*, a high-sterned sardine boat still in occasional use in Oman and the east coast of the UAE. This is a very ancient type of vessel with a rudder attached to the stern and operated with ropes. It is a rowing boat and two to four pairs of oars are used, but it does not carry a sail, so the ships of the bas-relief carvings, although similar in shape, cannot have been *badan*s.

The big two-pronged metal anchor was first introduced into this area by the Portuguese in the 16th century, but smaller four-pronged grapnels are known to have been in use some 200 years earlier. So all that can be said is that the boats with metal anchors cannot be older then 700 years, at the most. And even that is not certain, because on one of the ships the rope and anchor appears to have been added at a later date, judging by the different patination of the carving.

On the group of rocks nearest to the coast, on the far side of the road that runs to the east of the main *jebel*, are a number of detailed line-cut drawings, in which grooves have been pricked out using a pointed metal tool and a hammer. There are 17 line drawings. They are interesting because of the number of recognisable types of sailing vessels. The artists were careful to include such details as would enable a ship, when seen at a distance as a silhouette, to be identified. One, a *battil*, has the characteristic fiddle-head projection at the bow and a high stern (*fashin*). In addition, seven round-bladed oars are shown along one side and the ship carries both a triangular and a lateen sail, which may have been used in combination for certain wind conditions. The *battil* was a large, fast vessel, extensively employed in the pearling fleets but also useful as a warship. When a *battil* was on the pearling banks, the oars were used to manoeuvre it around. Photographs of the Qatar pearling fleet taken in 1929 show banks of oars with square-shaped blades.

A linear carving of a battil *with typical 'fiddle-head' projection at the bow, a high stern with a 'dog's head', round-bladed oars, and both a lateen and a triangular sail.*

Bas-relief of an oared boat trailing an anchor rope, with indications of internal structure.

Another illustration may be of a *baqqarah*. A characteristic of the *baqqarah* is its projecting stern frame which enclosed the rudder stock. The stern post had a raised part at the back and is decorated. Both *battils* and *baqqarahs* were of stitched construction, in a tradition which pre-dates the influence of European shipping on Arab boat design that began in the early 16th century. On this vessel, as in some of the others, the lantern holder at the back of the ship is shown. The hulls of both *battil* and *baqqarah* are divided by vertical lines to indicate the size and loading capacity of the ship – just the kind of information which would have been of importance to a sea-faring people. Not all the ships have their masts depicted, as these could be laid down when required.

Smaller vessels, some with sails, have been identified as *shu'i*, which were generally employed for fishing. At present we can only say that this group cannot be dated earlier than 1000-1200 CE, because that is when stern rudders were first developed in the Arabian Gulf. Before that time steering oars were in use and, indeed, continued to be used on some kinds of boats right into the 20th century. All of the anchors shown are the Arabian stone *sinn*.

The Portuguese were the greatest European naval power of their time and when they seized power in the Gulf the early 16th century their great galleons, with their high, square sterns and rich carving, impressed the local Arab ship-builders. The largest of the galleons had a row of five square windows in the heavily decorated stern, and these features can be seen in one of the carvings.

We can only speculate as to why such a large number of ship carvings occur at Al Jassasiya. It is remarkable that, with the exception of some depicted on Jebel Fuwairit, they are found on few other coastal petroglyphic sites in Qatar. Ships held a powerful role in the beliefs of ancient peoples, who saw them as a symbolic means of transit from this world to the next. Both the Babylonians and the Egyptians believed that the dead reached the afterworld upon a ship. Ancient Greek myths speak of the ferryman Charon, who carried the souls of the dead across the river Styx to the underworld. More recently, both the Norsemen and the Anglo-Saxons burned or buried their dead in ships, it is tempting to consider the bas-relief carvings at Al Jassasiya not merely as a record of the fishing activities central to the existence of the people of Qatar but as expressions of a belief shared by many ancient peoples. It may be that these strange, rather disturbing petroglyphs, which crawl across the surface of the rock like scorpions, represent the echoes of a folk memory reaching far back into pre-historic times.

Uncovering the Past at the World Heritage Site of Al Zubara

The old city of Al Zubara lies on the north-west coast of Qatar, approximately 100 km from Doha. It is Qatar's largest archaeological site, and the ruins within its boundary walls cover an area of 60 hectares. For a century the town lay empty and deserted, its walls slowly crumbling into mounds of sandy rubble, strewn with brightly-coloured fragments of Chinese glazed porcelain and humbler earthenware cooking pots.

Along the lonely shore, between the bright blue-green waters of the shallow bay and the ruins of the ghost town, the silence was broken only by the cries of sea birds. It was difficult to imagine that little more than a century ago a thriving community had occupied this windswept and waterless corner of the peninsula.

Aerial view of Al Zubara showing the extent of the settlement.

Al Zubara was settled around 1760 by members of the Bani Utub from the Nejd who migrated from what is now Kuwait. Later the settlers were joined by another branch of the Utub, the Jalahaimah. From a few kilometres further north the inhabitants of the old coastal settlement at Al Ruwaida abandoned their large fort and its surrounding buildings and migrated to join the townsfolk of Al Zubara, seeking safety behind its walls.

Stone diving weights.

Between 1775 and 1780 Al Zubara's commercial importance grew when the trading city of Basra in Iraq was attacked and finally taken by the Persians and this, together with an outbreak of plague, caused many merchant families from the town to emigrate and settle in Al Zubara. Houses were constructed from coral rock or *faroush*, the beachrock formed from compressed sea shells and sand, and from limestone quarried at Fraiha to the north of Al Zubara. Mud was used as mortar between the rocks and stones, and a layer of gypsum-based plaster, sometimes decorated with incised patterns, completed the whole. The roofs were made from mangrove poles, either locally gathered or imported from Zanzibar, which were sometimes waterproofed with bitumen. Over this was a layer of woven bamboo strips, topped with mangrove or palm branches and finally compressed mud. As well as the walls the floors were also plastered with gypsum. From the sea the rows of white buildings shone in the sunshine against the golden sandy floor of the desert.

Handmade jar of coarse clay with oxidized red painted decoration, made at Julfar in Ras Al Khaimah, UAE.

Ships sailed in and out of the wide, sheltering curve of the bay of Al Zubara: not only fishing *dhow*s and the pearling fleet for which Al Zubara was once renowned, but traders from far-off lands. The city was a hive of busy activity: potters, metalworkers, weavers and other craftsmen practised their skills, and traders haggled over the price of pearls and luxury imported goods, among them the Chinese porcelain.

Al Zubara is not the oldest town in Qatar. The settlement at Al Huwaila on the east coast pre-dates it as a pearling centre, and the ancient settlement at Murwab, not far from Al Zubara, is many hundreds of years older. However, during the 18th and 19th centuries, Al Zubara occupied a strategic position as a centre for trade, linking sea routes that ran both north and south along the coasts of the Arabian Gulf. Coins from Persia, India, Iraq, Turkey, Zanzibar and both

A Turkish terracotta tobacco pipe bowl found at Al Zubara.

German and British-ruled East Africa found at the site indicate the extent of the trade that flowed through Al Zubara. So important was the town that a contemporary European map simply labels the entire peninsula of Qatar as 'Zubara'!

The people, living a life-style that was comparatively wealthy, inevitably attracted the attention of raiders coming by both sea and land, and the jealousy of trading rivals in the region. A fortified settlement, Qalat Murair, was constructed in 1768 to guard the town's precious water supply within its walls, as Al Zubara, being built on *sabkha*, had no fresh water of its own. The following year a two-kilometre-long canal protected by screening walls, one of the most remarkable pre-oil era structures ever built in this country, was dug to link the town and the fort. Walls with cannon towers constructed at regular intervals on the land side surrounded the settlement at Al Zubara.

The 18th century town was laid out according to a plan, with narrow lanes running down to the sea and others running at right angles. A souq with rows of small shops stood near the shoreline, and a small fort guarded the harbour. In its heyday the population may have numbered between 6,000 and 9,000, although such figures are estimates. Some inhabitants would have lived in tents or *barasti* (woven palm leaf) huts, which leave little trace.

For the whole of its existence Al Zubara experienced constant strife. In 1780 it was attacked by the Persians. In 1809 it came under the control of the famous leader of the Jalahaimah, Rahmah bin Jabir, but again in 1811 it was sacked and burned to the ground by Saiyid Sa'id, the ruler of Muscat. Amid the screams of the women and children and the shouts of the raiders the town blazed, the roofs of mangrove poles and palm thatch burning quickly, the mud-walls blackening, cracking and crumbling in the heat. The town was left 'entirely in ruins', according to a British Resident in the Gulf who was eye-witness to the disaster. When the dust had settled the survivors, mainly from the Al Na'im tribe, returned and patiently re-built their homes, but Al Zubara never again regained its former size. A smaller wall was built to enclose the reduced settlement.

Many more raids and re-buildings followed. In 1842 it was re-constructed by disaffected members of the Al Khalifah as a base from which to attack Bahrain, and in 1878 it was again sacked and destroyed. In 1895 Al Zubara was occupied by the Al bin Ali tribe of Bahrain, together with a Turkish contingent headed by a *mudir*. A British gunboat, the *Sphinx*, attacked and destroyed all the ships in the harbour. Again, the Al Na'im returned and occupied the site of the old town. It survived as a small pearl fishing community, but it was gradually abandoned in the first half of the 20th century. Al Zubara's weakness had always been its lack of readily available fresh water, and by the time the last inhabitants left the wells at Qalat Murair had become so saline that they could no longer be used.

In the 1980s the first excavations took place at Al Zubara, conducted by archaeologists from the Department of Museums and Antiquities. Two large housing complexes and a market area beside the shore were uncovered. More recently, large warehouses for the storage of trading goods have been found in the same area. The variety of small finds – large, heavy silver coins from Iran, gold jewellery, incense burners, fine porcelain – was testimony to the relative affluence of the townsfolk. Part of the original city wall, with several of its large drum towers, was reconstructed. It had a 'fire-step' on its inner side where defenders could stand to fire their rifles over the top of the wall.

Between 2002 and 2005 more excavations took place by archaeologists from what was then the National Council for Culture, Arts and Heritage. In addition to Al Zubara they also investigated Fraiha, a contemporary settlement a short distance to the north. The area close to the shore line which was excavated in Al Zubara proved to contain an exceptionally large number of hearths. It became clear that the associated structures were not only of housing – this was a semi-industrial area. The association of the hearths with several small clay crucibles containing solidified burnt material indicated that here the smelting of metal used to take place. The discovery of fragments of iron, bronze and copper reinforced this. There was no separate 'Industrial Zone' in those days! The modest homes of the workers were crowded around the courtyards where the metal-working took place.

Various potsherds litter the site, including innumerable fragments of export-quality Ming blue-on-white and other porcelain, all from the Chinese province of Canton, which had strong trading links with the Middle East. A few pieces of blue-green celadon ware probably came from Thailand. There are large numbers of three-handled clay water jars.

The excavated area of walls and hearths shows three distinct areas of occupation. Layers of burned ashes bear mute witness to Al Zubara's turbulent past. The oldest occupation layer, presumed to date to the late 17th or early 18th centuries, appears to be of purely domestic origin. It is in the later occupation layers that the evidence of hearths and crucibles is found. *Tannur* ovens, made of clay jars half sunk into the ground, were used for the preparation of food, in particular for the baking of flat, round loaves of bread. Several date presses (*madbassa*), where the sweet, sticky syrup from the compressed dates trickled slowly down narrow channels to a collecting jar, were uncovered in the 1980s excavations and two more were discovered in 2002.

Restored area of the palace complex, Al Zubara.

An unusual find in the first season was of a quantity of very large pearl oyster shells piled up in the corner of what had been an open courtyard. These were from a species, *Pteria macroptera*, which was mainly gathered for mother-of-pearl. The trade in mother-of-pearl, used not only to make buttons but also in the elaborately inlaid furniture popular at the time, was controlled by Germany until the First World War. Among miscellaneous small finds in 2002 were several bronze coins, fragments of inlaid glass-paste bracelets from India and an attractive ring made of agate, probably of Yemeni origin.

Excavations the following year doubled the area uncovered in 2002 to 1,600 square metres. A street became visible, running between the house walls. More date presses came to light, and a number of small finds gave glimpses of the lives of the people of this remote town. One was a small, green-glazed toy horse, minus its head and legs, similar to those already found in Iraq, the UAE and Bahrain. A tiny clay jar was crammed full of brightly-coloured beads made of semi-precious stones, glass and metal. Clearly the treasured possession of some

girl or woman, its loss must have been mourned. A ten-centimetre-long boat-shaped object crudely modelled out of bitumen proved to be something of a mystery, and may have been used for holding ink. The barrel of a small cannon, one of the very few weapons ever found at Al Zubara, may have come from a ship.

In 2004 excavations continued, when a further 700 square metres was uncovered, and in 2005 the archaeologists concentrated on the settlement at Fraiha, north of Al Zubara, with its small fort and scattering of houses. It appears to have been a 'satellite' of Al Zubara, probably established in the early 19th century when space within the walls of

A small jar containing a collection of beads, some made of semi-precious stones.

Small Chinese cup or bowl of the type known as 'kitchen Ching', mass produced for export to Asian markets. Late 18th-19th century.

Beads made of coral.

Blue and white glazed porcelain bowl interior with yin and yang motif. Japanese, 19th century.

Glass and porcelain bottle containing khol (eye liner), late 19th century.

the larger town became scarce as the population expanded.

In 2009 the Qatar Islamic Archaeology and Heritage Project was established by the Qatar Museums Authority and became one of the largest archaeological, conservation and heritage project in the Gulf region, involving an international team of more than 40 specialists in archaeology, conservation, architecture, geology, heritage, oral history and museum studies. Large scale excavations at Al Zubara are continuing in collaboration with the University of Copenhagen, and when complete the remains of the town will be an important heritage site, open to visitors.

One of the areas more recently excavated has been dubbed the 'palatial compound': a conglomeration of structures surrounding nine interlinked courtyards, with large, square buildings and towers of plastered limestone in the surrounding walls. The whole complex covers 100 x 110 metres. Some of the rooms were domestic dwellings and contain cooking areas and *hamam* (bathrooms). These had floors with layers of tiny shells or clean white gypsum plaster, and walls whose plaster was sometimes decorated.

In the courtyards are holes where water or grain storage jars and *tannur* ovens were once half buried. But other buildings facing onto different courtyards were storerooms and places where some kind of manufacturing was carried out.

The whole complex was fortified, with towers from which the building could be protected from attack from either land or sea. The discovery of two staircases leads to the speculation that some parts of the palace may have had an upper storey. The doorway to the palace was screened to preserve the privacy of the family, especially the women, from public gaze.

Examination of the contents of a nearby midden, where domestic waste piled up, revealed that the inhabitants of the 'palace' enjoyed a high protein diet. The evidence, in the form of animal bones, is that they ate meat more frequently than the other inhabitants of Al Zubara, who relied on fish as their main source of protein, an indication that

Excavation of one section of the palace complex, 2013.

the 'palace-dwellers' were well-off. But despite its grandeur and the precautions for its protection and security, the 'palace' was occupied for no more than two or three generations.

Al Zubara was, above all, a pearling port and immense wealth poured into the town from its harvest of these treasures from the sea. There is a written record of a single robbery in the 19th century when pearls to the value of the income a pearl dealer could expect to make in three years were stolen! But trade was also a very important occupation for the citizens. The harbour was shallow, restricting the size of the *dhows* that could enter it, but fleets of these vessels carried pearls, dates and jars of dibs far along the trading routes and imported tobacco from Iran, fine coffee from Yemen, food stuffs and huge quantities of pottery, especially Chinese porcelain mass produced for the export market. Coins and trading tokens from Persia, India, Turkey, Zanzibar and British-ruled East Africa, indicate how widespread was the trade. The city was also the home of poets

and scholars, and it is known from documentary sources that many of the inhabitants were educated and cultured citizens.

The traditional-style 'Zubara Fort', which is a prominent landmark for the visitor approaching Al Zubara, was erected in 1938 as a defence post on the orders of the ruler Sheikh Abdullah bin Jassim Al Thani, and has been converted into a small museum.

In June 2013 Al Zubara Archaeological Site was inscribed onto the UNESCO World Heritage List, becoming one of 911 natural and cultural properties on the international register. Its importance has been recognised as the best preserved of the region's major pre-oil era trading and pearl-fishing coastal towns which flourished outside the control of the Ottoman, European and Persian empires and eventually led to the emergence of the modern-day Gulf states.

Information about the ongoing work at Al Zubara can be found on the website http://alzubarah.qa/en/ and on Facebook at https://www.facebook.com/AlZubarah.

Zubara Fort, erected in 1938 as a defence post, stands about a kilometre from the old town.

Islamic Coastal Settlements

The ruins of a large fort lie on the north-west coast, one of several between Al Zubara to the south and Al Ruwais on the northern tip of the peninsula. Its name, Al Ruwaida, is a diminutive of the Arabic, *rodat*, meaning a fertile area in a depression, and the area is still noticeably greener than the surrounding arid land.

Since a brief stop by a team from Beatrice de Cardi's British expedition to Qatar in 1972-3, which made a surface collection of pottery, no archaeologist had investigated the site of the fort and its surrounding settlement until 2008, when the first of several seasons of excavation began.

The plan of the huge fort, the largest in Qatar, revealed three main phases. The earliest was a simple square structure. Subsequently a tower was added on one corner, and later still the fortress was

A solid corner tower on the earliest fort, possibly constructed by the Portuguese in the 16th century.

massively enlarged to eight times its original size. Some years afterwards, it was reduced in size and the walls made much thicker, suggesting that a more defensive structure was required.

The largest fort had a tower on each corner and another one half way along each side. At the time of the construction of the most recent fort the longer walls of the second phase were demolished, leaving towers rather oddly sited a short distance from the corners. One corner tower is large and solid, rather than hollow as is usual, and was intended to support a cannon. The structure would have stood about four metres in height. The archaeologists theorize that the presence of this solid, round tower which could support heavy artillery may be an indication that the earliest fort was built by the Portuguese, as this was a European rather than an Arab fortification technique of the time. If this is true then it will provide the first evidence for the presence of the Portuguese on the Qatar peninsula.

Such a large fort must have protected a sizable population, and remains of buildings stretch along the coast for almost two kilometres, with the fort at the centre. The inhabitants of Al Ruwaida were engaged in fishing, pearl fishing and trading. Rich pearl beds lie only about ten kilometres away, and the remains of stone fish traps can be seen all along the coast. The sea is too shallow for boats to come close to the shore, so a shipping channel was dug, stretching out to sea. Its site is now indicated by the mangroves fringing the shore, which grow much higher in the channel than on either side.

The conglomerate stone known as 'beachrock' which was excavated from the shipping channel was used for the construction of the courtyard houses and other buildings. Limestone, which is plentiful in the area, was another source of building material. A semi-nomadic population would have joined the settlement to engage in fishing or pearling, living in tents or in *barasti* huts, simple wooden frames with walls and roof woven of palm fronds. A photograph taken in Bahrain a century ago shows a cluster of pearl divers' neatly built *barasti* homes, with steeply pitched roofs, clustered around the walls of a fort, and the divers of Al Ruwaida probably lived in something similar.

Two mosques have been located and one excavated, sited beside the beach at the northern end of the settlement. In fact, it is so close to the sea that the ground around it sometimes floods at high tide! Sailors would probably have made the mosque the first place to which they headed to after a voyage, to give thanks for a safe journey. The mosque has been rebuilt five times and its orientation adjusted slightly. On one side are steps which would have led to the *minbar,* from which the *imam* addressed the congregation. It was not inserted into the wall as is usual in later mosques, possibly indicating a date in the early 1700s. Pieces of dry mud imprinted with palm fronds are evidence that the roof was thatched and then coated with mud.

After visiting the mosque sailors may well have headed to the merchants' warehouses, or to the marine workshop which lies a short distance away. The remains of iron rivets and of bitumen, used to coat the outsides of ships, provided clues as to the purpose of this building.

Unlike Al Zubara, which was built on sand and had an inadequate water supply, Al Ruwaida had several wells, one of which has been excavated. The water table lay only a few metres below the surface. The area is so green that the inhabitants of the settlement may even have been able to grow some crops.

A small house in the corner of the courtyard within the fort was excavated and also other dwellings built against the outside of the walls. Small finds areas include fine Chinese ceramics from the 18th century, and colourful red and blue glazed fragments of pottery dating to the late 16th or early 17th century, made in Iran and imitating Turkish ware, which in turn derived its inspiration from Chinese designs. There were fragments of bowls made of a soft stone called chlorite schist or soapstone, and the inevitable pieces of glass paste bangles from India which litter almost every late Islamic site in Qatar, as well as a number of beads of glass and cornelian. There are the remains of clay ovens for baking bread, a ball of daisy coral which was probably used for grating food, a coarse pottery jar with bitumen inside it, and small flat stones pierced for use as fishing weights. The coral does not occur in the Arabian Gulf and must have been brought from some distance.

It is something of a mystery as to why such a large and apparently flourishing settlement should have been suddenly abandoned. Local people interviewed some years ago believed that the inhabitants of Al Ruwaida moved to Al Zubara in the 1760s. One reason may have been the silting up of the bay. Severe epidemics of cholera in the lands surrounding the Arabian Gulf broke out around this time, and if the disease reached Al Ruwaida and decimated the population the survivors may have been too few to continue living there. Whatever the reason, the fort and the village were left to the drifting sand, until the archaeologists arrived.

Excavations have also been carried out on Ras Al Sharig, the small peninsula south of the old town of Zubara, where a scatter of stones drew the attention of archaeologists working at Al Ruwaida. There was little to show on the sandy surface, just a few rocks and some low, wind-weathered mounds.

Above: Cache of Indian silver rupees in a cotton bag hidden in the wall of the fort. Al Rubaiqa.

Below: A large fire pit lined with a re-used storage jar, Al Rubaiqa.

Archaeologists excavating the warehouse complex at Al Ruwaida.

Unusually, the inhabitants of the little village were not fishermen, nor were they fishing for pearls – there are none of the signs that go with these two common coastal occupations. An indication as to the occupation of the villagers is Al Rubaiqa's proximity to deep water and also the remains of a small jetty. Another is the extraordinary number of date presses. Date presses (*madbassa*) are very common in Qatar and occur in almost every Islamic settlement excavated, including the large, early Islamic settlement of Murwab, not far from Al Rubaiqa. A date press consists of a rectangular or square area deeply grooved with parallel channels onto which sacks of dates were piled. The weight of the compressed dates caused the sweet, sticky syrup (*dibs*) to ooze out, which trickled down the channels and into a large jar sunk into the ground to receive it. But a curious fact about the date presses in Al Rubaiqa is that no two are alike. Some, but not all, are coated with fine white gypsum plaster. One press has holes and pits for two collecting jars. And one has such a convoluted maze of collecting channels that the archaeologists have no idea as to the purpose of such an extraordinary structure. It could be that the presses were made by people from other regions with their own way of doing things, or by individual local families each with its own traditional method of constructing a press.

The jetty and the deep water which would allow ships to approach the coast suggest that the inhabitants might have been producing date syrup on a commercial scale. It is not certain where the date plantations were located, but the dates may have been imported from the huge oasis at Al Hasa in Saudi Arabia. The name Al Rubaiqa is recorded in the 1760s, and the earliest pottery found on the site is 16th century 'Julfar ware' from Ras Al Khaimah in the UAE. Middens (refuse mounds associated with occupation) contain ash and layers of detritus including fragments of pottery and animal bone, indicating a long occupation period. Samples have been taken for Carbon 14 dating, and these should yield more definite information as to the age of the site. The ceramic remains indicate a wide trade with other countries: in addition to the

A selection of ceramic sherds made in China, Europe and Persia (Iran) found at Al Rubaiqa and Al Ruwaida.

The base of a small Persian fritware (stone paste) bowl. Early 18th century, Al Ruwaida.

A small Aali ware jug. Al Ruwaida, 18th century.

Julfar ware there are fragments of glazed pottery from China and Burma and pottery from Iraq and Iran. The ceramic tops of shisha – the local 'hubbly-bubbly' pipes – confirm that tobacco was being imported. Al Rubaiqa may have served as an entrepôt, importing goods and selling them to nomadic tribespeople from the interior.

Two areas of buildings were excavated, one of housing and another constituting a large, irregularly shaped walled area, designated a 'fort' by the archaeologists as it appeared to be defensive, with the remains of a single, well-constructed corner tower on the landward, not the seaward side. It had been demolished at some period and the stones removed to be reused, but the solid foundations remain. The fortified area appears to be older than the rest of the settlement.

Embedded in the rubble of the walls of the 'fort' was a large cannon ball! History records many instances of attack along this stretch of coast in the 18th and 19th centuries – some a response to piracy, others for political causes – and the discovery of the cannonball, with another in the courtyard, demonstrates that life was not always peaceful in Al Rubaiqa. Burnt roofing timbers collapsed on top of household objects suggest that the fires occurred suddenly while the buildings were still occupied. A cache of 19 fine quality Indian silver rupees was discovered, wrapped in a cotton bag and stuffed into a crevice in the wall of a mosque. The coins, which bear the head of Queen Victoria on one side, date to the 1860-1880s, but whoever hid their savings never returned to retrieve them.

Other coins found on the site include some from the Ottoman period of the 19th century, along with Iranian coinage, and the first Qatari coins from the 1930s, showing that site was occupied over a long period. In the remains of the mosque, which includes a large open prayer ground and another inner, smaller prayer room, was a fragment of plaster with a verse from the Quran written on it.

The archaeologists excavated right down to bedrock, and there they found a number of pits, presumed to be post-holes for buildings, cut deep into the rock. To cut these must have been a laborious task, and at present their date or purpose is unknown. Further excavations may provide an answer.

History was made at Ras Abrouq

The peninsula of Ras Abrouq, which lies north of Dukhan on the west coast of Qatar, is one of the most beautiful areas of the country. The entrance to it is dramatic: after driving across the featureless gravel plain which occupies the centre of the country, you leave the Doha–Dukhan road and at a large interchange take a newly-surfaced road north. The modern road passes a hospital and schools, but only goes as far as the village of Bir Zekrit. Founded in the 1930s, Zekrit played a minor part in history as the site of the first camp for workers after oil was located. Just beyond it lie the remains of a square fort and traces of its surrounding settlement. Local tradition holds that the fort, which was excavated by a French team in 2003-2005, was built by the famous Rahmah bin Jabir in the first years of the 19th century.

Limestone plateaux and free-standing pillars at Ras Abrouq.

Constructed of beachrock and limestone blocks, plastered with gypsum, the ruins are now rapidly returning to their pre-excavation condition of low sandy mounds.

Soon you enter into a different landscape, suddenly coming upon low, gleaming white cliffs of Miocene limestone, sculpted over aeons of time into strange contours. Besides numerous plateaux, their sides hollowed by the wind and topped by a harder layer of sand and gravel known to geologists as the Hofuf formation, there are many free-standing mushroom-shaped pillars. Here and there the limestone is pierced with arches, worn by relentless wind-blown sand over the millennia. Further into the peninsula a large, natural oasis lies in a shallow depression, sheltered on one side by a limestone plateau. It is always green, even after months without rain, and when it does rain a carpet of fresh green grass covers the ground within days. Bitter gourd vines trail their tennis-ball-sized fruits over the sand, which in the spring months is starred with small yellow flowers. Thorny bushes and trees used to surround an ancient well next to a group of tall date palms, but the well has now been filled in and a shallow, concrete-lined drinking pool was provided for a small herd of sand gazelle which were released a few years ago at the oasis.

Numerous remains left by the ancient inhabitants of Qatar have been found throughout the Abrouq peninsula. Between about 6000 and 3500 BCE a semi-nomadic population survived here by

Limestone plateaux by the coast at Ras Abrouq.

hunting, fishing and gathering shellfish and wild grains and fruits, besides herding sheep and cattle. Their flint tools still litter the ground, and dark, ashy patches on the plateau still mark the remains of their cooking fires. Pottery known as 'Ubaid ware' was imported, fragments of which survive on a few coastal sites.

In 2008 the first Danish expedition to work in Qatar for four decades arrived to excavate a site in the oasis first located by a British team led by Beatrice de Cardi in the early '70s. Beneath an Islamic layer the excavations revealed remains dating to the Bronze Age, with evidence of a structure built of large stone blocks and associated red-ridged pottery from Bahrain, known as Barbar ware. Lower still lay shards of Ubaid pottery dating to the late 6th millennium BCE.

Fine-quality Ubaid pottery, some of which is distinguished by elegant painted designs, predominantly geometric, was traded from Mesopotamia as far south as islands off the coast of Abu Dhabi, and has also been found in Iran. All the sites on which Ubaid pottery has been found so far are coastal, and the pottery was almost certainly brought from Mesopotamia by sea. Some archaeologists suggest that sites where remains of this pottery have been discovered provide evidence for the earliest known international trade; others believe that they represent sailors and fishermen from Mesopotamia travelling along the Gulf to exploit local resources such as pearls or particular species of fish.

Much later came the tent-dwelling pastoralists, the ancestors of the bedouin, moving through the area with their flocks of animals in search of water and pasture. There is little evidence of permanent housing anywhere on the Abrouq peninsula, with the exception of a small, fish-processing complex on the coast, dating to the early centuries CE, and the recent village at Zekrit and older fort and small settlement. The Gulf War in 1990-1991 resulted in the construction of some temporary military installations, while a coastguard station was erected some years ago near the northern end of the little peninsula.

For decades, the lonely peninsula lay almost deserted. Then, suddenly, everything changed. In 2001 hordes of picturesquely-dressed warriors mounted on Arab steeds charged across the landscape, their swords glittering in the sunlight. A village came under sudden attack, and before long the palm-thatched roofs of the huts were ablaze. Sleepy Abrouq had certainly never seen so much activity in the eight millennia since human beings first entered the peninsula. A flashback in time? Ghosts from the past? Not at all – Qatar Television was making a film!

The film, which was eventually broadcast as a long-running series, was entitled *Eial al Deeb: The Sons of the Wolf*. It was by far the most ambitious project ever undertaken by QTV, with a budget more than twice as large as for any other previously-made films. Actors, actresses, cameramen and technicians were drawn not only from Qatar but also from Kuwait, Jordan and Syria. The expert horsemen were recruited from Bahrain as well as Qatar, and several hundred soldiers were brought in to take part in lively battle scenes.

Painted pottery vessel from the Ubaid period, Marawah, UAE.

Loosely based on historical fact, the story was set in Qatar some four to five hundred years ago. Much of the plot centred on the inter-relationships of the families within a little town, soap-opera style, with some breathtaking action scenes to liven up the story. Hayat Al-Fahad, the well-known Kuwaiti actress, was one of those who played a star part in the film.

Three film sets were constructed: a group of thatched circular stone huts in a ravine encircled by a horseshoe of steep limestone cliffs, occupied by the 'enemy', a tented encampment on the coast, and a superb 'mini-town' on the northern side of the Abrouq oasis. It is a cleverly-designed conglomerate of recognisable features of traditional Gulf architecture: houses, minarets, wind-towers, *majlis*es and enclosed courtyards jostle together in a fashion which might look a little odd in real life but is ideal as a film-set. The effect of this rich architectural collection painted a pleasing honey-colour in an arid landscape which has never previously seen any construction at all, is surreal.

Nowadays the set, nicknamed 'Film City', makes a pleasant focus for weekend visitors to Ras Abrouq. The tented village has gone, and the thatched huts were set alight during the filming of an attack, so all that remains are the curious round stone-walled structures around the ravine. One of them is perched high on a giant mushroom of limestone, up which a stairway (now collapsed) had to be constructed. The traditional mini-town is kept under repair, and the caretaker allows visitors through the gate to take a look around and climb to the roofs of the buildings for a view of the landscape.

Given the extremely delicate and fragile nature of the unique landscape of Ras Abrouq, there were, inevitably, concerns as to the long-term impact all this construction and activity would have on the environment. QTV personnel were keenly aware of the problems of possible damage and sought advice from senior officials from the Supreme Council (now a Ministry) for the Environment and Natural Reserves.

Once filming was finished, the landscape was restored to its original state. Removing the thick, black carbon deposits from the limestone cliffs behind the fired village – the fires were fuelled with car tyres soaked in diesel – was a major exercise. But all was left as clean as before filming began. There was even a bonus that resulted from the filming – the cleaning up of the oasis. This beautiful area was, sadly,

often littered with rubbish left by careless campers and picnickers. Before filming, every last piece of trash was carefully collected from the landscape. Even car tyre marks had to be carefully swept out with a palm leaf brush before filming could begin. It would hardly do for a set of tracks, a cigarette butt or a soft drink can to appear in scenes that were supposed to be taking place five hundred years ago! Now the oasis is surrounded by a light fence to keep out vehicles, and the only tracks are the delicate hoof prints of the sand gazelle which wander to and from their drinking pool. It is a heartening example of how simple, inexpensive repairs to a damaged landscape have greatly improved it as an amenity for all who visit Ras Abrouq – one that, hopefully, will be followed in other parts of Qatar.

The film set of Eial al Deeb: The Sons of the Wolf.

Seeking the Angels' Teardrops

For thousands of years divers worked in exhausting conditions in the waters of the Arabian Gulf, seeking ornaments for the crowns and robes of kings and noblemen and women. Through the suffering of these humble men was born incredible shining beauty, the lustre of natural pearls.

Gulf pearls are found in two species of shellfish: *Pinctada radiata* and *Pinctada margaritifera*. An oyster shell is a casing consisting of several layers of hard material that grows along with the oyster. Inside the shell is a soft layer, the mantle. The outer layer of the mantle produces the hard material for the shell, and repairs the shell if it gets damaged. Under this is a layer that plays a vital role in enclosing and protecting the organs of the animal, and within it is another thin layer of tissue.

Shellfish such as oysters have many enemies. Predators such as parrotfish, sponges, crabs, worms, even other shellfish, all try to break into their shells. Some crush the shell or dissolve it with acid, others simply bore a hole, or enter through the mollusc's weakest point near the hinge that joins the two halves of the shell together.

If a small intruder succeeds in getting inside, the shellfish simply suffocates it by covering it with a pearly material called nacre. This cements the intruder to the shell, where it forms what is known as a 'blister' pearl.

Free-moving pearls occur when the cells from the outer layer of the mantle migrate into the internal cavity of the shell. Several things may trigger this movement. It might be an injury

An Arabian Gulf pearl oyster and pearl.

such as a bite from a fish, or a reaction to the intrusion of a predator or a parasite. The cells are genetically programmed to build the shell. Once they are displaced and get into the interior of the shellfish, they continue doing just that – producing shelly material. The cells come together to form a pocket known as a 'pearl sack', and around this nucleus the pearl gradually develops over a period of between three and seven years. Left to itself, the shellfish will eventually try to eject the pearl, which causes it discomfort.

Nacre is composed of hexagonal platelets of aragonite (a form of calcium carbonate) arranged in layers. The overlapping platelets of aragonite on the surface reflect different wavelengths of lights at different viewing angles, and this gives the pearls their characteristic lustre. Pearls come in many colours, ranging from creamy white to golden yellow or rosy pink, through to deep grey and gun-metal blue, known as black in the trade.

The simple process whereby pearls are formed was not understood until recently, and legends attempted to explain the seemingly miraculous appearance of pearls in oysters. They were said to be the teardrops of angels, or drops of rain which the oysters rose to the surface of the sea at night and opened their shells to receive. Until very recently, it was thought that they were formed by a grain of grit or sand acting as an irritant to the soft body of the oyster. But a shellfish is quite capable of squirting a grain of sand out of its shell without any problems. Oyster beds (*hayr*) are located in greater numbers on the Arabian coast of the Gulf than on the Iranian side, probably due to the shallower depths on the western coast, combined with sediments more suited to oyster growth.

The history of pearling in the Arabian Gulf goes back some 7,000 years, to the period of the New Stone Age, when man first occupied the eastern coast of the Arabian peninsula. Some of the oldest pearls yet identified have been found at sites dating to the 6th-5th millennium BCE, which were created by herding, fishing, hunting and gathering communities, generally referred to under the term 'Arabian Neolithic'. A pierced pearl from this period has been found in Kuwait, and other pearls are associated with burials in the United Arab Emirates, at a coastal site in Umm Al Quwain and an inland site in Sharjah.

In addition to pearls, mother-of-pearl artefacts were also found at some of these sites. Undoubtedly, these resulted from deliberate pearl fishing, rather than accidental acquisition during food-gathering activities. The discovery of huge middens of oyster shells at a site in eastern Saudi Arabia, together with microlithic drills used to pierce the shells and pearls, indicate an established industry, which may well have been the basis for trading with other communities.

There is a reference to 'fish-eyes' being imported into the Mesopotamian city of Ur in the early 2nd millennium BCE. This unlovely name may be a reference to pearls: when a fish is cooked its eye is circular, white and opaque. However, some authorities think the reference may have been to polished, banded stones. Later in the millennium a scribe recorded on clay tablets the legend of the semi-mythical hero king Gilgamesh and his search for immortality. Following directions from Utu-nipishtim, the Babylonian counterpart of Noah, Gilgamesh attached stones to his feet and dived into the sea to find the 'flower of immortality.' This technique is strongly associated with ancient pearl diving.

Some scholars consider that the magical 'flower' could have been a pearl, which had associations with the concept of eternal life. The quest was centred in Dilmun, the Bronze Age trading empire that extended from its focal point in Bahrain to Qatar and up the eastern coast as far as Kuwait.

The first unequivocal reference to pearling does not occur until the 1st century CE, after which references to pearling and pearls in the Gulf become more frequent. By this time pearling was an established industry in the Gulf, supplying the Roman market and later the ruling élite of the Byzantine, Persian and Early Islamic periods. The Roman writer Pliny, identified Tylos (Bahrain) as a specific locality associated with pearling. Pre-Islamic Arabic poets refer to pearl-diving and the dangers faced by the divers. In the 7th century, the beauty of pearls is referred to in the Holy Quran, where they are associated with Paradise.

Very early on, Bahrain became established as a leading pearling centre. The traveller Ibn Battuta, writing in the 14th century CE, said that boats with divers and merchants from Bahrain fished the banks in April and May. In the following century there is a reference to 1,000 pearling ships from Bahrain. Another important centre was Julfar, north of the modern town of Ras Al Khaimah in the Emirates.

Both these places had established populations, with good water supplies and a high agricultural input. Julfar was nearly 300 km from the pearl banks (hayr) in the middle of the lower Gulf and over 400 km from the dense pearl banks off the coast of Qatar. There is no reference to Qatar as a pearling centre at this time and it would seem that centres for the trade were not necessarily those closest to the pearl banks. Instead, the industry was dominated by coastal areas, which had large enough populations and resources to equip sizeable pearling fleets.

Brass sieves used by merchants to sort the pearls into groups of different sizes.

Divers about to descend.

The saibs (haulers) waiting to pull the divers to the surface.

The north coast of Qatar has the advantage of being located in proximity to the pearl banks. The Iraqi historian Al Masudi, writing in the 10th century CE, records that its waters were renowned for being rich in pearls. However, the population of Qatar at this time was not large enough to supply a major industry and significant pearling centres did not emerge on the peninsula until the 18th century.

The earliest centre associated with the pearling industry in Qatar was Al Huwaila on the north-eastern coast, which appears as Huali on the Niebuhr map of 1765 of the Arabian Gulf (see page 88). Now a ruined site, which remains largely unexcavated,

it was clearly a town of considerable importance from the 17th to the 19th centuries, judging by the extent of the ruined buildings and the variety of surface pottery. Another centre may have been at Al Ruwaida on the north-western coast, where a large fort dominates two areas of settlement. But from the mid-18th century onwards both these centres were eclipsed by the great pearling and trading port of Al Zubara, which rapidly increased in size and importance after the Al Khalifah clan settled there in 1766. The town, which frequently came under attack, was surrounded by walls and guarded by Al Murair fort, constructed in 1768 and linked to the sea the following year by a two-kilometre-long canal.

Besides the pearl oysters, another species, *Pteria macroptera*, smaller than *Pinctada margaritifera*, was gathered for mother-of-pearl. During excavations at Al Zubara, a pile of oyster shells the size of dinner plates was uncovered, stashed in the corner of a courtyard where presumably they were awaiting export. Until World War I, Germany was the principal importer of mother-of-pearl from the Arabian Gulf.

Contemporary pearling centres founded in the 18th century were Kuwait City (1710) and Abu Dhabi (1761). Unlike Al Zubara, no previous centres had existed there locally.

Al Zubara, Kuwait City and Abu Dhabi are all located in areas where an inadequate water supply and little potential for growing food crops had limited previous settlement and expansion. This indicates that, unlike the much earlier settlement at Julfar in the northern UAE, fresh water and an agricultural hinterland were no longer essential for a pearling centre to develop. All the new centres had to import water and food to supply their growing populations.

In 1810 a British naval captain, John Wainwright, reported of the Arabian coast that, 'Along its whole extent a valuable Pearl Fishery is carried on by the Arabs,' and many of the older pearling centres continued to flourish, headed by Bahrain. Other centres were at Dubai, Sharjah, Ajman and Umm Al Quwain. From the 18th century onwards, the families which controlled the pearl trade became established as local rulers. They were the Al Khalifah of Bahrain, the Al Thani of Qatar, the Al Nahyan of Abu Dhabi and the Al Makhtoum of Dubai, all of whom retain power to the present day. In 1863 a British traveller, William G Palgrave, spent some days in Qatar. Seeing the numerous forts and towers scattered around the landscape, he observed that although the land outwardly seemed barren and poor, 'Katar has wealth in plenty, and there are robbers against whom that wealth must be guarded.' He visited Al Bida'a (now the heart of modern Doha) as the guest of Sheikh Mohammed bin Thani, the founder of the ruling dynasty, who remarked to him, 'We are all, from the highest to the lowest, slaves of one master, Pearl.' All thought, all conversation, all employment turned on that one subject, commented Palgrave, and he describes the long lines of black boats drawn up upon the shore and the careworn appearance of the men

inhabiting Al Bida'a, who spend 'the one half of the year in search of pearls, the other half in fishery or trade.'

The following year Col. Lewis Pelly, in his brief study of the pearling industry, explained that, 'The beds along the Arabian coast are held to be the property of the Arabs in common… an Arab of Kuwait may dive along the Bahrain or Ras Al Khaimah coast and vice-versa. But no person other than the coastal Arabs is considered to have any right of diving.' He estimated that there were between 4,000 and 5,000 boats engaged in pearling along the Arabian coast, each boat containing from 10 to 32 men.

Diving occurred in the months when the warm water allowed repeated immersion. The diving season was divided into three. First came a 40-day 'cold dive' period beginning in the middle of April, called *ghaus al barid* in some regions but known in Qatar as *al khanjiyah*, followed by *ghaus al khabir* (local name: *al-oad*), a long, gruelling stint from the end of May until the second week of September, and finally *al raddah*, 'the return', a three-week period at the end of September and the beginning of October. Between these events there were breaks to allow the pearl-fishers to return to their home ports to re-provision and rest.

During bad weather the ships would sometimes make for the nearest shelter. The waterless Halul Island, situated 90 km off the coast of Qatar and adjacent to some of the best pearling banks, was often used as a haven by the pearl-fishers.

Pearls were also gathered in the winter, in a practice called *mujannah*, which involved wading and gathering oysters from the shallow coastal waters.

During the long periods when almost all the able-bodied men in Qatar were away at sea, their wives assumed the responsibilities of the head of the household, in charge of family finances and the care of children, the sick and the elderly. When they returned from the pearl banks the pearl-fishers handed over their earnings to their wives, if any remained after paying off their debts. It is evident that women at this time held an important role within the coastal communities.

Some pearl fishermen would spend as much as six unbroken months at sea, having taken out a loan from the boat owners to buy provisions for their

A pearl merchant's chest containing all the equipment needed for sorting, weighing and valuing pearls.

A collection of Gulf pearls on red velvet bag

families. An initial loan was usually paid in Indian rupees, the common currency at the time, and was known as *teskam*.

Each ship carried a captain (*nakhuda*), usually a man with a lifetime's experience of fishing for pearls who could locate the best pearl beds without the aid of maps, relying on the observation of stars, currents and the state of the surface of the sea. The depth at which an oyster bed lay was measured by means of a *bild*: a large piece of lead at the end of a rope which was smeared with grease and thrown into the water. The mud or sand which stuck to the lead yielded information about the state of the sea-bed.

The pearl divers (*ghais*) might be either free men or slaves. A diver's puller, who hauled him up from the sea-bed, was called a *saib*. A trainee diver was known as a *radif*. Boys (*tabbab*) as young as nine or ten came along on the trips, to learn the secrets of pearl-fishing from their elders. Their job was to catch fish, help with the cooking, and make the coffee. One old diver recalled that he learned to swim at this age when his father tied a rope around him and threw him off the side of the ship!

The *nakhuda* would announce the date of departure to the assembled men, after which those who wished to dive would step forward. They were then given an advance payment. On the day of departure (*al daasha*) the whole community turned out with songs and dances to bid their men farewell, and the *nakhuda* would sometimes hand out small gifts of money to the divers' families, which was thought to bring good luck.

Music, including singing and dancing and the playing of percussion instruments such as the drum (*tabr*) was an important activity on board, as a moral-booster and a distraction from the harsh and often dangerous working conditions. The lead singer was known as the *nahham*. A visitor to the pearling *dhow*s wrote that, 'the singing, clapping and beating of rhythms never stops from dawn until sleeping time.' Before deciding which pearling boat they would join for a season, divers would make enquiries about the *nahham*. A singer with a good reputation helped to ensure an enthusiastic crew.

In good weather, the average diver made between ten and fifty dives per day, depending on his stamina. But exceptional divers were reputed to make as many as ninety dives. The depth of the dives averaged from 12-15 metres, but could be even greater. Some boats anchored on one pearl bank and stayed there the whole season; others moved from bank to bank.

The divers prepared themselves each early morning by fixing pincers of turtle-shell (*futam*) to their noses, plugging their ears with wax, and donning leather finger stalls (*khabat*) for protection from sharp shells and venomous fish. Cotton suits provided protection against jellyfish stings, and some divers believed that they helped guard against shark attack. Attacks were always more likely to happen towards the end of the season, when sharks had overcome their natural fear of humans and had become accustomed to food scraps being thrown overboard.

When ready, the diver placed his foot in the loop of a rope to which were attached lead or stone weights, and dropped to the sea bed. There he collected the oysters into a bag (*dayeen*) hung around his neck or attached to his waist. When he could no longer hold his breath he gave the rope a tug to signal to his waiting puller to haul him up.

The usual method of retrieving the pearls was to leave the shellfish piled on the deck overnight to weaken and die, before prising them open with a sharp knife (*meflaka*). If a man found a pearl he lodged it between his toes. When the task ended the captain would retrieve the pearls. The shells, which often had tiny developing oysters attached to them, were then thrown back into the sea as 'nourishment' for the oyster beds.

This was the practice in the Arabian Gulf, but in other parts of Asia the oysters were taken to shore before opening.

A weight with rope loop used by pearl divers.

Excavations in 1981 and 2000 on a small island off the coast of Qatar revealed large shallow pits littered with fragments of oyster shell, dating to the 14th century CE. These may be evidence for an alternative method of retrieving pearls. Two large pierced stones which may have been divers' weights were also retrieved at the site.

Opening the oysters in the morning.

Divers and crew lived on a simple diet of dates, fish and rice, with dried limes to ward off scurvy. Working divers generally ate very little, to preserve their lean and wiry physique. Before the season began, some divers visited traditional healers, who would bleed them (*al hajamha*) using a glass cone. Divers often suffered from respiratory and ear problems and a popular form of treatment was cauterization with a hot iron (*al kaye*).

In the evening after a day's dive the crews of different ships visited each other to exchange news and drink coffee. Ships belonging to feuding tribes would peacefully anchor side by side, as there was an agreement not to quarrel during the season.

Buyers (*tawwash*) used to visit the fleet and go from boat to boat, bargaining for the catch. The name comes from that of the small rowing boat, also called a *tawwash*, which the buyers employed to get around the pearl fleet when it was anchored on the pearl banks. Another smaller boat called a *huri*, or a dug-out canoe known as a *ket*, was also used. However, sometimes the pearls were returned to land before being sold. In 1866 Col. Lewis Pelly, the British Political Resident in the Gulf, made a study of the pearling industry and recorded that pearls of yellowish hue were exported to Bombay (now Mumbai) whereas the Baghdad market preferred pure white pearls, including seed pearls.

Before bargaining began the pearls, which were kept in a red cloth bag, were graded for size by being passed through a series of circular copper or brass sieves with holes of various dimensions. The largest were known as *ras*, then came *batn*, in the third sieve, *zayl* and finally, *ruweiba*. The seed pearls which passed through the smallest sieve were known as *alsahtat*. Pearls were then further classified according to their quality, shape and colour. Those not perfectly spherical were called *barouque*. An expert could sometimes tell if a misshapen pearl contained a perfect one, and could peel off outer layers to reveal its beauty.

At the end of the season (*gaffal*), the money from the sale of the pearls was divided between the *nakhuda* and the crew according to a prearranged ratio. The *nakhuda* himself usually borrowed money from a businessman (*musaqqam*) at the beginning of the season to pay for provisions on board and give loans to the divers. The divers in their turn were often in debt to the *nakhuda*, who charged them high interest on the loans. After a poor season it often happened that a captain could not pay off his own debts, and so had to sell the entire harvest of pearls to the *musaqqam* at 20% below market value. A diver who did not earn enough to pay off his debts had to continue working, sometimes for years. Debts were passed on to a man's sons when he died until, in the 20th century, some states passed laws to end the practice. The system of debt-slavery was endemic throughout the Gulf region. It has been said to be less common in Qatar because many of the divers returned to a semi-nomadic existence at the end of the season, so that it was difficult to trace them, but there is no real evidence for this.

All kinds of boats were used for pearling: the most common were the big *baghlah* and *battil*, but *boum*, *sanbuq* and smaller vessels were also employed. The generic term in use in Qatar for a pearling boat with oars and sails was *ghawwas*. The oldest boat surviving in Qatar is a *jalbut*, which was still in use as a pearling boat in the 1940s and is preserved at the National Museum. Some were built in the boatyards (*wushar*) of Doha and Al Wakra, others were ordered from the UAE. While on the banks the pearling fleets had to be guarded against piracy, and large, well-armed ships patrolled the fleet to give protection.

In 1900, among the principal pearl merchants of Qatar besides the sons of Mohammed Al Thani, were members of the Al Sulaiti, the Al Khulaifi and the Al Attiyah families, and also the Al Mohannadi of Al Khor and the Al Khater family of Al Wakra.

The businessman, Hussein Alfardan, whose father was a pearl merchant, is today internationally regarded as a leading authority on natural pearls. Until 1990 the house of Al Haj Mohammed Al Majid, with an upstairs room overlooking the sea, still stood in Al Wakra: here the returning divers entered directly from the shore, to collect their salaries and repay any money they owed. Other merchants would gather to inspect and bargain for the season's harvest.

By the end of the 19th century, the demand for pearls was global. The British Empire was an insatiable market for pearls and the markets of Europe and the USA also fuelled the boom. During the first two decades of the 20th century New York became the second biggest market for Gulf pearls after Bombay. In 1907 J G Lorimer in his *Gazetteer of the Persian Gulf*, recorded that over 800 pearling ships sailed from 11 coastal towns in Qatar, the largest number (350) from Doha, with the majority of the adult male population engaged in pearling. But within three decades the industry had received its death blows, first from the recession following the First World War, culminating in the Wall Street Crash of 1929, which coincided with the development of the cultured pearl in Japan. Experts say they can easily differentiate between a cultured and a natural pearl, but the average customer cannot, and few were willing to pay the higher price for wild pearls, particularly at a time of financial depression in Europe and the States. The Second World War meant that less money was available in the West for luxury goods, and the trade suffered a further setback in 1947, when the Indian sub-continent gained independence from British rule. The spending power of the maharajahs, who had long been among the Gulf pearling industry's highest-spending clients, was curtailed.

The combination of these factors was a major setback for the economy of the entire Gulf region. Two decades of severe hardship, during which many families emigrated from Qatar, were to follow, before the fortuitous discovery of oil changed the country's future. Many of the finest pearl banks now lie directly beneath the oil rigs.

A few boats still continued to fish for pearls until the early 1950s. A retired diver, Jassim bin Qroun Ibrahim Al Dosari, in an interview published in 1984, recalled, 'It was a very difficult period. Of the dozens of craft which used to go out in search of pearls all but a few lay idle in the harbour, and the boat I had been working on was broken up and used for firewood.' But a few years later, divers who had been earning 60 rupees for six months' work were earning 25 rupees a month working in the growing oil industry. The days of bitter toil and hardship were over.

In conversation with an old pearl diver a former British ambassador to Qatar once referred, rather naively, to the 'good old days'. Fixing the diplomat with a look of withering disdain the old man responded, 'For you, young man, half an hour then would be like a lifetime of hell.'

Traditional Boats

The people of Qatar have been seafarers for countless centuries. Pearling, fishing and trading by sea were, before the advent of the oil era, vital to the existence of all the peoples whose lands bordered the Arabian Gulf. Along with their neighbours, Qataris were accomplished boat builders, creating their wooden craft from imported timber.

There were many different types of vessel, known collectively to Europeans by the generic term *dhow*. Unlike European ships and boats, which are classified according to their rigging, Arabian boats are distinguished by the shape of their hull. At one time there were some 80 names and sub-names of *dhows* in the Arabian Gulf and Oman, but only about six of these are still active today.

The most common fishing craft of the northern Gulf were the *sanbuq*, *shu'i*, *jalbut* and *badan*. The *sanbuq* and the *shu'i* are still in use today. The *shu'i*, distinguished by its simple and elegant lines, is now the universal fishing *dhow* of the Arabian Gulf and Oman.

Inshore fishing involved fishing with both nets and handlines, and inspecting the dome shaped fish traps called *gargoor*, formerly woven from strips of bamboo but nowadays made of steel mesh. For inshore fishing and for travelling short distances along the coast from one village to another, the *huri* and the *shasha* were in use until a few years ago. The former were small wooden sailing vessels, while the latter were of a very ancient design, made from bundles of palm-leaf spines lashed together with rope made from beaten date palm stalks. They had cross-pieces made from Zizyphus or Acacia wood. These little craft were cheap and easy to manufacture and a fisherman usually had at least two, as they were not waterproofed and when the palm stems in one became waterlogged he would return it to the beach to dry out. Although fragile, their flexibility allowed them to ride heavy surf with ease. A *shasha* could carry two to four men and usually had two wooden oars, one located in the middle and one at the back.

The *shasha* is no longer manufactured in Qatar, but in Fujairah, UAE, there was until recently a builder of these simple craft. He said that he obtained 90% of the material for building them from the date palm and the wood for the cross pieces from trees growing in the mountains. However, nylon rope replaced the traditional date palm stalk rope, and styrofoam blocks provided buoyancy instead of the sections of

A pearling dhow *leaving harbour.*

date palm stem that was formerly used. Building a *shasha* took the master and his assistants five or six hours, provided all the materials had been prepared beforehand.

Sanbuq, *shu'i* and *jalbut* also served as trading vessels and cargo carriers, but for many years they were the Gulf pearling vessels and turned the area into one of vibrant commercial activity. A *jalbut* is one of the *dhow*s in the care of the National Museum and was still in use as a pearling vessel until the 1950s.

The *sanbuq* has a high, square stern rather like the shape of a shield, which is embellished with flower and petal carvings. Some have blue and white decorations. They have a short keel, which old Qatari boat builders said was suitable for use in the shallow waters where the oyster beds were located. It also made the boat more manoeuvrable with oars. Some types of *sanbuq* were double-ended, and Bahrainis were renowned for manufacturing these.

Shu'i, referred to by Gulf seamen as the sister of the *sanbuq*, are almost identical, the difference being the shape of the stemhead: the *shu'i* has a straight stem (the main upright timber at the bow of the ship) ending in a double curve while the *sanbuq's* stem is cut off in a single concave curve. The tip of the *shu'i's* stemhead is usually painted blue. The stern has projecting strakes, which nowadays are often used to hold a platform on which fish traps can be carried.

Until the 1950s the *baggara* or *baqqarah* was used for pearl diving as well as for fishing and transporting goods. It was from 30 to 60 feet long and carried a cargo of between 10 and 30 tons. Another vessel much in use in days gone by was the *shahuf*, a fishing craft with a pointed stemhead and a long upright sternpost. A carving of a *shahuf* at the petroglyph site at Jebel Al Jassasiya shows the main features of this craft but without its rudder and mast. Today the *shahuf* is used for fishing with both lines and nets, but formerly it was also sometimes in use as a pearl-diving vessel.

Another large vessel was the *baghlah*, a stately craft which measured up to 135 feet in length, with its stem curved and topped with a distinctive rounded figure-head. The largest and most ornate of all the *dhow*s, it was rigged with two or three masts and had a low bow. A light superstructure attached

Illustrations from the Dhow Festival, Qatar, 2013.

Above:, a shu'i, *below a* boum *and bottom, a* sanbuq.

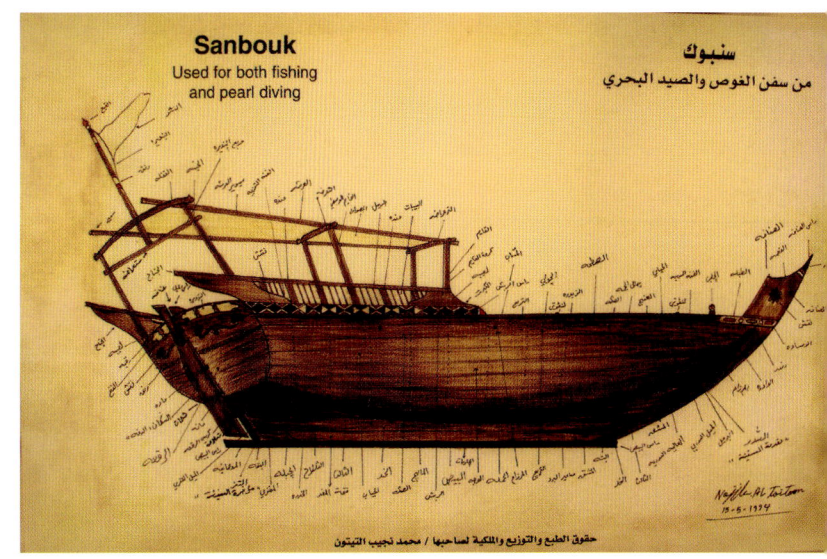

tothe stern served as living quarters for the captain and his family and some elite passengers. It is believed that the *baghlah* came into use in the beginning of the 17th century after Arab sailors visited the shipbuilding yards of the English East India Company in Bombay.

The *baghlah* was the traditional ocean-going vessel of the Gulf until supplanted towards the middle of the 20th century by the *boum*, many of which can still be seen in the local harbours. Its richly carved transom stern was decorated with elaborate foliar scrolls and arabesques and pierced with five windows, a design influenced by that of the Portuguese ships that came to the Gulf in the 16th century. Again, an example can be seen among the Jebel Al Jassasiya petroglyphs. The world's largest wooden sailing vessel is a *baghlah* built in Kuwait in 1998-9 as a floating hotel, the magnificent 'Al Hashemi II'. It has a length of over 269 feet and weighs 600 tons. In Qatar, the largest locally-built wooden *dhow* is currently a 90 feet long *battil*, constructed by the master builder Yousef Al Majid in the 1990s.

In former days *battils* were operated as pirate ships, coastal trading vessels and occasionally as pearling vessels. They were renowned for their speed. This made them popular long ago among slave traders, who often had to defend themselves against aggressors or escape patrol boats endeavouring to put a stop to the trade. A double-ended craft, the *battil* had a long, overhanging fiddle-headed bow, a high sternpost and double, forward-leaning masts. From the keel the after part rose up to form a thin stern-board, towering over the poop. A linear carving of a *battil* at Jebel Al Jassasiya shows clear

The earliest photograph of Doha, with pearling dhows drawn up on the shore, taken by a German traveller in 1904. A visitor to Doha in 1863 described 'line on line of huge black boats whose grooved edges showed where the divers' cords had been let down.'

evidence of this type of *dhow*, with seven round-bladed oars on one side and the characteristic bow and stern with the rudder in place. The carving depicts both a triangular and a lateen sail, which were possibly used in combination for different wind directions.

Because of their enormous size, *baghlah*s were very expensive to build and craftsmen sufficiently skilled to construct vessels of this size were becoming hard to find. They gradually became replaced, therefore, by *boum*s, and several examples of these can be seen at the jetties along the Corniche in Doha, and at Al Wakra, Al Khor and Al Ruwais. One of the finest ships in the maritime history of the Gulf, the *boum* is distinguished by its sharp, straight-pointed stemhead which is usually painted black and white. Though mainly used for trading, *boum*s were also used for pearl diving. In the days of sail they had two masts; the main mast was raked forward and the mizzen mast was vertical.

Although *boum*s were, in general, smaller than the *baghlah* they replaced, they were cost effective as they were lighter, with better cargo space. Their pointed sterns made them much faster ocean-going vessels.

Before World War II, some ocean-going *boum*s weighed as much as 400 tons and carried six sails, with a crew of 40 men. But the most common type of *boum* ranged in weight from 60 to 200 tons, with the length varying from 36 to 120 feet. They were frequently used to carry mangrove wood from East Africa and teak from India. Some transported rocks or stone, cement and even trucks to Gulf ports. They were also equipped with tanks to transport water, and in the pre-oil era many *boum*s were in use carrying water from Bahrain, which had a plentiful supply owing to its many natural springs, to thirsty Qatar. The *boum* is believed by some authorities to have derived its hull shape from the pre-Portuguese period, as there are marked similarities to medieval

illustrations of ships. A feature of the medieval ships is also the high, straight bow angled at 45 degrees, which is such an eye-catching feature of the modern *dhow*.

The shift from sail to engine power took place in the early 1950s, although some boats had engines much earlier than this and one Bahraini pearl merchant had an engine fitted to his boat as long ago as 1927! Although sails were replaced with engines the traditional shapes of the *dhow*s were retained. The awe-inspiring sight of a fleet of ships under full sail, setting out for the pearling banks, is now, alas, a thing of the past.

The change from wooden to fibreglass hulls is more recent, but some boat owners still prefer the traditional wooden hulls. Both have their advantages and drawbacks. Fibreglass *dhow*s are built up, layer by layer, inside a wooden mould. They lack the beauty and grace of wooden *dhow*s, but are economical to construct, since several *dhow*s can be made successively in the same mould. Fibreglass boats ride higher in the water, since there is no timber to be saturated, and require less maintenance. But if anything goes wrong and the *dhow* is damaged it is more complicated and expensive to repair than a wooden vessel. So it seems that the days of the wooden *dhow* are not yet over and, hopefully, they will continue to be built in Qatar for years to come.

Stern of the Hashemi II *in Kuwait, the largest wooden sailing vessel in the world.*

Fine examples of many of the above-named craft, from large pearling vessels down to the humble *shasha*, can be seen at the private museum of Sheikh Faisal bin Qassim bin Faisal Al Thani at Al Sheehaniya, which is open to the public by appointment. A comprehensive collection of traditional wooden ships will also be on display once the new National Museum opens.

Below: a large, ocean-going trading battil *built in Doha in 1992.*

Traditional Boat Building

Until the mid-20th century, boat-building yards flourished up and down the Gulf. Although many of these have now closed, the building of *dhow*s is still a living tradition. It is one of the most evocative images of the past, but is now having to survive against the onslaught of modern technology. Within a couple of generations, boats that were once widely in use have now become objects to be displayed in 'heritage' museums, along with the tools used in their manufacture.

Of all the craftsmen once associated with *dhow* building, only the master builder survives. The craftsmen with whom he would once have discussed the building of a new *dhow* and its various requirements: the blacksmith, ropemaker, flax spinner, weaver and sailmaker, are long gone, and only the *dhow* builder is left to hold together

A boat builder working with simple tools.

the art of building a *dhow*. Although it still survives in Qatar and traditional *dhow*s can be repaired here in a boatyard, the centre of *dhow* building is concentrated in the UAE and buyers from Saudi Arabia, Bahrain, Kuwait and Qatar now travel to the small Emirate of Ajman where the most extensive yards are to be found. The majority of the *dhow*s ordered are *shu'i*, used for fishing. A few *dhow*s are built in each of the other Emirates, with the largest boats being constructed in Dubai. The owners of the yards are nationals, but their workforce comes entirely from India, where there is also a very long tradition of building wooden boats.

Until the advent of the Portuguese in 1488, ships were constructed from hewn planks, fastened together with coconut-fibre cord held in place by wooden pegs. Later, iron-nailed framing was used in the hulls. The ancient Gulf craft were always double-ended, with a pointed stern, and would have carried a steering oar mounted close to the sternpost. Before the square stern was introduced, the earliest rudders were detachable and steered by ropes. The advantage was that the rudder could easily be unshipped if the boat was drawn up on a beach. They required a high stern post, which survived as a feature of boats such as *battil*s. Gradually, square-sterned boats with conventional tiller-steered rudders came into use, influenced by the design of Portuguese and Dutch vessels of the 15th and 16th centuries with their high, elaborately carved sterns.

One of the last 'sewn' boats to be constructed in this region was in Oman in the early 1980s, when the adventurer Tim Severin re-created the kind of vessel Sindbad the Sailor might have used, and sailed it to China. The boat, a *boum* named *Sohar*, belongs to the government of Oman and is on display on the roundabout near the Albustan Hotel in Muscat. More recently, in a joint effort by the governments of Oman and Singapore, a sewn *dhow* was built as a replica of the 9th century shipwrecked Arab trading vessel found off the island of Belitung in Indonesia, the remains of which had been preserved under sediment. The *dhow*, named *The Jewel of Muscat*, sailed from Muscat to Singapore in 2010 and is now in a maritime museum in Singapore.

The methods and tools of the boat builders have changed remarkably little over the centuries. In the *dhow* yards today it is still possible to observe boat-building skills that may well date back thousands of years, still practised in much the same way.

Construction work is carried out without the use of plans or drawings. All measurements for the variations are memorized by the builder. When discussing the building of a *dhow* with his customer, the master builder will sketch the ship in the sand with his finger, or on a plank with some chalk, detailing some parts. As a master craftsman, he would not be happy if the customer tried to pin him down to precise measurements. The whole business is based upon mutual trust: the builder and customer discuss the measurements of the *dhow*, a price and an estimated completion date are agreed, and then the transaction is sealed with a handshake. It is then up to the builder to provide the best boat he can for the price.

Dhow *under construction.*

The building season for *dhow*s traditionally begins in October, when day temperatures began to fall, and ends at the beginning of June. A relatively small *shu'i*, used for fishing, can take about 3 months to build, with bigger *dhow*s taking anything up to 9 months. Almost all Gulf *dhow*s follow the shell construction. The keel is laid first, with the ribs of the ship which run from the keel to the side rail being inserted after the planks on the outside have been fitted in. This is contrary to the method used in the West, in which the planks are fitted to a rib-skeleton.

In the past, the laying of the keel was an anxious time for the *dhow* builders, and a new keel was usually guarded or protected by a fence. There was a belief that if a woman who had had difficulty in becoming pregnant could jump across a newly laid keel she would conceive a male child, but that the *djinns* which watched over the *dhow* would inevitably take a life for a life. So the carpenters worked as quickly as possible to lay enough planks to make a barrier too high for any woman to jump over! In northern Europe there was a somewhat similar superstitious belief that if a witch could cross the keel she could

attack the boat at sea. So a piece of wood from an elder tree, long held to be efficacious against witchcraft, was sometimes inserted into the keel.

In a traditional boatyard, the first impression the visitor receives is of the pleasant smell of newly-cut timber, mostly teak, together with the more powerful odour of shark oil. Untidy piles of adzed branches of trees, known as *jangali* ('jungle wood') lie about here and there. In the height of summer the branches are sometimes piled into the sea, to keep them from splitting in the intense heat.

Teak (*Tectona grandis*) from North West India was always the preferred wood for the boat builders. It does not split, crack or shrink, is easy to work, durable and resistant to the toredo shipworm. Its use in Bahrain for the construction of seaworthy and durable vessels was noted by the Greeks more than 2000 years ago. Nowadays, teak is becoming scarce and prohibitively expensive. Teak is used for sections of the hull, especially for the keel, and *jangali*, usually Indian laurel, for the ribs. Other types of wood in use for various parts of the *dhow* are mangrove, jackwood and babul wood. Owing to the cost of these materials, many *dhows* today are being built from fibreglass in a wooden mould, but some owners still prefer to have a traditionally made wooden boat. While the master builder is a local, sometimes assisted by his sons who join him after school to learn the family trade, his highly experienced carpenters come from India or sometimes Pakistan. The master builder is

A boat builder working with simple tools.

called the *jallaf* and his employees are the *zarrab*, the carpenter who fastens the planks with nails, the *imzawri,* who carries the timber from the yard to the ship, and the *imleid*, the boy who clears up the yard and whose important task it is to keep the kettle boiling on a scrap-wood fire to provide tea and coffee for the workers.

The tools employed are basic. In Kuwait as late as the mid-1980s logs were still being cut into planks using a pit saw, which took days of concentrated skill in the exhausting heat. Despite the introduction of the electric drill in many yards some old shipwrights still prefer to use a bow drill to bore holes for the iron nails. They claim that an electric drill can burn the wood and that the bow drill is cleaner and safer. The carpenter uses an adze, a thin arching blade set at right angles to the handle, to fair off the planks with gentle strokes. The adze, saw, chisel and auger, little changed from their original design, have been in use in eastern boatyards for thousands of years, as ancient drawings and writings testify.

Once the adzing and planing of the planks is finished, they are carefully slotted into grooves along the keel, and into the stem and stern posts which have already been bolted to the keel. The first planks are the most difficult to fit, as they must have a pronounced twist to give the shape of the boat, and much hammering and tapping is required to get them just right. They are then nailed into place and small blocks of wood are fixed temporarily on the outside to help the planks keep their shape.

Only as the ship grows are the ribs, made of crooked lengths of wood, fitted inside it. Eventually all the planks will be nailed down to the ribs, the nail holes making neat lines running up the sides of the ship. The holes are made wider at the outside so that the large heads of the nails may be countersunk. If a bow drill is being used then the men have to chisel out the holes for the nail heads with an auger. Once the nail is in place the hole is stopped with mastic.

Nails to fasten the planks are still manufactured locally by ironsmiths in Bahrain and Kuwait, along with the hinges for doors and the gudgeons and pintles which hold the rudders. Some carpenters prefer galvanized factory-made nails from India, although they are more expensive,

A toilet box hung on the stern of a boat.

rust which eats into the wood and spoils the appearance of the boat.

Once the planks are all in place, a piece of soft cotton string impregnated with fish or coconut oil is driven into the joints and then the whole boat is oiled with fish oil, or sometimes coated with hot pitch, to make it waterproof. Below the waterline a coating made from boiling oil and animal fat mixed with burned lime is applied, to deter barnacle growth and give protection against the wood-boring worm, teredo. Shark oil is applied to the topsides and the interior. The oil intensifies the rich colour of the mahogany.

because they are harder. The nails come in many different lengths, each for a different purpose; the longest are the ones used in the keel.

Yousef Al Majid, the Qatari master shipwright who built the beautiful *battil* which can sometimes be seen at its moorings by people driving or walking along the Doha Corniche, said that he preferred iron nails to the galvanized factory-made type because they were firmer and more durable. In his boatyard the nails were carefully wrapped in oiled fibre before they were inserted, to help ward off the

Then the finishing touches are added: the deck, the cabin and, nowadays, the engine and propeller. *Dhows* with engines are known as *lanchaat*. Finally the toilet, a round box with a hole in the floor, is hung over the stern of the boat.

The larger *dhows* may have carved decoration. The carved rosette or 'eye' amulet design, elaborate on large boats and usually painted red, blue and white, has degenerated to a simple eye painted on the prows of some *shu'i*.

Finally, the *dhow* is ready for launching. This is always an occasion for celebration and feasting. In the old days the whole village would turn out for the launching of a boat, and in the yards in Ajman, UAE, everyone lends a hand to help get the vessel into the water. A path to the sea is cleared, rows of logs are greased to act as rollers and truckloads of old tyres are placed on the left side of the *dhow*. Props are knocked away until it subsides onto the tyres, and, rather inelegantly, it is pulled and pushed by a bulldozer until it slides into the sea on its side.

A carpenter using a bow drill.

Once it has reached deeper water the *dhow* rights itself and glides proudly out over the blue-green water, accompanied by singing, dancing, the beating of drums and hand clapping from the excited watchers on shore. In the days of sail, the last job to be done before the *dhow* could start on its maiden voyage was the fitting of the masts, rigging and sails and this was always done while the *dhow* was afloat.

Fascinating Forts

A notable feature of traditional architecture in Qatar is the number and variety of its forts, especially those along the northern coastline. In days gone by, when attacks on settled populations by marauding desert tribesmen were a constant threat, it was essential for people to have strongholds to which they could retreat in times of emergency. Sometimes these were no more than isolated, windowless round towers, with an entrance half way up the wall, which could be reached by a ladder or a rope that could be pulled inside.

William Palgrave, who in 1863 was the first European traveller to visit the interior of the Qatar peninsula, wrote: 'the villages of Katar are each and all carefully walled in, while the downs beyond are lined with towers, and here and there a castle huge and square makes with its little windows and narrow portals a display of strength.' He went on to describe the towers: 'Towers of refuge line the uplands, they are small circular buildings from twenty-five to thirty feet in height, each with a door half-way up the side and a rope hanging out...the Katar shepherds, when scared by a sudden attack, clamber up for safety...and once there draw in the rope after them, this securing their own lives... whatever may become of their cattle.' A drawing made in 1823 of the view of the landscape from Doha bay shows several of these little towers dotted

The reconstructed fort of Al Rekayat.

around on the low hills, with a couple of substantial forts guarding Doha and the neighbouring village of Al Bida'a. Few of the towers of refuge have survived (although plenty remain perched on the craggy hill tops of Oman) but there are still a number of forts.

In addition to attacks by robbers intent on plunder, there were many disputes between neighbouring tribes over territory and water, so communities had to be constantly alert to the possibility of danger. The forts should not be viewed simply as a co-operative defence system against attack from the sea or by hostile bedouin tribesmen. Rather, they were individual symbols of power and prestige, and would have been visible for many miles across the flat desert terrain, both to people on land and to the crews of ships out at sea. The chief and his family resided in the fort, which was surrounded by the humbler mud-plastered stone dwellings, *barasti* huts and tents of his followers.

The typical desert fort was rectangular and built of rough blocks of limestone or flat slabs of beachrock (the Arabic name for this is *furoush*), to a height of two metres. Above this, solid walls of small mud bricks were built, and the whole structure was then given a thick, smooth coating of mud or gypsum plaster. Obviously, such a type of building required constant maintenance, particularly after the rainy season. After they were abandoned in the first half of the last century, most quickly fell into ruin.

Each fort had a combination of round and rectangular or square corner towers, apparently entirely at the whim of the builder. On the north-west coast, for example, Al Thaghab has three round corner towers and one rectangular, whereas Al Rekayat, less than three kilometres away, has three rectangular and one round corner tower.

Inside the forts villagers would need to store food and water in case they were besieged, and usually a well was dug in one corner. There would be a storeroom for dried dates and larger forts often had a *madbassa*, a room for processing dates. This had a ridged floor which was covered with palm leaf matting, on which sacks of dates were piled. Their weight caused the *dibs*, the sweet sticky juice of the dates, to ooze out and run down the channels into a collecting jar set into the ground in one corner.

Some forts, for example the one at Al Wajba west of Doha, had slit spaces in the wall under beak-like projections from which arrows or guns could be aimed downwards when the enemy got close enough.

Wajba Fort dates to the 19th century and is thought to be the oldest standing fort in the country, although remains of the very earliest forts, which have been dated to the 8th and 9th centuries CE, lie among the ruins of the settlement of Murwab in the north-west of Qatar. Al Wajba was the headquarters of Sheikh Jassim bin Mohammed Al Thani on the famous occasion in 1893 when he and his men routed the Turkish occupying forces, who were forced to retreat to their own fort in Musheirib. (The present 'Doha Fort' in the Al Bida'a area of Doha was built in 1880 as a police station and later used as a jail.)

The corner towers at Wajba Fort have simple external buttressing which is typical of some styles of fortified building; other examples of this can be seen on the two fortified houses built in 1910 by

The Barj Barazan, above before reconstruction and below after reconstruction, showing buttressing.

Sheikh Jassim's son, Sheikh Mohammed, at Al Umm Slal Mohammed, about 20 km north of Doha city.

Visible from the main road leading to the north of Qatar are the recently restored towers known as the Barj Barazan. These were also constructed on the orders of Sheikh Mohammed bin Jassim, possibly as surveillance towers, although the number of rooms within the towers suggest that they were also used as a residence. 'Barazan' means a high place which can be seen from far off, and it is said that pearl divers could see the towers from their ships when they returned home.

Forts had narrow openings in the wall which widened out on the inside; here the defenders could stand and aim their arrows or firearms in all directions. Gates, always a weak spot in the defences, were made of thick wood studded with heavy nails, into which a small door was inserted, just big enough to allow one person, stooping, to enter at a time. Some forts had a recess just above the gate from which stones could be hurled onto the heads of the attackers.

Although in some cases reduced to little more than low piles of crumbled mud and stones, with a surface scatter of potsherds, the string of forts around the coasts are instantly recognisable because of their shape. Between 2002 and 2005 two were excavated by archaeologists: Zekrit Fort in the south-west, and Fraiha Fort, a few kilometres north of Al Zubara. There is a local belief that Zekrit Fort was constructed on the orders of Rahmah bin Jabir, the famous chief of the Al Jalahaimah who harried Gulf shipping for 40 years. If this is so it can be accurately dated to between 1809 and 1812.

Zekrit Fort is unusual because, apart from a similar ruined fort at nearby Bir Hussein, also popularly attributed to Rahmah bin Jabir, there are no other surviving forts on the southern coasts of Qatar. It appears to have had gypsum plaster on the lower levels of the walls and around the south-facing gateway, which was framed by solid pillars of palm-tree trunks. It has a scattered settlement of small

Doha Fort in the 1950s.

Al Zubara Fort, built in 1938.

houses around it, and in 2005 the archaeologists uncovered the remains of a substantial building between the fort and the shore, housing three date presses.

Fraiha Fort appears to date to the 19th century, and has a small settlement around it which may have been a 'satellite' of Al Zubara to the south. Al Zubara was surrounded with substantial walls when it was established as a pearling and trading city in the 18th century. The walls were strengthened with drum towers that could support cannon at intervals, and there was a fort within the walls to guard the harbour, so the place was protected against attack from both sea and land.

Murair Fort, the barely visible remains of which lie just south of the modern fort, was built in 1768 to guard the wells which provided the settlement's precious water supply. In 1769 a ship canal, flanked by parallel structures on each side, was dug to link the fort to the sea.

The Al Zubara Fort which today forms a spectacular landmark on the coast is comparatively recent, and stands a kilometre north of the old town. It was constructed on the orders of the Ruler, Sheikh Abdullah bin Jassim Al Thani in 1938, as a response to the claims of Bahrain on Al Zubara and the construction by the Bahrainis of defensive fortifications on the nearby Huwar Islands. This square, honey-coloured structure, with its crenellated parapets and sturdy corner towers and an old cannon standing beside the entrance, is one of the best-known of the peninsula's buildings, ever popular with tourists and photographers. It was occupied by the police until 1987 and was then taken over by the Department of Museums and Antiquities. It has recently undergone major restoration and is now a visitors' centre and museum housing finds from the excavations at Al Zubara.

The archaeologist, Geoffrey Bibby, describes a visit to Al Zubara Fort in 1957. 'We pulled up at a more modern fort, a white-washed stone building with the flag of Qatar flying above it. It was a police post and we were greeted by the police detachment as a welcome break in the monotony of their lonely watch. Our escort had many friends among the little garrison and we were immediately given mugs of hot sweet tea, to last us while coffee was being brewed.'

When my family came to Qatar 30 years later, the police at the fort were still hospitably entertaining visitors with tea and biscuits. Our children were impressed when informed that dangerous prisoners were incarcerated in the upper rooms of the corner towers, reachable only by ladders, whereas lesser felons enjoyed the comparative freedom of the courtyard during daylight hours!

Al Thaghab Fort lies, or rather lay, until a new fort was recently built on top of the ruins, about 10 km north of Al Zubara on the eastern side of the road. The fort was 19th century, as can be determined from the pottery fragments and scraps of Indian glass bangles scattered around. However, the remains of a scattering of houses which surround it may be of earlier date. There is a deep well to the west of the fort, inside a barbed-wire enclosure, which J G Lorimer mentions in his *Gazetteer of the Persian Gulf* as in use in 1911. It is still in use today, although nowadays the water is pumped out rather than hauled up in buckets. Lorimer also said the fort was in good condition on the occasion of his visit, but all trace of it is now lost.

The new fort is a somewhat fanciful 'restoration' with stained glass panels over the brass-studded doors. Just north of Al Thaghab is the small fort of Al Rekayat, reconstructed by the Department of Museums and Antiquities in 1988 in a more authentic manner than at Al Thaqab. It is smaller than Al Zubara fort, but no less picturesque. Before reconstruction it was partially excavated, and in the date store a number of coins were found, including a 19th century 'fils' from a Baghdad mint, presumably contemporary with the construction of the fort. An intriguing find was a coin from the Abbasid period, bearing an Arabic inscription, 'There is no god but God, and Mohammed is the prophet of God,' and a date which translates as 1315 CE. It was found near the surface, and may simply have been an old coin in the possession of a 19th century inhabitant of the fort.

Going north again, we come to the ruins of the huge fort of Al Ruwaida, the largest in Qatar and situated beside the shore. The name of the fort and settlement is a diminutive of the Arabic word *rawda*, meaning a fertile area in a depression. The fort and its surrounding settlement are now a major archaeological site currently under excavation, and are described in detail in on page 45.

Camping with the Bedouin

Nowadays many people in Qatar, both locals and expatriates, regard camping as a pleasant weekend pastime. It is hard to realise that within a short space of time, well within the memory of many citizens, setting up home in a tent was the normal way of life.

For thousands of years, the nomadic population of the country, known as *bedu* or *bedouin*, travelled the desert sands, always moving on in search of fresh pasture for their camels, sheep and goats. The term *bedouin* derives from the Arabic *badawi*, meaning 'without a settled home', and is in fact a double plural as *bedu* in Arabic is already a plural form, the singular being *bedui*. However, Westerners commonly speak of *bedouin*, and then compound the error by adding an 's'!

There are still people living the life of pastoral nomads in many parts of the world: the Turkoman, Kirghiz and Mongols of Central Asia, the Pashtun of Afghanistan , the Lur of Iran and the Tuareg of north-west Africa are among them. Although their lifestyles and customs differ in many ways, all nomads share the same necessity to move according to the seasons and the availability of water and grazing. Such journeys recognise no national boundaries, but with the introduction of modern borders and such tiresome necessities as passports and visas, the nomadic way of life becomes difficult to maintain.

Many countries actively discourage nomads from trying to cross borders.

In the Arabian Gulf, the fixing of national borders coincided with the oil wealth that changed the lifestyle of entire peoples and rendered the harsh life of the bedouin unsustainable, once people began to want the amenities that go with a settled lifestyle. More and more men found employment in oil-related work. For a while their wives and children and the old people continued the lifestyle of tent dwellers, with the oilfield workers returning to their families at weekends. During the 1960s the practice gradually died away, as the government built villages and encouraged families to settle so that the children could attend school. Some tribes settled earlier than others, but in Qatar, within two decades of the first oil-derived cash which flowed into the country at the end of the 1950s, almost no families were following the old way of life. A lifestyle which had continued without a break for at least three thousand years had disappeared without a trace.

In 1959 a Danish ethnographer, Klaus Ferdinand, together with a noted documentary film-maker, Jette Bang, armed with notebooks, tape-recorders, cameras and film cameras, arrived at just the right moment to record the old way of life before it vanished. For three months, from January to the end of March, they travelled and camped with the bedouin. Both took thousands of photographs, both in colour and in black and white, and Jette Bang also made a colour documentary. The original film footage was two hours, but it was considered at the time that 20 minutes was the maximum length of time a TV audience would watch a

Loading the camels at the Al Murrah camp at Uglat Al Manasir, south Qatar, 1959.

documentary, and sadly, all that remains is 18 minutes of film footage.

Many years later, between 1991 and 1993, Ferdinand put together the best of his and Bang's photographs into a superb book, with the text based on material from their notebooks. He also drew on material and information collected by some of his Danish colleagues, the archaeologists and historians who were working in Qatar in the 1950s and '60s. The book was published in English by the Carlesburg Foundation in Denmark as part of their extensive Nomad Research Project.

While in Qatar, Ferdinand and Bang went first of all to the north, near the old ruined city of Murwab, to spend some weeks with the hospitable Al Na'im people, and later shifted south to travel with the Al Murrah. The two tribes had very different lifestyles; the Al Na'im were only semi-nomadic by this time, and kept chickens and pigeons, which would have been an inconvenience to people constantly on the move. They also used donkeys rather than camels as beasts of burden, as well as motorised transport.

In the hottest part of summer, the Al Na'im lived in simple houses constructed of sea-rock or limestone blocks, or in palm-leaf huts known as *barasti*. The tents would be set up beside the permanent dwellings, so that when the temperature soared the families could retreat to the comparative coolness and shade of the houses.

During the cooler months of the year the Al Na'im set up two other camps. One was an autumn camp and the other was used during spring. All the camps were in the same area. The people explained to Ferdinand that in former years some of them used to migrate to Bahrain for the hottest months, transporting their camels by *dhow*. Water was always available in Bahrain, owing to the plentiful natural springs both on and off shore.

It was not long after the beginning of the oil era before modern artefacts turned up in bedouin encampments. Most useful of all were the inner tubes of large tyres, which could be used to transport water, looking rather like giant black sausages. Telephone wire was handy for tying goods to pack animals, and proved stronger and lasted longer than the traditional hand-made ropes. The Al Murrah people, whom the Danish researchers joined after spending some weeks

A storage bag, possibly Dawasir.

Above: A woman's dress of woollen fabric, Al Murrah, 1959.

Below: A leather-covered basket used for storing coffee pots, Al Murrah, 1959.

Al Murrah camp at Uglat Al Manasir, south Qatar, in 1959.

with the Al Na'im, considered themselves to be one of the purest of the bedouin groups and were fiercely proud of their way of life. They were camel breeders and kept saluki dogs, which were often treated almost as members of the family, as well as falcons. During the autumn months they made short migrations, which gradually became longer once the winter rains arrived, their journeys taking them through wide regions of desert.

Pitching or dismantling the heavy striped woollen tents was strenuous work, undertaken by the women, while the men busied themselves with making coffee and caring for the falcons. Not surprisingly, for short stays the travellers sometimes simply erected a temporary shelter, made from one of the wall panels of the tent, or a tarpaulin.

Cooking was done in a shallow hole dug in the sand in front of the kitchen section of the tent. The pots and pans were kept in coiled, leather-covered lidded baskets. Other articles in daily use, including babies' cradles, were slung from the tent poles.

Besides the kitchen area the tents had separate sections for the men and their guests, and for women and children. There were one or two sections where everyday family life went on, but many daily activities took place in the area in front of the tent. A section of the main area of the tent was used as a store, and also by anyone wanting to take an undisturbed nap during the day. Additional woven partitions to give extra privacy could be quickly put in place. Very young animals were sometimes penned in a section of the tent at night for safety.

A mother and child of the Al Murrah tribe, in 1959.

Side cloths extending from each end of the tent, sometimes curving around in front to semi-enclose an area, gave some privacy and protection from blowing dust and sand. If the wind shifted direction these could be quickly moved.

When visitors arrived by vehicle, it was considered good manners for them to drive up to the back of the tent, to allow the women time to cover themselves with their *abaya*s and withdraw to their own part of the tent if necessary.

Not only did the women set up and dismantle the tents, they also made them, weaving the long, dark brown and cream sections and the strengthening bands which were sewn onto them, as well as sewing or pinning the sections together once the tent was pitched. 'In ordinary daily life everyone had a job to do, especially the women, who worked all the time,' commented Ferdinand. The women spun wool or goat hair as they walked, and wove small articles such as udder-covers for the milk camels on simple hand looms held between the toes as they sat on the sand.

The milk camels and their foals were taken away from the camp around mid-morning by the herdsmen, in search of grazing, and returned to the camp just before sunset or sometimes later. Milking took place in the evening. Pack camels were simply hobbled and allowed to wander around in the vicinity of the camp in search of their own grazing.

A family might stay a week in one place, or a month or even six weeks, depending on the amount of the surrounding vegetation and how long it lasted. When preparing to move, everything had to be packed into bags which were slung onto the camels. Ferdinand and Bang were glad to have the opportunity of helping their friends by using their vehicle to assist with the moves, and also with fetching water when needed.

The grandchildren and great-grandchildren of the bedouin with whom Ferdinand and Bang spent such a pleasant stay only half a century ago, still enjoy camping during the cooler months, but nowadays a desert camp is likely to have a generator and electric lights, and even air-conditioning and a TV! The desert campers of the 21st century enjoy the pleasures of the outdoor life without any of its hardships.

Al Nai'im tribesman and calf with a suckling-preventer of hedgehog skin fastened to its noseband.

The Camel and the Bedouin

For thousands of years the bedouin of Arabia and their camels lived in a symbiotic relationship in which each was important to the existence of the other. The bedouin name for *Camelus dromedarius*, the one-hump dromedary, is *Ata Allah*, which means 'Gift of God'. Their camels provided the desert-roaming nomads with everything from milk and meat to wool for weaving and leather to be made into a whole range of useful articles. Small wonder that their owners regarded them as a gift from God, helping them to survive in a harsh world that gave them little else.

The story of the gradual development and domestication of this animal is a very ancient one. The earliest prehistoric relative of the camel lived in North America some 65,000,000 years ago and was the size of a hare. Later, from the Middle to Late Miocene era, it evolved into a tall creature called *Aepycamelus*, with long legs and an S-shaped neck. Like its modern descendants, this proto-camel

moved both legs on one side of the body at the same time, a movement called pacing.

Around 5,000,000 years ago prehistoric camels migrated from North America to North-East Asia via a land bridge which existed then. The ancestors of the humpless New World camels spread southwards to South America, where they evolved into guanacos and vicunas. From this wild stock the llamas and alpacas were domesticated. In North America the early camels disappeared about 10,000 years ago, probably hunted to extinction by the indigenous peoples.

The development of the Old World camel is harder to trace. It used to be thought that both the one-humped camel and the two-humped camel (*Camelus bactrianus*) derived from the same wild species (*Camelus ferus*). But recent research has shown that each of the two species has a separate ancestor. Over the last few years archaeological excavations in the UAE

have provided new information about the wild ancestor of the domesticated dromedary. The earliest camel bones found were unquestionably those of wild animals, and there were signs that they may have been hunted and butchered. But later finds, of bones dating to around 1000 BCE, correspond to the period when some researchers think that one-humped camels began to be domesticated in Arabia. Others consider that it may have been even earlier. One theory is that it could have been frankincense traders, as far back as the 3rd millennium BCE, who first trained camels to make the long and arduous journey from southern Arabia to the northern areas of the Middle East. Others theorise that they were first domesticated as milking animals before they were employed as beasts of burden. Later, they became used as riding animals. There are accounts of ancient battles being fought by camel-riding Arab warriors, the Amorites, as long ago as the 9th century BCE.

The grave of a warrior dating to the Sassanid period, after 224 AD, was excavated some years ago at Al Mazrouah, north of Doha, and an intriguing feature was the discovery of remains of camels around the grave. Early literature refers to the hamstringing of camels around the grave of a hero.

Among non-desert dwellers, camels have the reputation of being bad-tempered and obstinate creatures which spit and kick. In fact, nothing could be further from the truth: camels are, on the whole, docile, patient and intelligent. The moaning and groaning noises they make when they are loaded up and trying to rise to their feet, which sound to human ears like grumbling, should be compared to the grunting noises and heavy breathing of a weightlifter in action. Nevertheless, camels can bite and kick when angry, and a male camel in 'must' should always be approached with caution during the breeding season, when the bellowing animal inflates a red skin 'balloon' and projects it from its mouth.

The mutual affection of camel and bedouin owner is legendary, and the bedouin are said to have loved their camels on a par with their children. The famous British explorer, Wilfred Thesiger, who crossed the Empty Quarter in southern Arabia with his bedouin companions in the 1940s, described how, several times a night, a female camel would approach her sleeping owner to sniff gently at him as he lay beside the camp fire, carefully stepping over the bodies of his companions as she did so.

The body of a camel is perfectly adapted for survival in the harsh extremes of the desert climate. Although it loses moisture through the skin, just as humans do, the camel has a unique and extraordinary method for conserving water loss. It can close its nostrils to conserve moisture and keep out sand and dust, and in addition, experiments revealed that it is also able to extract moisture from expired air. The camel can minimise the quantity of water lost by the natural processes of urination and defecation. Camel urine is intensely concentrated – four times that of humans. Camel droppings are dry, powdery balls containing almost no moisture. For that reason they have long been used by desert-dwelling peoples as fuel for fires.

A newborn camel feeding from its mother.

Although camels, superbly equipped with bodies able to minimise water loss, can go for long periods without drinking, when given the chance they take on board vast quantities of water, far in excess of what their bodies have lost. In one experiment some camels were denied water for three weeks and then provided with an unlimited water supply. The camels drank at the rate of 60 litres per minute, and one animal managed to put away 186 litres! Normally such rapid ingestion of liquid would result in the swelling or even rupturing of red blood corpuscles, but the red corpuscles of camels are apparently able to withstand the strain.

The brains of mammals are heat sensitive and under extreme conditions the brain can heat up: this causes heatstroke in humans, which can be fatal. But the camel has a unique inbuilt air-conditioning system, lacking in other mammals, enabling it to survive in the soaring temperatures of an Arabian summer. As the camel inhales, air flowing over its large nasal surfaces forms a layer of dried-out mucus. This mucus absorbs moisture when the animal exhales, which cools a network of small blood vessels around the jugular vein. When the cooled blood reaches the brain and eyes it lowers the temperature of the most sensitive cells by more than 4° C.

The Danish anthropologist, Klaus Ferdinand, and the photographer and documentary filmmaker, Jette Bang, when travelling with the Al Murrah in the south of Qatar in the spring of 1959, observed how their companions made use of practically everything from the camel, even its urine. The camel, Ferdinand observed, was the focal-point of their occupation and central to their way of life. When people from different families met, the subject of their conversations was often the welfare of their camels and the possibilities of grazing. A British anthropologist, Roger Webster, who studied the bedouin of Qatar for his doctoral thesis, described how, whenever the herdsmen worked with the camels they stroked them, talked to them or sang to them constantly.

In *Arabian Sands,* published in 1959, Wilfred Thesiger, who journeyed into the vast and waterless Rub Al Khali, or Empty Quarter, of the deserts of Arabia, said of the Bait Kathir who were his travelling companions, 'They could tell at a glance from the depths of the footprints whether a camel was ridden or free, and whether it was in calf. By studying strange tracks they could tell the area from which the camel came. Camels from the Sands, for instance, have soft soles to their feet, marked with tattered strips of loose skin, whereas if they come from the gravel plains their feet are polished smooth. Bedu could tell the tribe to which a camel belonged, for the different tribes have different breeds of camel, all of which can be distinguished by their tracks.'

The camel was the bedouin beast of burden, riding animal and a source of rich, nourishing milk. Its urine was used for washing hair, to which it imparted a rich shine, and it was said to help keep down lice. In addition, urine was used in tanning leather. It was the job of the little girls to follow the camels around with collecting bowls, and Ferdinand describes them 'leaping in like cockroaches', whenever a camel obliged!

Dried camel manure made excellent fuel, and it had another use, as a dry absorbent lining for babies' nappies. Jette Bang, who formed a very close and affectionate relationship with the bedouin women, describes how mothers of young infants had a supply of the light dry balls of manure on hand, which they crushed into powder. This was used to dry and clean the nappy area, before handfuls of the powder were used to line a clean cloth wrapped between the baby's legs.

Camel wool was spun and twined for a wide range of articles: cords of all thicknesses, socks to wear in summer for protection against the searing sands, bags, blankets and all kinds of equipment used on the camels themselves. Camel wool comes in all shades of natural colours, from cream through every shade of brown to almost black, and so was often used undyed. The wool used for the long striped tents, however, was dark brown goats' hair with bands of cream-coloured sheep's wool.

The skin was turned into leather, again used for a variety of useful articles, in particular for large transport bags. It also provided water containers, but by the time Ferdinand and Bang travelled with the bedouin, these were being superseded by the inner tubes of tyres.

Although men, women and children all had their roles to play in relation to and in working with camels, ultimately they were the responsibility of the men. The owners and herdsmen had the true responsibility for breeding and daily care, and an important part of their work was milking their camels.

All lactating camels wore – and still wear – an udder cover to prevent unchecked suckling by their foals. Ferdinand wrote that it was necessary that the foal was nearby or was even suckling during the milking. Milking normally took place from the left side, while the foal suckled from the right.

If the foal died, its skin was stuffed and used as a dummy during milking. Sometimes another foal was put to the mother and her nose was blocked so that she could not tell by scent that it was not her foal. A good mare would give two to three litres of milk at a time. Camel milk could be drunk fresh, or put into tea, or made into a kind of yoghurt called *laban,* which was kept in a skin bag.

Pack camels were only assembled for moving camp; the rest of the time they were hobbled and turned loose without supervision. The result was that when the decision was made to strike camp and move on, it often took a day or two to locate the pack animals.

Female camels with foals were kept separate from the male pack animals and generally cared for by herdsmen. Young girls also sometimes looked after the camels and little girls were often given the job of putting hobbles on the legs of the camels. When on the move, women and girls rode in a large, cushioned wooden litter called a *hawdaj* or *maghbat*. It had a curved framework which could be covered with cloth to provide shade from the sun and to conceal the passengers from passers-by.

Although camels are no longer essential to the way of life in Qatar, many families still like to keep herds of camels. Until recently the animals could be seen wandering in search of vegetation, particularly on the southern and western coastal regions, with their herdsmen never far away. But overgrazing by an increasing number of animals was resulting in damage to the natural environment, and now all camels are kept in pens in the camps and their food is brought to them. Camel racing is a popular sport in most Gulf states, including Qatar, and a pure-bred animal can fetch the same kind of astronomical price as an Arab racehorse. It seems that the day of the camel, at least in the Arabian Gulf, is far from over.

What's in a Name?

Recording the Place Names of Qatar

The place names of a country can yield a wealth of information, not only about geographical features but about the people who gave the names, and what they considered important about a particular location. Maps of the Arabian Gulf made by Europeans from the mid-18th century onwards recorded, for the most part, only the coastal pearling and trading ports. The famous map of the Gulf made by Carsten Niebuhr in 1765, lists a number of place names in Qatar, but Niebuhr, who derived his information second-hand from a sea captain, hadn't realised that Qatar is a peninsula, and the place-names are strung out along a straight coast and read the wrong way round! Gattar (Al Bida'a) is placed opposite the islands of Bahrejjn (Bahrain), and Huale (Al Huwaila), Iusofie (Yusufiyya, possibly an alternative name for Al Ruwaida) and Faraha (Fraiha), all significant pearling ports, are located from west to east instead of east to west.

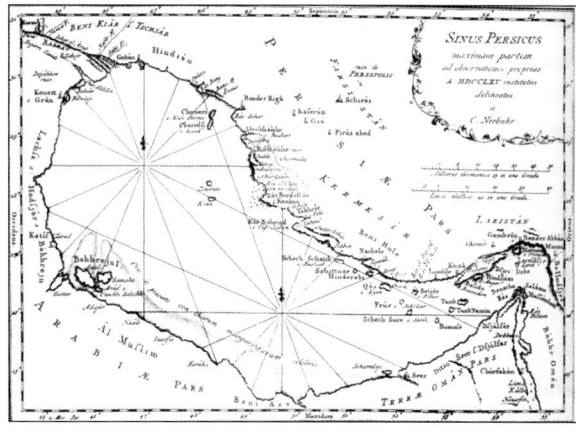

Carsten Niebuhr's map of the Arabian Gulf made in 1765 shows the coast of Qatar as a straight line!

It was not until oil was discovered in the 1930s and oil production in Qatar began after World War II that there was a need for more detailed cartography. But until September 1995 only 700 place names had ever been recorded, and many were wrongly transcribed, often because the cartographers were foreigners who in some cases were not even Arabic speakers. It was decided that this situation had to

be rectified, and so the Qatar Geographical Names Survey was set up.

In 1996-7 a team of researchers from the Geographical Names Survey set to work to make a complete record of the place names of Qatar, and in doing so came up with a wealth of fascinating sociological and cultural information. The researchers were recruited by the Centre for Geographical Information Systems (GIS), which was in the process of producing up-to-date and accurate maps of Qatar, using the very latest technology.

How do you go about organising such a huge information-collecting survey as this? Obvious sources of information about place names were the memories of elderly people, but getting in touch with the right people was initially not easy.

After some failures, the researchers hit upon the idea of approaching the seven different municipal authorities of Qatar for help. They prepared maps with the existing names and presented them to the local authorities. These proved extremely helpful in supplying the names of possible informants, and eventually a list of around sixty elderly citizens was compiled.

There was no time to be lost, because the researchers feared that some of the informants, who were in their eighties, might pass away before they had time to complete their survey. So, during the summer of 1996, despite the heat, the teams roamed the length and breadth of the country daily, from morning to night.

There were nine people involved in the surveys, divided into three teams. Each team included a fluent speaker of English and Arabic. Other team members arranged the appointments and took charge of the Global Positioning System equipment which recorded the precise coordinates for each site.

Team members soon discovered that the best time to visit the villages and gather information was the early evening when, like old people everywhere, elderly men and their friends met together at the *majlis* to chat, drink coffee and set the world to rights.

Obtaining precise information about place names took much time and patience, because the old folk often argued fiercely and at length about the exact pronunciation and derivation of each name. The researchers followed the disputes with interest, often gaining extra information that way. Getting to know the older generation of Qataris was a most rewarding and pleasant occupation for the researchers. They were overwhelmed by the kindness and hospitality shown to them by the local people, and by the enthusiasm shown for their work.

Old ladies were not directly interviewed by the male researchers, but sometimes, when they were talking to an elderly man in his home, his wife would listen and dispute with him about the correct names. In Al Khor one elderly lady who was known to be an authority on the area was sent a map and proved to be most helpful in identifying and naming new sites.

The usual method of checking the information, once a name had been decided on, was to ask the informant to accompany the team to the location, to be sure it was correct and to record the coordinates using GPS. This scrupulous attention to accuracy led to a dramatic incident in the searing heat of August 1996. One team nearly came to grief, together with their informant who had a reputed age of around a hundred years, when they got lost in the desert sands near Abu Samra, on the border with Saudi Arabia. The vehicle became bogged down in soft sand and the radio failed to work. The water supply ran out, and two members of the team set off to walk to Abu Samra to get help from the police. By the time they got there they were severely dehydrated. The police immediately launched a rescue operation and in the end the team members were none the worse for their adventure. They were, however, deeply impressed by the way in which the apparently frail old gentleman was little affected by the heat and thirst, whereas the researchers, whose average age was some 60 years less than his, were on the point of collapse. They had learnt their lesson, and on future trips into the remoter regions they never travelled without a second vehicle and plenty of water.

Within six months, working every day, the bulk of the survey had been completed. Along with the exact location of each site its particular features were recorded, along with the pronunciation of its name. The accurate recording of the place names of Qatar

Qurayn Balboul or Spinning-top Hill.

yielded a wealth of information on the closeness with which a desert-dwelling people observe the slightest variation in the landscape. An area of sand-dunes south-west of Al Wukair is named Naqa Abu Dolou. 'Dolou' means 'ribs' in English and the name refers to the rib-like ripples formed by the wind on the surface of the sand. In the north-east of the country is a sandy area with two low mounds called Al Nehaidat, and the name derives from *nahd*, the Arabic word for a woman's breast.

The name Al Zubara, in the north-west of the peninsula, rather surprisingly means a 'sand-mound'. Sand is not an especially noticeable feature of the place today when compared with other places in Qatar, but perhaps there was more in former times. 'Doha' derives from a word meaning 'roundness', a reference of course to the C-shaped bay around which the city is constructed. The name is found elsewhere on the country's coastline.

Other geographical features had been given fanciful names from their resemblance to everyday objects. A cone-shaped hill, Qurayn Balboul, would be

'Spinning-top Hill' in English. And an obviously tent-shaped hill in the south-west naturally received the name, Al Khuwaimat.

The deep cave which lies to the right of the Salwa Road opposite the Satellite Earth Station is named Dahl Al Misfir. 'Dahl' means a cavern, and 'Misfir' means brightness, because of the bright light in the cave entrance when seen from within. Charmingly, the term is also used to describe the beauty of a woman who has just unveiled her face.

An area with strangely-shaped stones bears the rather sinister appellation of Umm Al Jamajim – the 'Place of the Skulls' – and a craggy promontory with the profile of a cat's head is named Al Qita.

An interesting area in the centre of the peninsula has some unusually deep, natural holes in the rock: these were carefully kept covered by the bedouin with large, flat stones to conserve the precious rain water which collected in them. And so the place became known as 'Ummahat Al Maghati: the Place of the Covers'. Three surrounding fertile areas (*rawdat*s) derive their names from this feature, which was once an important source of water.

Some places had been incorrectly named on maps by oil company geographers in the years following World War II. One of these was Umm Said. It is now given its correct name of Mesaieed, which refers to a particular kind of soil found there.

Countless place names derive from trees, plants or shrubs. Umm Al Tuwaim Al Gharib, a fertile area in south-west Qatar regularly visited by the nomadic bedouin in former times, is named after a perennial shrub, *Aerva javanica*, called 'Tuwaim' in Arabic. Its fluffy seed heads were used for stuffing pillows and saddle pads. That attractive coastal plant, *Limonium axillare*, which bears stiff bracts of purple flowers and is known as Sea Lavender in English, is called *qutaif* in Arabic and gives its name to Al Qutaifiya Lagoon, near Doha.

A species of desert broom, *Leptadenia pyrotechnica*, with tough branches and small yellow flowers which dots the coastal areas is *markh* in Arabic and gives its name to Al Markhiya. Abu Samra itself is

Al Qutaifiya Lagoon north of Doha is named after the attractive plant Limonium axillare, *known as* qutaif *in Arabic.*

named after the *Samr* (Acacia) trees which grow there.

In a land where until recently land ownership by individuals was relatively uncommon, the concentration upon geographical or botanical features was inevitable, the names yielding important information to travellers. There are some place names derived from individuals associated with a particular area, but they are in a minority.

In a mere 18 months, the number of place-names recorded in Qatar jumped from 700 to an astonishing 3,500: a tribute to the diligence and perseverance of the research team members. The teams estimated that they covered 11,000 kilometres in their journeys around the peninsula. That of course, was only the beginning of the story. Back in Doha, the mass of material had to be studied, compared with existing information, discussed with experts and re-confirmed before being entered into the database.

Finally, the names were stored in a National Archive which is freely available to the public. They joined the 400,000,000 names from all over the world which are stored in Geneva by the United Nations, in a database which is constantly being updated.

Al Markhiya derives its name from markh, *the Arabic name for the firethorn* Leptadenia pyrotechnica.

Above: The fluffy seeds of Aerva javanica *were used by the bedouin for stuffing pillows and the plant gives its name to the rodat* Umm al Tuwaim.

Picnic at Singing Sands

No one could claim that the landscape of Qatar is renowned for its dramatic variety! There are no lofty mountains, no craggy hills, no tumbling rivers and shimmering lakes. But Qatar boasts a geological phenomenon which, globally, is very rare: the singing dunes.

There are two major types of sand dune in Qatar, the great crescent dunes known as *barchan* in Arabic, and the transverse or *seif* dunes, which are long and straight and usually lie parallel to the prevailing wind. The word *seif* means 'sword' in Arabic. They tend to form in desert areas where the wind blows mainly from one direction but where there are cross winds, whereas barchan dunes form in areas where the wind blows from one direction only. Barchan dunes also occur on Mars, but this chapter will confine itself to the dunes on Earth, and those of Qatar in particular.

The area of barchans known as the 'singing dunes', which lies between the Salwa Road and Mesaieed, has long been popular with both locals and expatriates for weekend picnics and fun, whether it is careering up and over the dunes in a four-wheel-drive vehicle, scrambling up their steep slopes to be rewarded by a spectacular view from the top, or sand-boarding down the sides.

Worldwide, there are only 35 known sites where the *barchans* make the extraordinary 'singing' which so fascinates the visitor, and we are privileged to have such a rare phenomenon here in Qatar. Not only do the dunes emit a most impressive humming and roaring as people slide down, but individual footsteps produce a strange squeaking sound. The sand has to be absolutely dry for this to happen, so late afternoon is the best time to try it out. It's guaranteed to keep the kids happy for hours!

The singing of the dunes has been known and speculated about for many centuries. The bedouin, the traditional nomadic inhabitants of the deserts, attributed the noise to the voices of *djinn* – spirits which inhabit the desert landscapes, and which also manifest themselves in the eerie 'dust devils' which sometimes rise up and whirl hither and thither across the desert floor.

In the 13th century Marco Polo, who was also a subscriber to the *djinn* theory, said that the dunes 'sometimes fill the air with the sounds of all kind of musical instruments, and also of drums and the clash of arms.' A bit imaginative perhaps, but one gets the general idea.

The intrepid desert traveller, Wilfred Thesiger, describes the sound rather more accurately in *Arabian Sands*, his account of his journey into and across the Empty Quarter in the late 1940s: 'While we were leading our camels down a steep dune face, I was suddenly conscious of a low vibrant hum, which grew in volume until it sounded as though an aeroplane were flying low over our heads. The camels plunged about, tugging at their head ropes, and looking back at the slopes above us. The sound ceased as we reached the bottom. This was the singing of the sands.'

In recent times, scientists have come up with various theories to explain the phenomenon, and in 2004, Bruno Andreotti, from the University of Paris set out in a determined attempt to solve the mystery once and for all. The French physicist took his equipment to the Atlantic Sahara in Morocco, which contains more than 10,000 *barchan*s. He and his team studied one of the large crescent dunes which are said to sing spontaneously all year long, sometimes two or three times in an afternoon, if it is windy enough. I have never come across dunes in Qatar which sing spontaneously, but evidently they occur in Morocco.

The wind forces the sand to accumulate at the top of the dune until the angle of the slope reaches a tipping point of about 35 degrees. The eventual avalanche of sand produces the singing noise. The best days for the phenomenon are when there is no wind, so that the sun can thoroughly dry out the dune face. Not having the time or patience to sit around and wait for the dune to start doing its stuff naturally, Andreotti's team induced avalanches by sliding down the dunes.

By measuring vibrations in the sand and air, Andreotti was able to detect surface waves on the sand that emanated from the avalanche at a relatively slow speed of about 40 metres per second. The dune acts as a huge loudspeaker – with the waves on the surface producing the sound in the air.

Andreotti explained these sand waves as resulting from collisions that occur between grains at about 100 times per second. In a kind of feedback loop, the waves synchronise the collisions, so they are all on the same beat. This is why the low pitch – between 95 and 105 Hertz – has so often been compared to the noise of a low-flying, propeller-driven aircraft. The maximum loudness of the singing is about 105 decibels.

So there you have it. The research is still not completed, because the sound seems in some way to be connected to the actual shape of the individual grains of sand. And there seems to be no satisfactory reason why some *barchan*s among the local 'singing dunes' will belt out a tune while their seemingly identical fellows remain obstinately silent.

It is fascinating to learn how *barchan*s form. Often, the perfect crescent-shaped hills of fine sand seem to simply appear by themselves in the middle of a dry, windswept floor. The explanation seems to be that the breeze carries billions of grains of sand as it blows across the desert floor and if the wind drops, so do the sand grains.

Eventually there is a little pile, perhaps snagged against a small rock or bush. When there is more sand arriving on the wind than is being blown away, the dune starts to form. It develops its own stability as its lee side grows steeper and steeper, until there comes a point at which fresh dry sand simply rolls down it. *Barchan*s most often form on gravel plains or salt flats.

Formed into crescents by the relentless pressure of the wind, the barchans, which can reach 30 metres in height, move steadily but imperceptibly across the landscape, driven by the prevailing shamal wind from the north-west.

A group of *barchan*s can transform into a long, transverse *seif* dune if the wind changes. A cross wind causes the barchans to become elongated, each extending a 'limb' at one end. If the wind continues in the same direction the limbs will continue to grow and join together and the barchans will change their shape completely.

Dunes beside Khor Al Adaid, the Inland Sea.

This process can be observed among the great rolling dunes which march relentlessly south, across the land between Mesaieed and Khor Al Adaid, the 'Inland Sea'. Once there, they continue into the water, and if they continue at the same rate it's estimated that, within the next three hundred years, the whole of that shallow lagoon will be filled with sand.

Seif dunes in other parts of the world have been known to form continuous ridges up to 160 kilometres long. Generally, they form sets of parallel ridges separated by areas of sand or gravel plains which create interdune 'corridors'. The long axes of these dunes extend in the resultant direction of sand movement. *Seif* dunes can be much higher than barchans, often reaching over 100 metres.

If engaging in the exhilarating sport of dune-bashing – roaring up and down the dunes that lie between Mesaieed and the Inland Sea — keep a sharp lookout for the changes in shape which can happen within a few days. Sudden precipices may form as the wind changes direction, and a dune which was quite safe to ascend and descend one month may develop a near vertical surface the next. Whether you are dune-bashing or enjoying the gentler pastime of exploring the singing dunes, either way the sands of Qatar are a great place to have fun. The best time to be on top of a dune is at sunset, when the red ball of the setting sun seems to hang above the desert, the golden sand is bathed in a luminous violet light and long, dark shadows form across the landscape, creating a delicate tracery where the wind has rippled the sand.

The Truffle Hunters

After the winter rains, the deserts of Qatar bloom. Wide swathes of silvery-green tasselled grasses form on the gravel plains, and in the shallow depressions where the thorny scrub bushes grow the ground is starred with tiny yellow, pink and blue flowers. They attract feeding butterflies and other insects, while birds and darting dragonflies come to feed on the insects.

A desert truffle.

The desert blooms too, with dozens of black or white-clad figures, all of whom walk slowly, their gaze fixed on the ground at their feet. Their faces wear the concentrated expressions of people who have dropped their car keys.

Whatever appearances may suggest, these searchers are not looking for lost possessions. No, they are treasure hunters, intent on finding a rare and expensive delicacy: desert truffles. Every year, if there is sufficient rain early in the winter season, truffles form just under the sandy or rocky desert surface, and searching for them is a time-honoured weekend family pastime.

Known as *fuga* in local Arabic, the desert truffles are botanically distant cousins of the truffles of Europe, which they do not resemble in taste or appearance. Yet they are locally as popular as the famous truffles of France and Italy are in Europe, where they fetch almost unbelievable prices at

auction. In 1993, Perigord truffles, sometimes referred to as 'black pearls', sold in London at $1,450 a kilo, and the same year Italian truffles reached a record high price of $2,200 a kilo. In 2007 a billionaire in Macau paid $330,000 at a charity auction for a single white truffle from Tuscany weighing 1.5 kilos. The truffles of the Arabian desert have never commanded quite such dizzying prices, but they are considered a luxurious delicacy and many local families prefer the challenge and satisfaction of finding their own.

Possibly it is the secret and mysterious nature of truffles which has fascinated truffle addicts for countless centuries. Theophrastus, a pupil of Aristotle, referred to truffles in the 4th century BCE as, 'one of the strangest plants, without root, stem, branch, bud, leaf or flower.' They grow out of sight, but in Qatar they are commonly found in the proximity of perennial *Helianthemum* plants, known as 'sun rose' in English.

Truffles appear to have been enjoyed by the rich and famous from the very earliest times: hieroglyphic texts on papyrus mention that desert fungi were served to the pharaohs of ancient Egypt. Three thousand years later, the tables of the Fatimid caliphs in Cairo were graced with truffles gathered in the nearby Muqattam hills. They have long been credited with possessing aphrodisiac properties.

Traditionally, the bedouin of Qatar, who were expert truffle hunters, believed that they were spawned by lightning and a clap of thunder, just as they believed that Arabia's other great treasure, pearls, were formed by oysters rising to the sea surface and receiving drops of rain. It is no coincidence that the precious winter rains should be credited with the creation of both these marvels. A local bedouin expert said that the number and size of the truffles are directly influenced by the number and strength of the crashes of thunder during a storm. As the growth of truffles depends on the amount of rainfall, there is a grain of truth in this belief.

Truffles are found in arid areas all around the Mediterranean, especially along the North African coast from Morocco to Egypt and further east across the great desert plain between Damascus in Syria and Basra in Iraq. In all these regions, people

Desert truffles of the genus Terfezia.

gather truffles for food. They go by different names in different places and many varieties are found in Arabia. In Qatar truffles of both the *Terfazia* and the *Termania* species are found and are known as *khalasi* and *huber*. The former are oval with a dark skin and a pinkish interior and have a robust, nut-like flavour. Some people prefer the second type, the creamy-coloured *huber*, with their more delicate flavour. *Zubaydi*, another popular truffle, is also found here and more are imported from Algeria, Morocco, Libya, Iran and Egypt, which sell for anything upwards of QR 200 per kilo. Truffles can usually be found for sale during the early months of the year at the back of the Salwa Road vegetable market and in a lane at the side of the nearby Omani market. Sometimes, Asian expatriates working in Qatar go out into the desert at weekends and offer truffles they have found for sale beside the main roads.

Usually no more than a few centimetres across but sometimes as big as a man's closed fist, truffles are light in the hand, weighing anything from 30 to 300 grams. The skin can range from a pale sandy brown to a deeper chocolate hue, and some have a reddish tinge. They are roughly spherical, but with a tendency to irregular lobes and bumps, and have a slightly spongey texture.

Experienced searchers for truffles know to look for truffles in slightly hollow areas that may dry out more slowly than level or hilly ground. They know, too, to look for certain plants that grow in symbiotic partnership with the desert truffle, especially varieties of the *Helianthemum* 'sun rose' species. Fungal filaments of the truffle penetrate the roots of the other plant, from which it 'steals' its nutrients, sometimes reaching as far as 40 centimetres to do so. It is thought that in return the truffle produces a substance that inhibits competing plants.

In Qatar *Helianthemum kahiricum* and *H. lippii* are common and can be recognised, even by those without knowledge of botany, by their narrow oval greyish-green leaves and small, pale yellow flowers. Small, shrubby plants, they reach from 10 cm to 30 cm in height. They are known locally in Arabic as *ragroug*.

The best time of day to look for truffles is either in the very early morning or at sunset, when any slight rise in the sand casts a shadow that indicates a truffle might be hiding a few centimetres below. I found my first truffles, many years ago, by shamelessly following a group of bedouin ladies hunting for truffles in the desert until they took pity on me and kindly showed me how to look for the slight rise and the faint cracks in the surface of the ground which are the clues to the presence of truffles growing beneath.

My first efforts were not a success; being unsure of exactly what I was looking for I threw away the first two I found, mistaking them for pebbles! I know better now, but lack the patience of the truly successful truffle hunter.

Once found and brought to the surface, desert truffles have two enemies, sunlight and humidity, so they need to be speedily taken home and prepared. They are not happy being kept in plastic bags, and storage in the refrigerator does not prolong their life. Better to keep them in a shaded room with an air conditioner blowing cool air over them, if they cannot be prepared and eaten at once.

Traditionally, the bedouin roasted truffles in the ashes of their campfires or boiled them in camel's milk. Lacking either a campfire or a handy camel, many western expatriates prefer to boil them in cow's milk. Occasionally, gifts of truffles from generous Qatari friends come our way. We find that they are also excellent sliced and fried gently in butter for a few moments, with a sprinkling of rock salt and black pepper. Whatever method you use, truffles require the minimum of cooking, like mushrooms. You should also recognise that, no matter how carefully you clean them and slice them, their method of growth traps pockets of sand in the folds of the fruit body. So be prepared for a slight crunchiness!

The Desert Blooms

The flat, arid desert lands of Qatar do not at first sight seem like a place where one would expect many plants to survive. Yet the vegetation of Qatar is surprisingly varied. There is no natural surface water, and rainfall is minimal and sporadic, with almost none occurring in some years. But because of the high temperatures and shallow seas around the peninsula the evaporation and consequent precipitation rate is high, and the heavy dew settling on the ground at night is enough to provide moisture for both plants and desert-dwelling animals to survive. During the cooler months, fogs are a reliable and steady source of water.

Halopeplis perfoliata, *the String of Beads Plant.*

Desert plants adapt in various ways to the extreme climate and soil conditions. Much of the ground in Qatar is saline. Just 2% of plants worldwide are halophytes (salt-tolerant plants) but Qatar has a much higher percentage. Plants like the Bean Caper (*Tetraena qatarensis*) and the String of Beads Plant (*Halopeplis perfoliata*) store both moisture and salt in juicy leaves which simply drop off the plant when the salt content becomes too high. Other halophytes like the beautiful Sea Lavender (*Limonium axillare*), with its dry, stiff bracts of purple flowers, excrete salt through their tough, leathery leaves.

Many desert plants have small narrow leaves which allow any moisture that settles on them to drip off and fall to the ground where the roots can

absorb it. Some plants, such as the showy yellow Desert Hyacinth (*Cistanche phelypaea*) do not photosynthesize their food at all, and have no leaves. Instead they tap into the roots of neighbouring halophytic plants, the Bean Caper among them. Many desert plants, from the humble, ground-covering Knucklehead Weed (*Sclerocephalus arabicus*) to the acacias, arm themselves with a range of prickles and sharp thorns to repel grazing animals.

In addition to its native plants, there are many species in Qatar which have been accidentally or deliberately introduced and have become naturalised, either as weeds or deliberately cultivated. Some survive in natural shallow depressions in the desert, known as *rodats*, where enough moisture collects to allow both trees and flowering plants to survive, but others are reliant on artificial irrigation. Other introductions like the unwelcome and invasive Mesquite (*Prosopis juliflora*), originating in central America, are completely independent of human support and have now reached the remotest stretches of desert, where their deep thirsty roots and low spreading branches prevent other vegetation from surviving near them. By contrast, the native Ghaf (*Prosopis cineraria*), is in decline, with less than a hundred trees remaining, some of them estimated to be over a century old.

Each kind of habitat in Qatar has its own specialised natural vegetation. The *hamada,* which dominates much of the interior of the country consists of flat or gently rolling desert plains covered with broken stones and small boulders of the underlying limestone bedrock, and windblown sand. Vegetation is sparse and is dominated by the common, orange-berried shrub *Lycium shawii* and a few halophytic plants. Other areas are covered with smaller coloured, wind-polished stones and gravel, carried countless millennia ago by an ancient river, where small flowering plants like the Sun Rose (*Helianthemum lippii*), host to the desert truffle or *fuga* (Chapter 15), raise their delicate yellow blossoms to the sky, along with species of grasses.

One of the most attractive plants in Qatar, the Caper Plant (*Capparis spinosa*), grows in such stony soils. Although not common, when it does occur there are likely to be at least a dozen small bushes growing quite close together. The blossoms of most desert plants are small and inconspicuous but those of *Capparis* flaunt big, four-petalled whitish/pink flowers, much visited by bees.

Around the long coastline are areas of low-lying *sabkha* which is inundated with sea water whenever a high tide occurs, leaving a glistening, salt-encrusted surface. Even the toughest halophyte cannot survive here, but around the drier edges they flourish, including *Limonium axillare*, species of *Salsola* and the ubiquitous *Tetraena qatarensis*, the commonest halophyte of them all.

The large natural depressions known as *rodats* contain fine sand and loamy soil, enriched by the droppings of the sheep and goats which seek food and shade in these areas. Besides the native species like *Acacia ehrenbergiana*, *Acacia tortilis* and *Ziziphus nummularia*, is the invader *Propopis juliflora*. In the winter these areas, where shade is provided by the shrubs, are often carpeted with a rich variety of annual and perennial herbs and grasses, among them species of *convolvulus* with their pale, delicate cone-shaped flowers, the bright yellow buttons of the shrub *Pulicaria undulata*, the blue-flowered Eyelash Plant (*Blepharis ciliaris)*, the small, starry white petals of Spurrey (*Spergula fallax*) and the trailing vines and tennis-ball-sized fruits of the deceptively edible-looking Bitter Gourd (*Citrullus colocynthis*), so acrid that even camels will not eat them, although apparently the Spiny-tailed Agamas find them palatable!

Capparis spinosa.

Artificial wetlands in several areas of Qatar include large lagoons taking waste water from various sources, and the surrounding areas of sewage treatment plants. The lagoons are surrounded by

Pulicaria undulata, *a bush-like plant common in* rodats.

thick tall stands of the reed *Phragmites australis*, providing shelter for many birds, and *Tamarix* shrubs. Marshy areas around the treatment plants themselves host such plants as the climbing vines of *Solanum humile* and *Solanum nigrum*, with their dark yellow or glossy black berries, many species of grasses, and the low-growing *Launaea procumbens*.

Some of the most attractive and interesting plants in Qatar can be found on the rocky hills in the south-west, particularly the range on the north side of the road a few kilometres before the border at Abu Samra. The summits, covered in river-borne gravel and sand, are rather bare but the sides and sheltered pockets are often rich in vegetation, including the Brown lily (*Dipcadi erythraeum*) which grows from a small white bulb buried almost a metre below the surface. This is one of only two lilies found in Qatar, the other being the Asphodel

(*Asphodelus tenuifolius*) which grows in areas such as the edges of desert tracks where moisture collects. Another beautiful plant found on these hills is the bush *Indigofera intricata*, instantly recognisable with its small grey-green leaves and scarlet pea-like blossoms.

Plants, along with birds, were among the first branches of the natural history of Qatar to be comprehensively studied, with a detailed and well-illustrated flora, in *Ecology and Flora of Qatar*, published by an Egyptian botanist K H Batanouny in 1981. This is now becoming outdated as plant names change and new species are discovered, and several new floras have been published since then, with more in preparation. In 1991, following an initiative by HH Sheikh Mozah bint Nasser Al Misnad, the annual programme, *A Flower Each Spring*, was launched, and each year since then a different native plant has been chosen for study by school children, with activities organized by experts from the Friends of the Environment Centre.

Asphodelius tenuifolius. *one of two lilies found in Qatar that grow from bulbs.*

Lycium shawii, *or Arabian Boxthorn, may well be the commonest desert shrub in Qatar. Above and right, the shrub before and after bearing fruit.*

In the winter months *Cistanche phelypaea* grows in abundance on the coast beside mangrove forests and on the dunes beside Khor Al Adaid

Footprints in the Sand: Foxes and Jackals

One of the least frequently seen of all Qatar's desert mammals is the Arabian Red fox. Yet to judge from the trails of fox footprints on beaches and in the desert and from the droppings atop every coastal jebel, foxes are widespread. Whenever we camp on a west coast beach, the next morning our tents are surrounded by trails of little foxy footprints, criss-crossing the sand. Quite recently at our regular camping spot a large dog fox has taken to lying quietly just out of range of the light from our fire, watching us and waiting for scraps, or sitting on the *jebel* above, its large ears outlined against the starry sky. Unlike the rarer desert mammals, the fox is unlikely to appear on lists of endangered species in the foreseeable future, owing to its ability to adapt to changing conditions and its varied diet.

During the cooler months we occasionally see Red foxes out and about during the day on the low hills in the central gravel plains of Qatar, but generally it is easier to observe them at night. If disturbed during the daytime they invariably dash away, but at night, if caught in the headlights of a car, they stare transfixed for a moment before quietly trotting off about their business, and don't seem to object to being followed at a distance.

Foxes usually come out at dusk, emerging from their burrows as the sun goes down. There is a chorus of high-pitched barking as they communicate with other foxes inhabiting the area. This lasts for around twenty minutes, before they set off on the hunting trail. Feral cats occupy similar habitats to foxes and compete with them for food. For some years at our camping spot on the Ras Abrouq peninsula we were joined, late in the evening, by a large ginger cat. We never saw it arrive, but a torch shone underneath our vehicle would reveal its eyes, shining like lamps. In the early hours of the morning, when everyone was asleep, it silently slipped out to forage for food scraps.

It is easy to tell the difference between fox footprints and those of a cat. Foxes walk in a straight line, placing each paw exactly in front of the last, whereas a cat's footprints are spaced slightly to each side of the line. Also, a cat's toes are more widely splayed than those of a fox, making the print round, whereas the print of a dog or fox is oval. Unlike a cat's footprints, the tracks of a fox have distinct claw marks.

There are two species of fox present in Qatar, the Arabian Red fox (*Vulpes vulpes arabica*) and Rüppell's Sand fox (*Vulpes Rüppelli*). Saudi Arabia, the Emirates and Oman are home to an additional species of fox, Blanford's fox (*Vulpes cana*), a small, mountain-dwelling fox with an enormous dark and bushy tail.

The Arabian Red fox is smaller, more slightly built, and is generally lighter in colour than its European cousin, although we have occasionally seen one with a reddish coat. The light sandy colour of these foxes is an adaptation to the desert environment – a small, slender body retains less heat, and the lighter colour provides camouflage. Its ears are larger, not only to assist with hearing but also to help cool the body during the hot months: as the blood circulates through the fine capillaries in the ears it is cooled by the breeze. The animal has a thin pointed snout, and the long tail is bushy and white-tipped. The Red fox inhabits the open desert as well as the coastal jebel of Qatar. We have seen them in the area of the 'singing dunes' between the Salwa Road and Mesaieed. Judging by the quantity of droppings, a substantial colony of foxes inhabits the area, dotted with outcrops of rocky jebel, between Al Zubara and Fraiha Al Gharbiya a short distance to the north. Like European foxes, our local foxes will adapt to living alongside man, often visiting the outskirts of settlements and scavenging from litter bins and skips. In Oman, a vixen made her den within metres of a busy supermarket!

Foxes are not only adaptable as to their habitat, but are also opportunistic hunters. They will eat anything they can catch – all the small desert

Golden jackal tracks near Khor Al Adaid.

Rüppell's Sand fox.

Above, a young fox and, left, an adult in very pale summer coat.

Arabian Red fox tracks.

creatures such as jirds, gerbils, jerboas, reptiles and insects, as well as fallen dates, desert fruits and plants. They also eat young birds and eggs if they can get them. This adaptability partly explains why foxes continue to thrive in many countries, including Qatar, despite the huge increase in human population.

Judging by the number of fox trails along the beaches, they are scavenging for anything the sea may have thrown up. A survey of nesting Hawksbill turtles conducted a few years ago concluded that, until rangers were installed to guard the nests, foxes were responsible for the destruction of 80% of the eggs laid on the northern beaches of Fuwairit and Umm Tais. They probably also kill and eat small crabs. Despite this occasional salty diet, foxes are able to survive for periods of up to a year without drinking water, although they will drink water if it is available. Presumably they get enough moisture from their prey and by licking the heavy dew from the leaves of plants.

Fox burrows are not always easy to see, but we sometimes come across their shallow-roofed, oval-shaped tunnels among the *jebel* outcrops. In the open sandy areas they tend to be where mounds of sand have built up around vegetation, and the burrows are often surrounded by the tiny starry tracks of cubs. There are also several burrows deep inside the large cave known as Dahl Al Misfir which lies to the right of the Salwa Road. The smell of fox as you enter the cave is quite noticeable!

On the west coast of the country, in the Ras Abrouq peninsula, the prominent features of the landscape are white limestone 'mesas' with a hard, compacted layer on the surface. Here fox burrows can be seen at the edge of the low escarpments, where the animal is able to tunnel into the soft limestone just below the hard surface and have the benefit of a good solid roof overhead.

Vixens give birth to an average of three cubs, in February to March. The mother suckles them for a month before introducing them to solid food, and the father helps in finding food for his hungry cubs. The babies' coats of soft, woolly brown fur soon change to thin coats of reddish-coloured short hair.

An Arabian Red fox in full pursuit.

Early one hot April morning we were taking a stroll over the big dunes beside Khor Al Adaid (the Inland Sea) when an animal suddenly sprang out from the shade of a large clump of saltbush ahead of us and raced over the sloping dune. At first we took it to be a hare, as we often see them in this area, but a glance at the footprints showed it to be a small fox, and our binoculars confirmed it.

It was a Rüppell's Sand fox, half the weight of the Red fox, and indeed not unlike a hare in size. Its colour was exactly that of the dune sand. We had a good view of the little animal as it descended our dune, sprinted across a stretch of *sabkha* and ascended the next dune, to disappear over the summit. Just before it vanished it turned to look at us, giving a glimpse of the enormous ears and black cherry nose. I felt sorry we had disturbed it on such a hot day, as presumably it had planned to lie up until nightfall in the shade of the bush.

Unlike the ubiquitous Red Fox, the shy, nocturnal Rüppell's fox is never found near human settlements. It is unlikely to co-exist with the Red Fox, which would undoubtedly hunt it for prey. It weighs only around 1.5 kg and has large ears, a bushy white-tipped tail and golden-brown eyes with dark markings leading downwards to the snout from the inner corner of each eye. The fur is paler than that of a Red fox, short and very thick, and the legs are shorter and the ears broader. Colouring seems to vary considerably from winter to summer, as can be seen from the accompanying photographs, with some animals turning almost white in the summer. Family groups tend to stay together. They communicate with a variety of sounds, ranging from barks and yaps to bird-like whistles. Nothing is yet known about the population of Rüppell's foxes in Qatar, but it seems likely that their main area of occupation is the far south and west, where the lonely dunes are seldom visited by man except at weekends.

A few years ago, some people camping on the shores of Khor Al Adaid were much alarmed by what they took to be some wolves skulking around their tents in the middle of the night! The Arabian

Wolf is not found in Qatar; what they had seen were some rare Golden jackals, and their mistake was understandable, because the animal closely resembles a small wolf. In fact, it is more closely related to wolves and coyotes than to other species of jackals. It has a tawny brown coat speckled with black, and long legs on which it can trot long distances in search of food.

Like Arabian Red foxes, Golden jackals are omnivorous, exploiting a large number of food resources including small birds, birds' eggs, rodents, reptiles, beetles, carrion – and of course anything they can scavenge from humans! We have followed their tracks leading in a straight line for more than a kilometre across the barren area of *sabkha* at the inner end of the Inland Sea, going from their dens among some low rocky hills to the beach where they were feeding on dead fish, crabs and shellfish. Besides the area around the Inland Sea they have also been seen on the Abrouq peninsula and at Ras Laffan. In the 1930s an Englishman camping on the north-east coast near Al Zubara described hearing jackals calling at night. They remain uncommon, and are seldom seen as they are nocturnal.

Arabian Red fox , showing the diagnostic dark grey behind the ears that helps distinguish the Red from the Rüppell's fox.

Footprints in the Sand:
Gerbils, Jerboas and Jirds

One of the pleasures of exploring the desert in Qatar is coming across a dozen or more sets of little footprints in the sand, all quite different, and trying to work out which animal made them and what it was doing at the time. There are the long, narrow slots made by hares, the single lines left by foxes, the alternating claw marks with an undulating line between which are unmistakably lizard, and the strange S-shaped patterns left on the slopes of dunes by sidewinding snakes. Commonest of all are the myriad little footprints left by the patterings of tiny desert rodents, the jerboas, gerbils and jirds.

These little mammals, which are often broadly classified as 'mice' by the non-expert, breed prolifically, and this is fortunate, because there can be few animals with more predators. Monitor lizards will crawl down burrows and eat baby rodents, foxes will dig for them, a rodent meal will last a snake a fortnight, and constant danger looms from owls, hawks and other raptors.

Worldwide, there are some 1,700 species of rodents, ranging from large, bulky Indian and African porcupines down to the African Pygmy mouse, the smallest mammal on earth, about the length of your first thumb joint. Of these, about 50 are found throughout the Middle East, of which around 20 inhabit the Gulf region.

The number of species is not as high as in some other parts of the world, but the diversity of forms is wide, owing to Arabia's position as a 'zoological crossroads' which links the faunas of central Asia and India to those of Africa and Europe, and also to its climate diversity which means that sandy deserts, forests and even snow-covered mountains may be found in proximity, as in areas of Saudi Arabia.

There is no accurate record, as yet, of the number of rodent species present in Qatar. Lesser Egyptian jerboas (*Jaculus jaculus*) are widespread, as are gerbils, of which there are two, or just possibly three, species present: Cheesman's gerbil (*Gerbillus cheesmani*), the Baluchistan gerbil (*Gerbillus nanus*) and Wagner's gerbil (*Gerbillus dasyurus*). For the non-expert they are almost impossible to tell apart, and even the expert needs to catch them first in order to identify them.

The Cheesman's gerbil has hairy soles to its feet and is a sandy-orange colour, with a white chest and belly. Its tail is sandy-orange above and white underneath, with a small white hairy tuft. It is not colonial, living in solitary burrows in the sandy mounds that accumulate around vegetation. Its relative, the Baluchistan gerbil, is darker in colour,

The Lesser Egyptian jerboa, Jaculus jaculus, *is capable of making gigantic leaps on its long back legs.*

with white patches behind its ears. The soles of its feet are without hair, and it has a prominent dark tail tuft. It lives in colonies, preferring saline flats and semi-desert. The Wagner's gerbil is very similar in appearance to the Baluchistan gerbil, but favours rocky habitats. It has a grey-tufted tail, and the hind feet do not have hairy soles.

Gerbils are fast runners, and are occasionally active at dusk or dawn. This distinguishes them from jerboas, which hop rather than run and are mainly active after dusk.

Lesser Egyptian jerboas are a pale buff-colour on their upper parts, with a cream-coloured underside. They are charming little creatures, with a long, tufted tail, large, shining black eyes and a short, rounded nose. The hind legs are greatly enlarged, with three toes on each foot and a cushion of hair underneath. This is a feature common to both desert animals and those living amid snowy wastes. In both cases it helps the animal to maintain a grip and it insulates their feet from extreme temperatures. The front legs are short and are never used for running. The Lesser jerboa is popularly known as the 'Kangaroo Mouse' because of its spectacular leaps. When in flight from a predator, each leap may exceed a metre in length: the equivalent of a human jumping the length of a football pitch! Jerboas have been seen to

make vertical jumps to a height of almost a metre. I once kept a jerboa for a few days' observation, but I had to release it sooner than planned, as it was in danger of braining itself against the roof of its cage!

Lesser jerboas are nocturnal in their habits. We have sometimes had the pleasure of their company while sitting around a camp-fire at night, as they hop nimbly about and forage for our scraps. Down at Khor Al Adaid we have sometimes been joined by both jerboas and gerbils and that it may be that, owing to the influx of weekend visitors, they are losing their instinctive caution of humans.

The Lesser jerboa exists entirely without water and will not drink even in captivity. It gains all the fluid it needs from seeds, leaves and grasses. It is equally at home both in the deep, sandy desert and in the stony hills of the UAE and Oman. Like other desert dwellers, in the searing heat of July and August it survives through aestivation (summer hibernation) in deep subterranean burrows which it blocks with sand, thus keeping away predators and providing a steady micro-climate for itself. Their burrows are very deep, reaching to as much as a metre below ground. Jerboas always provide themselves with one or two escape tunnels: a wise precaution, as lizards can crawl down their burrows and foxes can, and often will, attempt to

Sundevall's jird, Meriones crassus, *is common in Qatar.*

A Lesser Egyptian jerboa, Jaculus jaculus.

dig them out. They line their sleeping chamber with camel hair or shredded vegetation and give birth to a litter of three to four young every three months.

Whereas jerboas will tolerate a variety of habitats, gerbils tend to specialise, with slightly differing species inhabiting different kinds of terrain. Gerbils in Arabia may be subdivided into two groups: the sand-dwellers (*psammophilae*) and those that inhabit rocky and hilly areas such as occur in the UAE and Oman.

Gerbils have larger cousins, known as jirds, of which two species may be present in Qatar: the Libyan jird (*Meriones libycus*) and Sundevall's jird (*Meriones crassus*). The only recognisable difference between the two species is that one has dark claws and the claws of the other are ivory in colour. Jirds are greyish-brown with a long black tuft on the tip of the tail. They are active in both day and night, living in colonies, and have elaborate burrow systems with many entrances, covering areas of several metres. When danger threatens, they run with their tails held upright while making clicking noises, perhaps as a warning signal to other members of the colony.

Worldwide, rodents continue to flourish, owing to their resilience and adaptability as well as their ability to reproduce themselves in large numbers. Provided that enough of the sandy wastes, salty flats and rocky hills of this region are left undisturbed by man, and the rainfall is sufficient to encourage the growth of the vegetation on which they depend, these harmless little creatures will survive, leaving the delicate tracery of their tiny footprints as they go about their business.

Cheesman's gerbil, Gerbillus cheesmani.

Footprints in the Sand: Sand Cats and Ratels

Within the last few years, positive identifications have been made within Qatar of two rare animals, whose presence had never previously been verified by scientists. They are the Sand cat (*Felis margarita*) and the Honey badger or ratel (*Mellivora capensis*).

The shy and beautiful Sand cat is the smallest of the Arabian cats, weighing on average around two and a half kilos. It is a stockily-built animal with short legs and a long tail. There are six sub-species, and the one found in Qatar is called *Felis margarita harrisoni*, after a British zoologist who made a tentative recording of its presence on the border of Qatar and Saudi Arabia in 1991.

Sand cat kittens at Al Wabra Wildlife Preservation.

The Sand cat has a cream-coloured or yellowish-brown coat and a broad face with low-set triangular ears. Faint reddish lines run downwards from both the outer and inner corners of each eye. There are faint striped markings on the flanks, and both the ears and the tail are tipped with black. The markings on the fur vary slightly according to the sub-species. The broad head encases an exceptionally large middle ear cavity, giving the cat acute hearing, augmented by the large outer ears. This enables it to detect its prey, even if the creature it is hunting is moving beneath the surface of the sand.

Like other desert dwellers, the soles of the Sand cat's feet are covered with a thick pad of wiry hair, and this means that its small footprints lack definition and leave blurred impressions. If you come across

A Honey badger.

a line of very small, circular, footprints, on which the pads of the toes are not clearly visible, the chances are that it might have been made by a Sand cat. It sleeps during the day deep in the heart of a thorny bush, or in a burrow, often a deserted fox den. A single Sand cat does not use one burrow all the time, but will swap burrows regularly with other cats. Almost entirely nocturnal, the cats prey on insects, small rodents and reptiles as well as the occasional bird, eggs or chicks, obtaining all the moisture they need from their prey. They are reputed to be fearless snake hunters, tackling vipers by stunning them with rapid blows to the head and killing them with a neck bite.

Although they are mainly nocturnal, they often start their activities at dusk. A friend of mine had the good fortune to get a clear sighting of a Sand cat one winter morning, just as the sun had appeared over the horizon. He was out bird watching near a farm in central Qatar when he saw the little cat hunting among some reeds. It looked at him for a startled moment before vanishing into a burrow.

Outside the mating season, Sand cats lead solitary lives, and like all cats they communicate by leaving scent markings. Their calls are similar to that of domestic cats but they also make a high-pitched barking sound especially when seeking a mate. There are usually three kittens in a litter.

The Sand cat is believed to be widespread in the sandy deserts of Africa, Arabia and Asia, but much more remains to be learned about the private life of this shy and elusive animal.

The story of the Honey badger in Qatar is somewhat mysterious, because until recently, no live specimen had been seen by natural historians. Some years ago one turned up in the central deserts, near a farm, and was battered to death by the farm workers, who claimed, no doubt with justification, that it had been attacking their chickens. A photo of the creature was taken and sent to the *Gulf Times* for publication, and was identified as a Honey badger, also known as a Ratel (*Mellivora capensis*). It caused some surprised speculation at the time, as the animal was not known by zoologists to exist in Qatar. Since then two dead animals have been found as road kills on the road past the singing dunes that leads to Al Kharana village and in 2004 one was reported in the Arabic press as having been caught, alive, near Al Sheehaniya.

In November 2005 I identified the long-clawed tracks of Honey badgers in a *rodat* not far from the area where the road kills were found the previous year. A live sighting has been reported from Ras Abrouq. Within the last ten years the discovery of a colony of Honey badgers in Abu Dhabi was announced, and a specimen captured and photographed.

Honey badgers are heavily built, black and white animals. They have a reputation for strength and ferocity and for more than ten years the *Guinness Book of Records* has named them 'the world's most fearless creature'! The South African army actually named a heavily-armoured Infantry Fighting Vehicle after this voracious predator, which has been filmed standing its ground in the face of a lion and tackling large, extremely venomous snakes that few other animals would venture to take on. There is footage of a Honey badger attacking a four-wheel-drive vehicle it regarded as trespassing in its territory.

 Sand cat tracks.

Despite their name, Honey badgers are not closely related to other badgers and are anatomically more similar to weasels. The head, with its inconspicuous low-set ears is flat, and small in relation to the length of the body, and the muzzle is black, as are the cheeks and the area around the brown eyes. The claws on the front feet are massive. Its tough loose skin enables it to wriggle free from the grip of an attacker, and it can also defend itself by squirting a foul-smelling spray from its rear end.

The animal's diet mainly consists of termites, lizards, snakes and small mammals. It gets its name from its partiality for honey, which it takes from bees' nests whenever it has the opportunity, devouring honey and larvae and ignoring the stings of the enraged bees. In other countries it has a well-deserved reputation for breaking into chicken houses and, like foxes, killing far more birds than it can eat.

Honey badgers are solitary animals, although they may hunt in pairs during the mating season. For that reason cameramen filming the BBC Two programme *Wild Arabia*, first broadcast in 2013, were surprised to encounter a pack of no fewer than six Honey badgers in the Dhofar mountains of southern Oman.

With ever-increasing encroachment on the desert, whether because of the demand for building land or from activities connected with the oil and gas industries, the pressure on creatures like the Honey badger is inevitable. It would be a tragedy if, its presence in Qatar having just been confirmed, it became yet one more statistic of extinct wild fauna of this country, along with the wild ass and the Arabian ostrich.

An adult Sand cat.

Footprints in the Sand: A Prickly Survivor

Within a week or two of arriving in Qatar from Britain in August 1985, I encountered a hedgehog in the desert not far from the Salwa Road.

The pleasure of meeting such a familiar animal was mixed with surprise at seeing it in what seemed an alien environment. I knew nothing about desert animals and had always associated hedgehogs with damp woods, long wet grass and the leaf-strewn bottoms of ditches where they searched for slugs and snails. Yet here was this little fellow, trotting along through bone-dry sand which was almost too hot to touch. It was obvious that my previously-held image of hedgehogs needed updating.

I did not realise then that Arabian desert mammals are always smaller than their European counterparts, and assumed from its size that it was a juvenile. I now know that it was not a juvenile at all but a full-grown Ethiopian hedgehog (*Paraechinus aethiopicus*). Ethiopian hedgehogs are in fact one of the smallest species in the world. Although its name is linked to Ethiopia, this hedgehog species is not endemic to that country but is distributed across the Saharan region from Morocco and into the Arabian peninsula. Unlike the European hedgehog it has a pale band across its face, with a darker muzzle and a bald patch on its forehead. The animal is light in colour with long, white-tipped spines, which gives it an overall speckled appearance, and the legs are dark. The ears are prominent and slightly rounded at the tip.

As in several other species of desert mammals, the large ears of the Ethiopian hedgehog serve to lower its body temperature as blood circulates through the fine capillaries just under the surface of the skin and is cooled by the movement of air. It has

Pictured right, the Ethiopian hedgehog, Paraechinus aethiopicus, is a solitary animal.

longer legs than European hedgehogs, so that it can raise its body off the sand to allow cooling air to pass underneath. They also enable it to run very fast. A zoologist at Qatar University, who was radio-tracking an Ethiopian hedgehog at night, thought at first that someone had picked up his hedgehog and was carrying it! He had not realised that a hedgehog in a hurry can cover a kilometre in less than 15 minutes.

Since that first happy encounter I have often come across hedgehogs in the late afternoon, just as evening is drawing in, and at night when driving

across the desert. The little animal can put on a surprising turn of speed over a short distance, but its ultimate defence is to curl up into a tight, prickly ball. Not a single part of the body is left unprotected.

Like desert foxes, hedgehogs are omnivorous and this ability to eat almost anything and everything contributes to their survival success. Hedgehogs in Qatar have almost no enemies except man, as some fall victim to speeding cars. Their habit of curling up when danger threatens, which has been a successful method of defence for millions of years, is useless in this new situation.

A desert hedgehog survives on insects, grubs, wild fruits and seeds and will take young rodents such as jerboas and gerbils if it can get them. It will also eat the eggs and chicks of ground-nesting birds. In the wadis of the UAE and Oman they will eat frogs and toads, and they are not averse to carrion, no matter how rotten. Large domestic rubbish dumps attract many hedgehogs. Wadis and oases where there is plenty of vegetation are the preferred habitat of hedgehogs, although they can survive in the true desert provided there are some plants present. They are often found in date plantations, and in gardens and cultivated land on the edge of settlements.

Hedgehogs apparently have no fear of venomous snakes and will attack with all their spines erect. When the unfortunate reptile attempts to bite its predator, all it does is to injure itself on the needle-sharp spikes. The hedgehog waits for an opportunity to seize the snake and kills it by biting through the spine. An unfair contest, but one that gives hedgehogs additional popularity with those who fear snakes. Although not immune to snake bites, hedgehogs have a remarkable tolerance of their venom and are able to withstand stings from insects such as bees and wasps and also from scorpions.

There are two other species of hedgehog in Arabia: the Long-eared hedgehog (*Hemichinus auritus*) and Brandt's hedgehog (*Paraechinus hypomelas*).

Brandt's hedgehog, a large, dark-coloured animal, generally prefers a mountain habitat and is not found here, It is just possible that the Long-eared hedgehog may inhabit Qatar, although it has not yet been recorded and is rare in the UAE.

The Long-eared hedgehog is smaller than its two relatives. It has longer and more pointed ears than the Ethiopian hedgehog, and it lacks the bald patch on the head. In the UAE it inhabits the margins of deserts and is found on cultivated land, where many fall victim to pesticides. It spends the day secreted in a burrow or under a rock, emerging at sunset to spend the night hunting for food. An agile, fast-moving animal, the Long-eared hedgehog can cover several kilometres. Hedgehogs have poor vision but good hearing and rely on that and their acute sense of smell to help them locate their prey.

Although the spines of a hedgehog are an excellent defence against any predator, they are poor insulators against the cold, and so, even in Arabia, hedgehogs hibernate during the cooler winter days. They retreat into burrows or into deep clefts between rocks, or into thick vegetation. Hibernation is thought to last for up to six weeks, and the sleeping animal defends itself by remaining tightly curled into a ball with all its spines erect.

Much has yet to be learned about the distribution and lifecycle of Arabian hedgehogs, but studies show that in Qatar most produce their young between March and September. The average number of babies in each litter is four. The spines, which are soft at birth, soon harden. Surprisingly, juvenile hedgehogs do not open their eyes for about 20 days and so, unlike other small mammals, they remain helpless for a comparatively long period. Gradually the babies begin to feed on solid food, although they will continue to take their mother's milk, and by six weeks they are small but fully developed versions of the adult hedgehog. Soon the mother will drive them away, to begin the solitary life of a desert hedgehog.

Hedgehogs are not afraid to tackle venomous snakes such as this Horned viper (left) and they prey on the eggs of ground-nesting birds such as Plovers (right).

Footprints in the Sand: Hares

Like several of the other mammals inhabiting Qatar's desert landscape, the Cape hare (*Lepus capensis*) is a smaller version of its European counterpart, the Brown Hare, weighing only around 1 kg, as opposed to an average 3.9 kg for the Brown Hare. Perfectly adapted to life in the dry savannah grasslands of East Africa, it also flourishes in all the Arabian Gulf countries and appears to be plentiful in Qatar. Within Arabia there are a number of sub-species.

The metabolic rate of the Cape hare is lower than that of its European counterpart, it can survive temperatures of 45° C and above, which would be fatal for hares from temperate climates, and it can tolerate water of a high level of salinity.

I have seen Cape hares in every corner of this country, from the great dunes of the far south to the gravel-strewn plains of the north, and also atop the coastal jebel, but have probably walked or driven unseeing past many times the number actually sighted. They are remarkably numerous on Saffliyah Island, not far from Doha. When faced with potential danger the hare instinctively crouches and freezes, relying on its perfect camouflage for protection, and will only flee at the last possible moment. This habit makes it hard to make an accurate calculation of the hare population in a given area, because clearly it is not limited to the number actually sighted.

On one occasion I was with members of the Qatar Natural History Group who were walking across the high plateau at Ras Abrouq on the west coast, inspecting ancient burial cairns. In the midst of one excavated cairn was a clump of salt-bush and Sea Lavender, and as people gathered around it someone suddenly spotted an adult hare crouched in the middle of the bush. Its colour blended perfectly with its background, and it remained motionless, watching us with its wide dark eyes. We moved away to allow the poor creature to recover from its stress.

Like desert foxes and hedgehogs, the Cape hare, which is also known as the Desert or Arabian hare, has extra large ears. The relatively small body of the hare is easier to keep cool than a larger frame, and its ears are an efficient cooling system. The hair on its ears is shorter and sparser than on the ears of its European cousin, and this probably helps to expose the skin to the desert breeze. The blood that circulates through thousands of tiny capillaries just below the large surface of the ears is thus cooled before returning to the body.

Being so much smaller than their European cousins, Cape hares are sometimes mistaken for rabbits, which are not found in Arabia. Unlike rabbits, hares do not dig a burrow. They spend their day in shallow depressions, known as forms, which they dig in the ground or in the wind-blown sandy hummocks that accumulate beside clumps of vegetation. In the summer, as the sun moves across the sky, the hare will change its position, moving to a form on the other side of the bush to obtain maximum shade. In the cooler months hares may not go to the trouble of digging a form, but simply shelter inside a bush, like the hare I described above. In the UAE they have been recorded as occasionally making use of abandoned fox or lizard burrows.

Small Cape hares are alert to their surroundings. Note the large ticks on this hare's ears!

Above: Cape hare resting in the shade of a bush.

Left: Tracks of a hare and a fox.

Like the two species of fox and the Sand cats that inhabit Qatar, and also the Lesser jerboa, hares have stiff tufts of hair between the pads of their feet, to give a better grip on loose sand. Their soft brown and greyish fur provides perfect camouflage, to help them blend in with their desert background. However, as in rabbits, the underside of the tail is white and this is raised while running, perhaps to act as an alarm signal or to make it easier for young hares to follow their mother at night.

In the past, hares were often hunted by the desert-dwelling bedouin and were a valued source of protein. Both falcons and saluki dogs were employed by hunters when after gazelle, but falcons were not generally used for catching hares because the chances of a bird damaging its feathers while fighting to subdue a struggling hare were too great.

It was more difficult to catch hares in winter than in summer, because when food was plentiful the animals were very fit and would bolt for safety at the slightest disturbance. In summer, when running wasted valuable energy and water, the hares would try to rely on their camouflage until the last possible moment. A hunter, on his camel, would follow fresh hare tracks until he had located his prey, often crouching among vegetation. Taking his saluki in his arms, he would ride his camel slowly around the area where the hare was hiding, each time coming a little closer. When he was within ten metres or so he would throw the dog towards the bush where the hare was in hiding, causing it to bolt. If the dog failed to catch it within 50 metres the man would call the dog back and go in search of another hare.

Hares when pursued will stop from time to time and sit up with their ears erect, making themselves as visible as possible. A hare can only be caught by a fox or a dog when it is taken by surprise, as given a few seconds' start it can easily outrun its predator, and both animals know this. So when a hare sits and faces its pursuer the signal it is giving is, 'Don't

113

waste your energy. I've seen you.' This avoids a futile chase for both. Hares in Europe and in Qatar behave in exactly the same way, sitting up after the first mad dash to take stock of the enemy and to make clear that they are well beyond pursuit.

Desert hares give birth to an average of two young, known as leverets. Breeding tends to take place during the cooler months. The babies are born fully furred and with their eyes open. Within a few days they leave their birthplace, which may be nothing more than a shallow scrape under a bush, and find their own shelter, each remaining within 100 m or so of its siblings. This reduces the chances of an entire litter being wiped out by a predator such as a fox. The mother visits each baby regularly to let it suckle, but young hares are able to eat grass and shrubs almost as soon as they are born. They quickly become independent of the mother, which helps to increase their chance of survival should the mother be killed. At eight months they are sexually mature.

What of the future of the Cape hare in this country? Among its predators are foxes, snakes, Monitor lizards and Desert Eagle owls, but the main danger faced by hares is, inevitably, loss of habitat. In addition, some die under the wheels of traffic, But on the other hand, cultivated land, vegetable gardens and the great stretches of green grass of the golf course at West Bay are irresistible to hares. So, while human disturbance of the landscape is infringing on their natural habitat, at the same time they are being provided with a source of high-quality nutrition. Hares, despite their shy and solitary nature, are able to adapt quite well to life in a landscape that has been extensively altered by human activity.

A survey that took place in the 1980s in the UAE revealed that ticks brought to the desert on imported livestock weakened hares so much that they could no longer out-run their chief predator, the fox. That might also be the case here. However, hares are resilient animals. There are still areas of desert in Qatar that are rarely frequented either by humans or their livestock and it seems likely that the Cape hare will continue to survive here in the foreseeable future.

A Cape hare sheltering in its form.

Serrated Wings at Sunset: Bats

Bats are the only true flying mammals and are found all over the world. The forelimbs in bats are developed as wings like those of birds, and the forelimb provides the supporting structure, with the skin on the upper and lower surfaces fused to form a very thin, elastic wing membrane. This is kept stretched during flight by the five elongated 'fingers'. The wing membrane extends along the sides of the body to the ankles, and the interfemoral membrane lies between the hind limbs and the tail.

There are about 900 species of bats known to science. Within Arabia, comprehensive studies have been made of bats in Saudi Arabia, where 29 species are recorded, and in the UAE where 18 species have been identified to date. Here in Qatar the flat, low-lying desert terrain and dunes are not particularly

The first image ever taken in Qatar of a Sind Serotine bat, 2012.

favourable to bats, which require dark places such as caves, sink holes, old, long-abandoned buildings and deep crevices in rocks in which to roost during the day. No comprehensive study has yet been made of these mammals in Qatar, and fewer than half a dozen species have been identified. The cave known as Dahl Al Misfir always has a few bats roosting in cracks in its roof, and bats favour old-established farms, where there are plenty of insects, and old date gardens with mature trees such as the one at Umm Slal Mohammed. We have also seen a few very tiny bats flitting at dusk over the craggy limestone plateaux not far from Umm Bab.

Probably the most frequently seen bats here are those we came across roosting in a windowless

A Trident Leaf-nosed bat roosting.

Bats in flight at sunset.

inner room in the small restored fort at Al Rekayat in north-west Qatar. Around sixty small, greyish-pink bats were clustered along the mangrove poles in the ceiling. They were identified as Trident Leaf-nosed bats, *Asellia tridens*. This species is found all over north Africa and the Middle East, and is particularly heat-tolerant – in Iraq a colony was found roosting under the iron roof of a shed in June when the temperature was estimated at 38° C! In cooler climates these bats will hibernate during the winter, but in Qatar it is rarely cold enough for them to do so.

They derive their curious name from a feature on their nose of folded membranes resembling a trident, with a triangular central part and three spear-like projections. The colour of their silky fur varies, from a sub-species commonly found in Egypt which has medium brown fur, to the lighter colour of the bats found in Qatar. They have large, pointed, almost hairless ears and pale faces. Bats in flight are very difficult to identify, but when roosting the presence of a tail projecting beyond the flight membrane helps to identify this species.

An exceptionally agile species, Trident Leaf-nosed bats have the most diverse diet of all the bats found in the Middle East, and can catch moths and butterflies as well as wasps, bees, flies, crickets and beetles. They will also skilfully snatch up prey from the ground. Like all bats, Trident Leaf-nosed bats hunt and catch their prey using echolocation, and experiments have proved that this species can detect and avoid wires with a diameter of only 0.65 mm.

Farmers welcome bats, because they consume vast numbers of insects which may harm crops or carry disease. The roost in Qalat Al Rakiyat was located near several long-established farms. But when we went back on a subsequent occasion accompanied by a zoologist armed with a detector which records the ultrasonic echolocation sounds made by bats, the colony of bats had vanished.

Another species recorded here is Hemprich's Long-eared bat, *Otorynctus hemprichii*. The latter is a very different animal from the tiny Trident Leaf-nosed bat – at 11 cm in length it is almost twice the size, with big pointed ears, chocolate brown fur and a dog-like muzzle with a rounded end. The fur is greyish-white, giving the bat a somewhat ghostly appearance. The population in the Arabian Gulf is widespread but scattered, with only a few individuals in any one location. Unlike the Tridents, these bats prefer a solitary existence although as many as twenty females may gather during the breeding season to rear their pups. The young bats become independent at about five months of age.

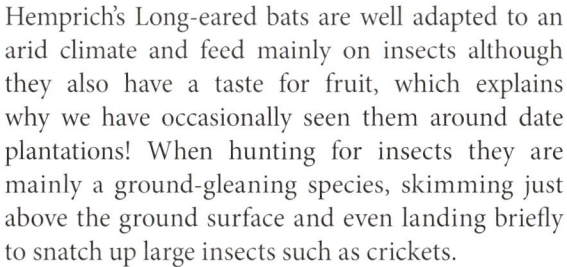

Trident Leaf-nosed bat in flight (above) and roosting in Al Rakayat Fort (right).

Hemprich's Long-eared bats are well adapted to an arid climate and feed mainly on insects although they also have a taste for fruit, which explains why we have occasionally seen them around date plantations! When hunting for insects they are mainly a ground-gleaning species, skimming just above the ground surface and even landing briefly to snatch up large insects such as crickets.

A bat that is recorded in Bahrain and is probably present in Qatar is the Kuhl's Pipistrelle, *Pipistrellus kuhli*, the smallest of the Arabian bats at barely 6 cm in length. The females are slightly larger than the males. It lives in colonies, often in crevices in the walls and roofs of buildings as it tolerates proximity to humans more readily than other species.

It belongs to a group known as 'Vesper' bats, which have blunt noses and lack a nose-leaf. The short fine fur is brown, and paler under the body, and there are distinctive stripes on the back of the wings. Although bats usually have single pups Kuhl's Pipistrelle females occasionally give birth to twins.

In July 2012 some photos were taken of a hitherto unrecorded species of pale-coloured bat flying over a waste water lagoon, which has identified as being almost certainly Sind Serotine bats (*Eptesicus nasutus*) rather than P*ipistrellus kuhli* as the pale stripe on the wing membrane between the fifth finger and foot, present in Kuhl's Pipistrelle, is absent. But to make a positive distinction between the two species would need an examination of the teeth.

Bats on the move are notoriously difficult to identify, flying at great speed and often in complete darkness. There is a famous story that the Arabian mammals specialist David Harrison was having dinner out of doors one evening in 1954 with Sheikh Zayed, who was at that time the ruler of Abu Dhabi's representative in Al Ain. Observing some bats flying around, Harrison remarked that he would very much like to have a specimen to identify.

Whereupon the Sheikh called for a rifle, and in a remarkable display of marksmanship brought down a bat with a single shot. It proved to be a hitherto unknown sub-species of the Sheath-tailed bat, *Taphozous nudiventris*, and Harrison named it *Taphozous nudiventris zayedi*, after the Sheikh.

Bats navigate by making a continual series of calls, too high for human ears to detect, which bounce off solid as well as moving objects and enable the animal not only to avoid collisions but to detect its insect prey. Lacking a crack shot, zoologists today rely on a handy gadget which records the individual echolocating calls and reproduces them in visible form as a series of 'pulses' known as spectrograms. The calls of each species are different, enabling them to be identified.

Land Snakes

Many terrestrial reptiles have successfully adapted to the harsh climate of sandy and rocky deserts. Their scaly skin, which is regularly renewed, helps to prevent them from dehydrating in arid environments. Their main limitation is their reliance on external heat: reptiles cannot control their own body temperature and require a level of around 25-30° C before they become fully mobile and active.

In Qatar, with its high summer temperatures and warm winters, reaching the required temperature is rarely a problem, but reptiles also have to ensure that they do not overheat. For this reason many species leave their burrows or hiding places, under rocks or in deep sand only in the early morning and late afternoon. Some are entirely nocturnal.

Among the reptiles of the Qatar desert are several species of snakes. Many people on first coming to Qatar wonder about the risk of encountering venomous snakes when out camping at weekends. In fact, the danger is very small. Of the nine species of land snake that may be present in the peninsula, only one is sufficiently venomous to cause harm to a human. Two or three others are mildly venomous and the others are completely harmless to humans, though not of course to their prey!

Non-venomous snakes have short teeth solidly embedded in their jaws. As they have no venom glands, the purpose of the teeth is simply to enable the snake to keep a grip on its prey. In addition to short teeth, mildly venomous snakes have one or more pairs of slightly longer grooved fangs, through which venom trickles into the wounded prey. They are sometimes called 'rear-fanged', as the fangs are located to the rear of the mouth and are only used when the reptile wishes to subdue its prey before swallowing. Since the fangs are not used for biting, people are in little or no danger from a mildly venomous snake.

Another group of snakes has long erectile fangs, which hinge back when not in use. In fact, they are so long that the snake cannot close its mouth when the fangs are erect. These long teeth allow the snake to inflict a deep wound into which they inject a large quantity of venom. In Qatar the only representative of this group is the Horned viper (*Cerastes cerastes gasperettii*) also known as the Sand Viper, which is found throughout the Arabian peninsula and eastwards to Iran. It is a short, rather thick snake, reaching a length of approximately 80 cm, and is light brown with cream

Toxinologist Dr Zoltan Takacs holding a Horned viper, Cerastes gasperettii, *caught in south Qatar.*

and darker brown markings. There is a distinctive dark stripe through the eye and a small projection, the 'horn', over each. In Qatar, many of the Horned vipers in fact have no horns. It's said that in Egypt, snake-charmers used to remedy the deficiency by driving a couple of hedgehog spines through the snake's upper jaw! When moving over loose sand, the Horned viper achieves minimum contact with the surface by 'side-winding', a movement in which only two points of the body are in contact with the ground at any time. It is this movement that leaves the curious pattern of parallel S-shaped tracks which can sometimes be seen in soft sand or on the sides of dunes. All 'side-winders' resume their normal sinuous movements when on firm ground.

Horned vipers are not aggressive snakes and, although they commonly bury themselves just under the sand, the thudding of approaching feet gives them plenty of time to disappear. If approached, they rub their scales together to make a loud 'hissing' sound. A few years ago an expatriate woman who was picnicking in the 'singing dunes' area of Qatar, near Mesaieed, was bitten because she put her hand under a rock beneath which a Horned viper was sheltering. She made a full recovery.

The venom of vipers is haemotoxic, causing bleeding in internal organs and kidney failure. The average person is highly unlikely to encounter a viper in Qatar, unless they spend much time in the desert, as these venomous snakes stay well clear of settled areas. In more than 20 years of walking the deserts of Qatar I have only once seen a Horned viper, although I have often come across their side-winding tracks on dunes. Although they are generally nocturnal, one was recently photographed coiled up on a path at Ras Laffan in broad daylight.

In neighbouring UAE, the most common venomous snake is the Oman Saw-scaled viper (*Echis omanensis*), which is found both in sandy deserts and in the mountains. Its bite is extremely dangerous and recovery from it is often both long and painful. A rarer relative, the Carpet viper (*Echis coloratus*), equally venomous, occurs in the mountains. Although a complete survey of the reptiles of Qatar has not yet been made, it is thought to be very unlikely, although not impossible, that the Saw-scaled Viper occurs here.

Rat snake, Platyceps ventromaculatus.

A reptile you are more likely to come across is the Rat snake (*Platyceps ventromaculatus*), which can reach almost a metre in length and is sandy-coloured with dark brown barred markings. Rat snakes are active during the day and will climb trees in search of small birds, to vary their diet of reptiles and rodents. It may turn up in your garden, and has alarmed many a Doha householder, quite unnecessarily! Some years ago, a British ambassador to Qatar noticed from an upstairs window what appeared to be a length of thin rope dangling from a tree in the embassy garden. While he was looking at it, it dropped to the ground and slithered away!

Another snake commonly seen in the daytime is the Sand racer or Sand snake (*Psammophis schokari*) which can reach a length of 1.5 metres. It is sometimes seen in Doha gardens. I have encountered Sand snakes sunning themselves on jebel outcrops on the north-east coast and among the ruins of the old north-western city of Al Zubara. Sand snakes are mildly venomous, but are highly unlikely to give a human a bite.

Once, at Al Zubara, a startled Sand snake streaked away from us along a ruined wall and into a crevice. Almost instantaneously a lizard shot out of the crevice like a cork from a popgun, sailing right into the air in its panic. It looked comical, although of course a matter of life and death for the lizard.

Sand snakes are slim and fast-moving. They are dark grey or olive brown with black and white lines at the side of the head. Some have longitudinal stripes along the whole of their body. Being a snake that is out and about during the day, it has round pupils in its eyes, which are a conspicuous red colour. Nocturnal snakes have pupils that narrow into slits in daylight. They are the longest of all the Arabian snakes, reaching a length of approximately

A Sand snake, Psammophis schokari, *devouring prey.*

Amphisbaenids are rarely seen nocturnal reptiles.

1.5 metres. If you see a long, thin, dark-coloured ribbon streaking away from you when you are out trekking, it is probably a Sand snake.

From time to time there are reports of people claiming to have come across cobras in the desert. What they are seeing is probably the Hooded malpolon (*Malpolon moilensis*), which is sometimes called the False cobra. If alarmed it will rear up and hiss and spread the skin of its neck in a cobra-like manner. The Hooded malpolon is another diurnal snake and has yellow eyes with round black pupils. It is a light, sandy brown with a pattern of darker brown spots. It inhabits the gravel plains in the centre and north of Qatar, and prefers areas where there is some vegetation, so it is not found in the areas of sand dunes to the south of the country. Like the Sand snake, the Hooded malpolon is mildly toxic, but with its fangs at the very back of its mouth it is very unlikely to cause harm to a human.

One morning recently we watched a Hooded malpolon venture out of its hole in the sandy mound under a thorny acacia bush and set off to retrieve the body of a jird it had killed the night before and left some 15 metres away. Every so often it stopped and lifted its head, flicking its tongue in and out to pick up the scent and adjust its direction. On reaching the bloated corpse of the rodent it took a firm grip with its teeth and proceeded to drag the animal back to its hole by whipping the whole length of its body and tail backwards, curling the last few centimetres into a 'hook' and anchoring itself to the sand with the hook while it eased its front half back over the ground. It then had to drag the jird up through the tangle of thorny branches of the bush, a

difficult process which took more than half an hour and must have been exhausting. Finally, the dead jird was parked beside the hole and the snake went inside, no doubt to rest after its efforts! A snake has to dislocate its lower jaw when swallowing its prey, leaving it temporarily vulnerable, so to have consumed the jird on the spot would have been too risky during daylight. When darkness fell it would emerge to enjoy the result of its labours. The meal would last it about two weeks.

On another occasion we were out in the desert, star-gazing, our telescope and binoculars trained on the heavens, when a snake slithered over someone's sandaled foot! It was a harmless little Leaf-nosed snake (*Lytoryhnchus diadema*) and the snake was photographed, rasping its scales indignantly, before being allowed to proceed on its way. The incident was a reminder to us to always wear closed shoes when walking in the desert after sunset, not just on the off chance of meeting a viper, but also because scorpions are on the prowl.

The Leaf-nosed snake, also called the Awl-headed snake, is a small snake, measuring only about 40 cm when fully grown. It is attractively patterned, with around 40 dark brown blotches on a light brown body and the dark brown 'diadem' on its head gives it its Latin name. Unlike snakes that hunt above ground, the Leaf-nosed snake will investigate burrows and other holes, and may well catch most of its prey underground.

We have come across the Leaf-nosed snake on a number of occasions since that first encounter. Once, on an early morning stroll on the high

ground near Salwa, we found one, barely alive, that had been bitten through the spine by a fox and left half-paralysed. Curiously, the fox had made no attempt to eat it.

One of the most attractively-patterned of the Arabian snakes is the Diadem snake (*Spalerosophis diadema cliffordi*), which can reach a length of 1.3 metres and has large, dark spots on a light brown background. It is harmless to man, and is indeed beneficial because of its preferred diet of small rodents. It is widely distributed in Arabia, Pakistan and Uzbekistan and has been recorded in the UAE and Qatar, where it is found around cultivated areas, but it is absent from the open sandy desert.

The only truly constricting snake found in Qatar is the Sand boa (*Eryx jayakari*). A nocturnal reptile, it lives almost permanently under the sand, but when it surfaces it leaves an easily recognisable undulating 'serpentine' track. We have sometimes noticed these tracks on the mounds of sand dotted around between the 'singing dunes' near Mesaieed, and on the area of dunes adjacent to the road leading to the Sawdaa Natheel border post. The Sand boa is perfectly adapted to its life under the sand, with its smooth glossy scales and its eyes and nostrils located on the top of its head, so that it can lie buried just beneath the surface with only these organs protruding. It preys on lizards and small rodents, coiling around its victim to asphyxiate it

A Sand boa, Eryx jayakari.

A Hooded malpolon.

121

and crush the bones before swallowing. Although it has no venom, the snake will still try to defend itself if disturbed by making 'mock' strikes. The Sand Boa has eyes with black pupils which narrow into slits in daylight, and can reach up to 40 cm in length. Its thick, strong body is yellowish in colour, with an irregular pattern of brown bars and blotches.

Occasionally we have come across most peculiar tracks in an area of scattered vegetation, forming sandy hummocks, on the interdune plains at Khor Al Adaid, and also on the west coast of Qatar. It looks as if a small snake had tried to move by tying itself in writhing knots, each leaving a roughly triangular coiled imprint. I was much puzzled when I first came across them as to what could have left such odd marks, but then I saw a photograph of the tracks of a creature called an Amphisbaenid (*Diplometopon zarudnyi*), and recognised them. Neither snake nor lizard, this strange little reptile lives mainly underground, feeding on insects and their larvae. It seems to surface only at night. Occasionally it can be found under pieces of wood, where presumably it feeds on termite grubs, and we came across one a year or two ago under an old piece of carpet that someone had abandoned after camping. The Amphisbaenid has a thick, pinkish-purple ribbed body with a pattern of small dark spots. It is about 20 cm in length, although larger specimens have been found. Another very

curious and harmless little reptile found in the Gulf states, including Qatar, is the Hooked Thread snake (*Leptotyphlops macrorhynchus*), which is one of the smallest snakes in the world. Rarely seen, it could easily be mistaken for an earthworm. It burrows in sand, only emerging at night, and is a specialised feeder on termites, although it will also eat ants. A good place to look for one is under the termite-riddled pieces of wood lying around in construction waste dumps, as it sometimes stays close to its food source during the day rather than go underground.

Although the chances of being bitten by a snake in Qatar are extremely small, it's important to know what to do, should it happen. First of all, forget all that dramatic cutting and sucking business, because all that will achieve is further pain and shock for the victim. Venom is so rapidly absorbed into the bloodstream that little or none would remain at the site long enough to be sucked out. The victim must be reassured and the limb that has been bitten should be immobilised at once. This is important. The injured person should lie down with the site of the bite lower than the heart. Then a broad pressure bandage should be applied if possible above and below the site, but not so tightly as to impair circulation. It can be made of clothing torn into strips. A splint made from a stick should keep the limb immobile. The injured person must then be carried to a vehicle and taken to the nearest hospital. Ice should never be applied to the site of a snake bite, as the reactive dilation of the blood vessels when the ice is removed can result in the venom being spread around the body more rapidly.

Authorities at the Accident and Emergency Unit at Hamad Hospital say that they see few genuine cases of snake bites. Far more common are the people who feel a sharp jab on the ankle from a twig or thorn and rush to the hospital in panic! For this reason a simple test for the presence of venom is always given before treatment.

Avoiding a snake bite is a matter of common sense: wear shoes rather than open sandals in the desert, and never put your hand under a rock when turning it over. Keep the fly-sheet to your tent closed at all times, whether you are inside or not. And if you are a golfer, don't fossick through clumps of long grass with your bare hands in search of a lost ball. Use a golf club instead.

A Hooked Thread snake, Leptotyphlops macrorhynchus.

Desert Sun-Worshippers

Anyone driving along smaller roads through Qatar's desert landscape will have noticed large lizards sunning themselves on the warm tarmac or, if the animals have any sense, streaking for their burrows at the sound of the approaching vehicle. All too often, the ones that leave it too late end up as road-kill.

These are the Spiny-tailed agamas (*Uromastyx aegyptia microlepis*), known as *dhub* in Arabic. They are the second-largest species of lizard in Qatar and present a fearsome appearance, with their heavy, spiked tails and sharp claws. They look more like something out of Jurassic Park than any other local reptile I can think of, but they are, in

fact, harmless herbivores. If cornered, they lash out strongly with their armoured tails and are capable of giving a nasty bite, although their strong jaws have no teeth. The naturalist and writer, Marijcke Jongbloed, who was based in the UAE for 25 years, had a passion for *dhub*s and occasionally handled them, but I have always kept a respectful distance!

*Dhub*s can grow to a length of 65 cm and live in burrows in a colony. Each burrow has an entrance twice as wide as it is high, with a convex top and level floor. The burrows are normally about 20 to 50 metres apart, with as many as thirty or forty individuals inhabiting each colony. It is possible that more than one *dhub* inhabits each

A Spiny-tailed agama warming up in the morning.

A juvenile Spiny-tailed agama.

burrow which may extend downwards as much as two metres. These colonies occur all over Qatar, but seem to be most common on the central gravel plain, although they also inhabit sandier areas and are present on the small island in the bay of Al Khor. We often see *dhub*s on the road between Al Wakra and Umm Bab and also in the area around Al Zubara in the north-west.

An active *dhub* colony can be quickly spotted by the droppings scattered around: they consist of large, elongated dry pellets, followed by a drop of white urea and, on fresh droppings, a blob of orange jelly lubricant. This quickly evaporates in the heat.

These lizards never drink water; obtaining all the moisture they need from their food plants. They have a gland near the anus which extracts all the liquid from the faeces and recirculates it within the body, while a special gland in the nostrils separates the salts and discharges them.

It was believed until very recently that *dhub*s were entirely herbivorous, but research conducted in 2010 by scientists at Qatar Foundation, who examined the contents of faecal pellets, proved that they also eat insects, dead skin from their own and other reptile species, and scavenge on the remains of mammals. All other lizards in Qatar are insect-eaters, with the exception of the Desert Monitor which takes larger prey. Like all reptiles, lizards and geckos regulate their body temperature by adapting it to the ambient air temperature. They only become active when they have warmed up. The terrain of Qatar, with its warm and dry climate, provides ideal conditions for this. In fact, in order not to overheat, many species have become nocturnal and are rarely seen.

Dhubs hibernate during the cooler winter months

124

and become more active from March onwards. When a *dhub* emerges from its burrow, it sits at the entrance to warm up, as being a reptile, and cold-blooded, it is reliant on the sun's warmth to provide it with energy. To begin with its colour is slate-grey all over, a colour which absorbs heat, but as the sun's rays take effect it becomes a pale mottled yellow. This colour reflects the rays of the sun at the hottest time of the day and helps to prevent the dhub from overheating. The face has an ancient look about it, like that of an elderly tortoise, and the large eyes are a deep amber hue. The heavily folded skin on the neck and body allows the animal to inflate itself with air when threatened. If cornered by a would-be predator, such as a bird of prey or a Desert Monitor, a *dhub* will inflate the loose skin that lies in folds around its neck and body to make itself look bigger and strike out with its spiny tail. It will also hiss loudly to create an impression of aggressiveness. But *dhub*s generally rely on their speed and make a dash for their burrows if alarmed. Their principal

The Toad-headed agama (above in close up) in an extraordinary mating ritual, in which one is repeatedly flipped upside down while remaining 'hooked' to the other.

The Short-snouted lizard, Mesalina brevirostris, *is an active daytime hunter, moving with great speed. It is common on the gravelly plains in central Qatar.*

enemy used to be humans, as the roasted tail of a *dhub* was formerly a popular dish among the tent-dwelling bedouin and is still considered a delicacy by some people. It has a reputation as an aphrodisiac!

The usual method of catching them is to place a long, narrow, nail-studded piece of wood with loops of fishing line attached to it besides the food plants near a burrow. The *dhub* gets entangled in the loops and when it dives into its burrow the piece of wood jams against the entrance, preventing it from reaching the depths. It can then be hauled out by means of the fishing line. They were formerly occasionally seen be seen for sale in the pet *souq*, which was sad, because they are almost impossible to keep alive in captivity, refusing to eat and dying of starvation and stress.

The size of *dhub* populations is directly related to heavy rainfall which has an effect on the plants on which they feed. Plentiful rain in 2005 resulted in an increase in the *dhub* population over that of the previous few years when rainfall was less, but recent years have seen very low rainfall and, once again, the population of *dhubs* and other desert inhabitants has fallen.

Another, even larger lizard inhabiting Qatar is the grey Desert Monitor (*Varanus griseus*). The Arabic name for it is *wirral*. Reaching a maximum length of 1.2 m, it has a back and tail banded with stripes of a dark colour, interspersed with lighter spots, and a long tail tapering to a thin point. Interestingly, the name *wirral* means the same as the English name 'Monitor': someone who keeps a regular check on

something. Presumably the reptile got its name from the concentrated expression it appears to wear.

Like all Monitors, this lizard is a carnivorous hunter and eater of carrion. It will also take the eggs and young of other reptiles and of ground-nesting and tree-nesting birds alike. It will dig for its prey and is reported to be cannibalistic. It has strong, sharp teeth and swallows its food whole. The roof of its mouth is made of thick bone to prevent damage to the brain by large mouthfuls of prey. Monitors are solitary animals, unlike *dhubs*, and each requires a wide area of territory.

We occasionally see Monitors on the central gravel plain, but they are less common and less widespread than dhubs. Environmental officers at Ras Laffan report that they are present within the large fenced area around the industrial complex.

An attractive little lizard to be found living in the great sand dunes of southern Qatar is the Sand skink (*Scincus mitranus*). It is commonly known as the 'Sand Fish' because of its ability to dive beneath the surface of the sand in a fraction of a second and then 'swim' underneath it, showing no trace on the surface. Beautifully marked, with a glossy skin like glazed porcelain and a row of rectangular dark spots on its flanks, it is a relative of the Ocellated or

Garden skink (*Chalcides ocellatus*), rather darker in colour, which inhabits Doha gardens. Once, we watched some herdsmen from a camel camp nab a Sand Fish on a 'singing dune' near the old road to Mesaieed; they assured us it had a 'very good taste'. We took their word for it! Later, we managed to catch one ourselves, down at Khor Al Adaid, and photograph it. We released it on the sand and then tried to recapture it, but the Sand Fish had instantly vanished.

A similar lizard, which is less common here, is *Scincus scincus conirostris*. It looks, to the amateur eye, almost identical to the Sand Skink except for the absence of the dark spots on its sides.

A small lizard which inhabits the central gravel plain of Qatar is the Blue-headed or Yellow-spotted agama (*Trapelus flavimaculatus*). Adults measure up to 20 cm in length. Brown, with mottled lighter markings, the Toad-head has long legs in comparison with the length of its body, and if feeling threatened will rear up and hiss with its mouth open. It gets its name 'Blue-headed' from its colour-change when alarmed or excited, the head becoming a deep blue and the tail orange.

In soft sand, and particularly on sand dunes, you are more likely to encounter its relative, the Arabian Toad-headed or Yellow Toad-headed agama (*Phyrnocephalus arabicus*). Adapted to life in the sand, this small lizard has fringes of scales to keep sand grains out of its eyes. Its body colour varies to match its environment: the Toad-headed agamas of the pale golden sands of Qatar being much lighter than those inhabiting the red sand dunes found inland in the UAE. The markings are black and white, with yellow patches on top of the head. On the underside of the tail is a black tip, used for signalling, which is highly visible when the lizard raises and curls its tail.

The Toad-headed agama has long legs, and uses them to raise its body above the sand surface on very hot days. It will stand poised and motionless for minutes on end while hunting, and then suddenly dart at an insect. When threatened, this lizard can sink vertically into the sand in a split second by rapidly vibrating its body, a process that has been nick-named 'shimmy burial'.

Away from the gravel plain, among the rocky areas of coastal jebel, tiny lizards dart at lightning speed, zipping under a bush or rock when danger threatens. These are Dwarf Rock geckos or Rock Semaphore

A Blue-headed agama, Trapelus flavimaculatus, *in display colours.*

A Desert Monitor, Varanus griseus, *the largest lizard inhabiting Qatar.*

A Spiny-tailed agama inflating itself in a defence posture.

A Baluch Ground gecko, Bunopus tuberculatus.

A Sand skink, Scincus mitranus.

geckos (*Pristurus rupestris*), delicately made little creatures with long tails and a mottled brown coloration that provides perfect camouflage. In fact, if they stayed still they would probably remain unseen, but that is not the way of these geckos. Their feet have long, thin, finger-like toes, typical of geckos. Dwarf Rock geckos have a number of signals that they can make with their tails, ranging from submission and appeasement to threat and aggression, hence their alternative name of Rock Semaphore geckos. The Rough-tailed Bowfoot gecko (*Cyrtopodion scaber*) is common in Qatar and like all geckos is an expert climber. It is nocturnal and can often be seen on the walls of buildings where it picks off insects attracted to lights.

Anyone living in Qatar, whether they go out exploring in the desert or prefer to stay closer to home, is bound to encounter the Yellow-bellied House gecko, *Hemidactylus flaviviridis*. In Indonesia a similar species of house-dwelling lizard is known as '*tjitjak*', and that exactly describes the chacking noise they make, like two pebbles being knocked together, during the summer breeding season.

Geckos are, apparently, the only lizards in Qatar with vocal chords. In May and June their eggs appear, like tiny oval white capsules, tucked into crevices in floors and walls around the house. The harmless House geckos do a good job catching cockroaches, mosquitoes and other insect pests, so it is a pity they are considered venomous by some local people. We once watched one swallowing a cockroach almost as big as itself, it took half an hour! The underneath of the gecko's toes are specially adapted to adhere to smooth surfaces such as walls and glass, with rows of lamellae covered with minute hairs called setae. A similar but much smaller house gecko is the Turkish gecko (*Hemidactylus turcicus*), which also has vocal cords.

For anyone interested in learning more about the reptilian inhabitants of the Qatar desert, the months of March, April and May are the ideal time to go lizard spotting. Cool weather keeps them indoors, but once the temperature begins to rise, and plants and insects are abundant, the reptiles are out and about and, like all of us, enjoying the sunshine.

Scorpions and Camel Spiders

Surprisingly, there are people who live for years in Doha without ever setting foot in the open desert, which they are convinced is full of hidden dangers. Some years ago our neighbours solemnly cautioned us about quicksands! They warned us that if we went off-road our vehicle would be in danger of being swallowed up. It was clear that they did not believe our assurances that no such terrors exist here.

One perceived hazard which worries some newcomers is the possibility of being stung by a scorpion. Scorpions are found here, as they are in all but the colder regions of the world, but being mainly nocturnal they are rarely seen during the

day. Still, everyone knows what a scorpion looks like even if they have never seen one. Their highly distinctive body shape seems ingrained in our minds from earliest times and conjures up images of an evil-intentioned, aggressive little creature scuttling around and lashing out with its tail in all directions. However, in common with other venomous creatures, scorpions avoid humans and will only sting when threatened. They hide under rocks and in clumps of vegetation, but what they really seem to prefer are pieces of old rotten wood, metal or even expanded polystyrene, of which, alas, there is no shortage, even in the remotest areas. Once, when we were camping, we threw a big piece of driftwood on to the bonfire and a

Fat-tailed scorpion, Androctonus crassicauda.

130

Deathstalker scorpion, Leiurus quinquestriatus, photographed at night in ultraviolet light.

A small, greeny-yellow scorpion, Buthacus nigroaculeatus.

on other arthropods, especially beetles and spiders, but some have been known to kill and eat vertebrates such as small lizards, rodents and snakes, injecting neurotoxins to immobilise their prey.

Unusually for arthropods, scorpions are viviparous, giving birth to live young that are miniatures of their parents. Mother scorpions care for their young, known as 'scorplings', carrying them massed on their backs, and the care can continue for several months. The lifespan of scorpions is generally from two to five years but in one species it is estimated to exceed 25 years.

The staff of the Accident and Emergency Unit at Hamad Hospital say they treat between one and three cases of scorpion stings per day. This seems a surprisingly high incidence, but similar figures are available from a hospital in Saudi Arabia. It is probably due to the high number of people here who make their living herding animals in the desert and working on building sites where scorpions may hide under building materials. A survey carried out in the Hail region of Saudi Arabia in 1994 recorded 820 cases of scorpion stings in 6 months of which one, to a small child, was fatal.

scorpion ran out and over someone's bare toes. It was a reminder to us that one should always wear closed shoes, not sandals or flip-flops, when walking around after dark.

Although scorpions have a reputation as dangerous killers, it is largely undeserved. As with snakes, another perceived desert hazard, many species are harmless, some are mildly toxic, and only a very small minority have stings that require medical attention. Even with the most venomous species, the sting is only likely to prove fatal to children, the elderly and those with an impaired immune system.

Scorpions belong to a very large group of arthropods – animals with a hard external skeleton, segmented body and jointed legs. They have four pairs of legs, but unlike insects they have no antennae or wings. The front pair of legs, called pedipalps, look dangerous, like the claws of a miniature lobster, but are harmless and are used for holding and tearing up food. The end segment of the tail carries a little sac of venom with a needle-sharp, curved sting.

Worldwide, there are between 1,270 and 1,300 species of scorpions, belonging to 16 families. They have existed on the earth for over 400 million years and are capable of surviving in the toughest conditions. In fact, desert scorpions are said to be able to withstand temperatures several degrees higher than other desert arthropods. They prey

If disturbed, a scorpion curves its tail over its back and circles, flicking its tail. It moves with surprising speed and agility. No work has yet been undertaken in Qatar to determine which species of scorpion occur here, but over 40 species have been recorded in Oman and the UAE and it is likely that several of these are present in Qatar.

The chunky-looking black scorpion, *Androctonus crassicauda,* is the largest of the scorpions so far recorded here. Adults can measure up to 15 cm from head to sting tip. Its name means 'Fat tail'. It is found in rocky areas and looks fearsome. Its sting is highly venomous and the smaller greeny-yellow scorpions which inhabit sandy areas including beaches are equally dangerous. Like *Androctonus,* they are members of the *Buthidae* family and a common species found here is *Buthacus yotvatensis nigroaculeatus.*

North Africa and Middle Eastern countries, including all the Gulf states, are home to what is said to be the third most venomous scorpion in the world, *Leiurus quinquestriatus*, commonly known as the Deathstalker. It inhabits both desert and scrubland and is small and a distinctive dark yellow which is different from the pale greeny-yellow of the locally common species mentioned above. Like them it is a member of the *Buthidae* family.

There are two types of scorpion venom. One is local in effect, causing swelling and discoloration of the tissues. The other is a neurotoxin (nerve poison) and the venom of the Deathstalker is of this type.

An interesting feature of scorpions is that they fluoresce in the dark when exposed to ultraviolet (UV) light. Scientists have not yet discovered why this happens, but it is used by biologists when estimating scorpion populations in a particular area without having to capture them. It is also an effective way of doing a quick scorpion count when camping, although in some locations it can be disconcerting to see just how many there are.

When hunting prey such as beetles, minute hairs on a scorpion's body can detect the faintest movement, and they can also detect chemical traces left by their prey. Just before moonrise the air is full of ultraviolet light, invisible to humans and other mammals, and this is when scorpions are aware that it is time to go into hiding to avoid being eaten in their turn by foxes, hedgehogs or owls.

There is no need for anyone to experience the pain and shock of a scorpion sting if simple, commonsense rules are followed. Never turn over a rock without keeping your fingers well clear of what might be hiding underneath. When camping, keep the fly screen on your tent firmly closed at all times. Scorpions seem to make a bee-line, if that is the right expression, for tents. A few years ago a school camping party on a beach near Mesaieed found no fewer than 11 small, greeny-yellow

A male Camel spider, Galeodes arabs.

scorpions underneath the ground sheet of the tent in which they had spent the night! Be careful when picking up boxes of food and equipment, you don't know what may have crawled under them or into them during the night. Always shake out your shoes in the morning before putting them on.

In the unfortunate event of a sting, reassure the victim, wash the wound with clean water and apply a firm supporting bandage but not a tourniquet. Keep the site of the sting below the level of the heart and get the injured person to hospital as soon as possible. In hospital a local anaesthetic will be administered by injection to relieve the pain, followed by an oral analgesic. The injured person is normally kept in for observation for six hours and then discharged if no deterioration in his or her condition occurs.

Camel spiders, also known as wind scorpions because of their speed, or sun spiders, are voracious eaters with enormous appetites. They eat any living thing they can catch – insects, desert rodents, lizards, snakes and even small birds. Some people believe that they also eat humans… but more of that later.

Their speed and aggressiveness make Camel spiders fearsome hunters, and ounce for ounce their body-crunching jaws deliver one of the most powerful bites in the animal kingdom. Using their massive jaws like a combination of pincers and knives, they chew their victims into pulp and then exude an enzyme that digests the flesh, before sucking it into their stomachs.

Camel spiders aren't true spiders, as they belong to a large order called *solfugida,* which numbers around 1000 species. As members of the arachnid family they are related to spiders, scorpions, mites and ticks. They appear to have ten legs, but the first pair are actually pedipalps – used as sensory organs in feeding, fighting and mating. They hide under rocks or in their burrows during the day, emerging at night on their high-speed hunting missions. In fact the name solfugida means 'avoiding the sun.'

On one occasion we were camping at the side of a dry, rocky wadi in Ras Al Khaimah, UAE. Soon after sunset in the light of our camp fire the ground seemed to ripple with movement as scores of Camel spiders raced around, the shadows cast by their bulky bodies and long, jointed legs making them seem even bigger and scarier than they were. We made very sure that the fly screen on our tent was securely fastened!

Camel spiders are less common in Qatar as in the Emirates, but nevertheless they do exist here and are occasionally seen by desert campers. Their legs are covered with short, stiff hairs, which help traction as they race around. Their bite is non-venomous, but they are capable of giving anyone who disturbs them a nasty nip. That intrepid Arabian traveller Wilfred Thesiger described in his famous book, *Arabian Sands,* the account of his crossing of the Empty Quarter, the horror with which these fast-moving creatures filled him: 'They were common in all but the most arid places. They were as much as three inches across, with hairy, reddish legs, and pendulous bodies, and they scuttled about in the firelight.'

Three of the ten known families of camel spider have been identified in Abu Dhabi: *Galeodidae*, *Solpugidae* and *Rhagodidae*. It seems likely that more than one of these families is present here. *Galeodidae* and *Solpugidae* are both long-legged with sandy-coloured bodies, whereas the *Rhagodidae* are smaller and darker coloured.

Not only are camel spiders ferocious predators, they are equally violent in their relations with each other. Males risk being killed and eaten when approaching a female to mate. If mating is accomplished the female will lay between 50 and 200 eggs in a burrow, and will feed the young with prey until they can hunt independently, but young camel spiders have been known to kill and eat each other.

Among the nomadic, tent-dwelling peoples of the Middle East, Camel spiders are reputed to creep up on sleepers, inject them with a powerful anaesthetic and eat their fill. A few years ago a British nurse in Qatar who had worked in Abu Dhabi told me of a bedouin woman and her baby who had been brought to hospital with fearsome wounds, attributed to a Camel spider. The woman had had part of her face eaten away, and the poor baby had bled to death after a vein in its neck was severed. The nurse believed that the injuries were the result of Camel spider attack, having heard of other instances while in the UAE. When consulted

A female Camel spider, Galeodopsis cyrus.

about this, an entomologist said that the bites were almost certainly made by rats, although it seems rather unlikely that a person would continue sleeping while a rat was biting them. I have also heard reports of workers on a desert construction site in Saudi Arabia who slept under their vehicles when it was cold, in order to benefit from the residual warmth of the engine. They would sometimes wake in the morning with wounds which they attributed to Camel spiders.

The experts assure us that such stories belong strictly to the realms of folklore. Unfortunately, these bedouin old wives' tales received a new lease of life from American soldiers who fought in the Gulf War of 1991 and took part in the invasion of Iraq in 2003. A photo posted on a popular website showed a soldier holding up a couple of Camel spiders which appeared to be the size of lobsters. It was the camera angle which made them look so large, but the picture received wide publicity in the United States, and the tale that Camel spiders

anaesthetise their human victims before eating them was repeated more than once by ill-informed narrators of TV documentaries.

Other popular stories doing the rounds at that time claimed that Camel spiders can grow to the size of dinner plates, and race across the desert making a high screaming noise as they run. When not dining off the American infantry they were said to feed on the stomachs of camels – some rumours even held that they did it from the inside.

Of course the size of the Camel spiders was grossly exaggerated, but all the same, they can reach impressive dimensions. One website states that they average about 2.75 inches (70 mm) in length. However, when I was living in northern Nigeria we managed to catch one and confine it in a glass tank. It was covered in ginger-coloured bristles. We measured it, and from the tips of its jaws to the rear end of its body it was 7.5 inches (190 mm) long.

Wings over Qatar: the Birds

Many people in Qatar, both citizens and expatriates, enjoy watching birds. This chapter provides a general introduction to the local birdlife, followed by two detailed chapters on birds of special interest, the Socotra cormorant and the Osprey.

The bird population of Qatar varies from month to month and from day to day, as migrants come and go. Some species reside in Qatar all year round, even during the searingly hot summer months of July and August. A number of these are introduced: birds that were brought to Qatar by the pet trade and have escaped, bred and established themselves as residents. A few birds, such as larks, survive in the desert during the summer despite the lack of available water, obtaining the moisture they need from the dew that falls on the ground surface at night. Of the migrants, some stay for weeks or months at a time, others are just 'passing through' and might make a stopover of only a couple of days.

Worldwide, human activities and above all the rapid increase of human population, have had a devastating effect on wildlife in many countries,

Common mynah, an introduced species now well established in Qatar.

driving some species to extinction. In Qatar, as far as birds are concerned, it is encouraging to note that the opposite is true. There is no record of the range of species on the peninsula a century ago, but it's likely to have been a fraction of what it is now.

Within the settlements, swimming pools, parks, gardens and golf courses provide sources of water which attract birds, and on the outskirts sewage effluent lagoons give shelter to thousands, some nesting or fishing, others simply stopping to feed, rest and renew their energy before continuing their long journeys. Rare migrants are regularly spotted in the gardens around the Sealine Resort south of Mesaieed, making their first landfall after flights covering vast distances. Date gardens and farms all over the country ensure a good supply of water and seeds, and attract the insects on which many species feed.

Residents in parks and gardens all year round include the colourful Rose-ringed (*Psittacula krameri*) and Alexandrine parakeets (*Psittacula eupatria*), introduced decades ago and now firmly established. Of these bright green species the former is the more abundant and is slightly smaller than its relative. Noisy but wary birds, small flocks fly screaming across the sky or congregate shrieking on rooftop aerials and in tall trees, feeding on fruit, seeds and nuts. They rarely venture down to ground level, but no parakeet can resist sunflower seeds so they are sometimes seen raiding gardens for these delicacies!

Another noisy resident, also introduced from the sub-continent, is the Common myna (*Acridotheres tristis*). Over the last three decades numbers have considerably increased and they are now common in gardens, parks and farmlands. A colony roosts in the date palms on the Doha Corniche and at sunset small groups follow each other homewards in looping flight along the sea front, loudly squawking as they go. As well as laying their clutches of 4-6 turquoise-coloured eggs in holes in trees or walls, some Common mynas in Doha choose to breed in the hot metal tubes of overhead traffic light gantries above main roads, the roaring traffic below being apparently no deterrent.

Rose-ringed parakeet, a noisy city-dweller.

Among the commonest land birds in Qatar, along with White-eared bulbuls (*Pycnonotus leucotis*), must be the soft grey-coloured Laughing doves (*Spilopelia senegalensis*) and slightly larger Eurasian Collared doves (*Streptopelia decaocto*). They are found everywhere, in gardens, parks and plantations, as well as on farmlands and in oases and even in the arid desert. Their numbers are surprising when one considers that doves, like their relatives the pigeons, are exceptionally casual nest builders and their flimsy constructions of twigs, balanced on thin branches or narrow ledges, frequently become dislodged by the wind, with disastrous results for eggs and chicks.

Among the most beautiful of the passage migrants visiting parks and gardens during the cooler half of the year is the Eurasian hoopoe (*Upupa epops*). Equally at home on grassy lawns and even landscaped traffic roundabouts, the hoopoe also frequents shallow wadis and rocky areas in the desert – anywhere that it can find insects. Its long slender beak is used for digging up insect larvae. On sandy ground its peach-coloured body blends into the background, but in flight its broad black-and-white wings are conspicuous. When landing, or when excited or alarmed, Hoopoes raise and lower the long crest which normally lies flat and projects behind the head.

Among other colourful migrants are the European (*Merops apiaster*) and the Blue-cheeked bee-eaters (*Merops persicus*) which pass through Qatar between late March and the end of May and again in September and October. The brilliantly-coloured European bee-eaters circle high in the sky above city gardens, farms and oases, hunting insects, and only when they perch on aerials and fences and occasionally at the tops of trees can their bright colours be seen. Blue-cheeked bee-eaters, rather less common, frequent settled areas and also mangrove and reed beds.

The peninsula of Qatar has an exceptionally long coast line in comparison with its landmass, and is frequented by thousands of sea birds and waders. Qatar has no natural open fresh water, but the

Opposite and right: Large flocks of Greater flamingoes inhabit the east coast of the peninsula, with smaller numbers on the west coast and at Khor Al Adaid.

Above: White-eared bulbuls are cheerful songsters seen all over Qatar, originally introduced to the country as cage birds many years ago.

Above: Common redshanks can be seen both on the coast and at grey water lagoons inland.

Below: Large numbers of Lesser Crested terns over-winter in Qatar, with a few staying over summer.

Below right: Great Crested grebes breed in Qatar and the adults perform elaborate pairing ceremonies.

construction of waste water lagoons, where reed beds quickly establish themselves, means that many birds also spend some of their time inland or even abandon the coast altogether. In the lagoons flocks of elegant Black-winged stilts (*Himantopus himantopus*) pick their way through the shallow water on their long, thin, bright red legs and are sometimes joined at sunset by flocks of Greater flamingoes (*Phoenicopterus roseus*) and Great cormorants (*Phalacrocorax carbo*) which fly inland to roost overnight. Flocks of Common moorhens (*Gallinula chloropus*) paddle in and out of the reed beds where they nest. They are quarrelsome birds and territorial disputes frequently break out, resulting in much noisy chasing and splashing. Another

source of noise in the reed beds are the aptly-named Clamorous reed warblers (*Acrocephalus stentoreus*). Their cacophony of screeching sound can be heard as one approaches the lagoons during the winter months, but the small brown birds hide in the reeds and only occasionally can an open-beaked songster be spotted, clinging to the top of a swaying reed. They do well to be cautious, as raptors sail silently over the lagoons on widespread wings, waiting for the chance to snatch a meal. These include Western Marsh harriers (*Circus aeruginosus*), Greater Spotted eagles (*Aquila clanga*) and even the odd visit from an Eastern Imperial eagle (*Aquila heliaca*).

Out on the coast, a passage migrant that is a 'must' for all serious birders is the Crab plover (*Dromas ardeola*). They are not common but small flocks are occasionally seen at low tide on the sandy flats on the east and north coast, keeping so far from solid land that good binoculars are essential. More easily seen and appreciated are the terns which glide and swoop over the water, making spectacular vertical plunges when a school of fish is spotted. The largest is the Caspian tern (*Hydroprogne caspia*) with its massive bright red bill and long pointed wings. A common winter visitor and occasional resident breeder on small offshore islets, it will not hesitate to attack any human venturing too near its nest sites! Around a dozen other species of tern inhabit the coast of Qatar, some are winter visitors and others, like the Lesser Crested tern (*Sterna bengalensis*), stay all year round. Among the waders are six species of heron. Some like the Grey heron (*Ardea cinerea*) and Western Reef Herons (*Egretta gularis*) feed out in the open, whereas the more secretive migrant Black-crowned Night herons (*Nycticorax nycticorax*) and Squacco herons (*Ardeola ralloides*) prefer the shelter of reed beds and mangroves.

Two young Little owls (Athene noctua) *locked in a mid-air fight over a mouse.*

As the tide goes out dozens of birds can be seen scurrying along the uncovered coastal mudflats, each species feeding in a slightly different way and so avoiding competition with others. Common (*Tringa totanus*) and Spotted redshanks (*Tringa erythropus*) are abundant winter visitors, along with Common greenshanks (*Tringa nebularia*) and both Terek (*Xenus cinereus*) and Green sandpipers (*Tringa ochropus*). Their relative the Wood sandpiper (*Tringa glareola*) prefers inland lagoons. Little Ringed (*Charadrius dubius*) and Common Ringed plovers (*Charadrius hiaticula*) are easily identified by their dark breastbands, and the Little Ringer plover also frequents farmlands and effluent lagoons.

Way offshore between the west coast of Qatar and the Huwar Islands great flotillas of Grebes sometimes congregate in the winter, with more than one species

A pair of majestic Desert Eagle owls, photographed in central Qatar.

joining the flock, which can include Great Crested (*Podiceps cristatus*), Black-necked (*Podiceps nigricollis*) and Little grebes (*Tachybaptus ruficollis*).

Four species of owl inhabit Qatar, of which three, the Barn (*Tyto alba*), Little (*Athene noctua*) and Desert Eagle owl (*Bubo ascalaphus*) are resident all year round. The fourth, the Eurasian Scops owl (*Otus scops*) is occasionally seen during the winter months, but is difficult to spot when roosting as its mottled grey-brown plumage is perfectly camouflaged against tree bark. Desert Eagle owls are one of the largest owls in the world, and a few pairs of these majestic birds nest among the tumbled rocks of limestone plateaux, far from human habitation. Although nocturnal they can occasionally be seen moving during the day near their roosting sites, and their prominent ear tufts and large orange eyes make them instantly recognisable.

Very few birds can tolerate the summer heat in the desert, and so true desert dwellers are few. But anyone exploring the desert landscapes is almost bound to see and hear one of the larks which live among the sand all year round, either small, grey-brown Desert (*Ammomanes deserti*) and Crested larks (*Galerida cristata*) or the more conspicuous slim and long-legged Greater Hoopoe-lark (*Alaemon alaudipes*), so named because its black and white wing pattern as it flies looks like that of a Hoopoe. Hoopoe-larks often approach quite close to humans, perhaps because they hope that the visitors' movement will disturb the insects on which they feed.

Undoubtedly, the most beautiful of all desert birds, and one which all birders hope to see, is the elegantly marked Cream-coloured courser (*Cursorius cursor*), which has been adopted as the logo of the Qatar Birds Records Committee. It is a passage migrant and winter visitor but occasionally breeds in Qatar. The plumage is a warm beige colour, blending in with the sandy terrain in which it hunts for insects, and the head has spectacular black and white stripes through and above each eye. Coursers, as their name suggests, are fast runners, and only as a last resort will they take to the wing.

Grey herons are the largest of the herons in Qatar and can be seen fishing in harbours, mangrove forests and tidal shallows.

Ancient legends say that the Eurasian hoopoe carried messages between King Solomon and the Queen of Sheba.

European bee-eaters constantly call to each other as they circle high.

Above: Squacco herons are solitary birds, usually hiding among vegetation, although they occasionally fish in the open.

Below: Clamorous Reed warblers are noisy singers, more often heard than seen.

A pair of Cream-coloured coursers with a juvenile.

A Socotra cormorant juvenile.

Socotra Cormorants

Anyone familiar with the coastline of Qatar will have noticed long, wavering strings of dark-coloured birds flying fast and low over the water, or drifting in dense flocks which constantly change shape like puffs of smoke as they move. These are Socotra cormorants (*Phalacrocorax nigrogularis*), known as *lohar* in local Arabic.

Unique in being the only bird species endemic to the Arabian region, they are intensely social creatures, and can easily be distinguished from the Great cormorants which visit our shores in the winter months. Great cormorants can be seen perched on buoys and fishing boats in local harbours and on the floating rubber booms around the Gulf Marina.

The Great cormorant is an altogether larger and heavier bird, with white patches on the head and neck and a jaunty orange bib on the throat. Socotra cormorants are slimmer and more streamlined, with very dark plumage, iridescent in sunlight, and are built for fast flying and, above all, diving. It has been officially recorded that these cormorants can dive to a depth of 18 metres. Unofficially, that depth was verified by a commercial diver who worked for some years in Qatari waters. He was finning along a pipe-line at 18 metres when he received a sudden and painful blow to the head. Thinking his last moment had come, he looked up to see a Socotra cormorant swimming away from him! During their dives for fish, inevitably, some birds get entangled in nets, or caught in fish traps, and drown.

The cormorants we see around the Qatar peninsula almost certainly all come from the great nesting sites on Suwad Al Janubiyah, a small, flat, sandy island with sparse vegetation, visible through binoculars from Ras Abrouq on the west coast of Qatar.

It is part of the Huwar Islands archipelago which is part of the territory of Bahrain. In the winter of 2002-3, more than 24,500 breeding pairs congregated in two nesting areas on this island, each pair laying an average of two large bluish-white eggs in a circular scrape on the rocky ground. There are two sub-populations of Socotra cormorants. The northern one breeds on Suwad Al Janubiyah and islands off the UAE and possibly Iran. The smaller southern population breeds on islands off Oman and Yemen. It is not known whether birds move between the two populations.

90% of the world population of Socotra cormorants breeds on small offshore islands in the Arabian Gulf. Extremely sensitive to human disturbance, over the last 30 years, 12 colonies have become extinct around the Gulf as sites have been encroached upon by development or subjected to prolonged human disturbance. Today, only 13 breeding colonies remain, of which the colony on the island of Suwad Al Janubiyah is the largest. Suwad means 'blackness' in Arabic, an echo perhaps from the days when the entire island was covered with breeding birds.

In January 2003 I joined a team from UNESCO, which was conducting a survey on the Huwar Islands. The boat I was travelling on passed windward of the cormorant colony. The smell was truly fearsome, inevitable when nearly 50,000 fish-eating birds congregate in a small area. Wherever one looked the sky was full of the black, drifting skeins, clouds and trailing wisps of cormorants skimming over the waves.

On the island the birds are packed as tightly together as a penguin rookery. Fights and squabbles are unavoidable, and the predatory Yellow-legged gulls are ever on the watch for unguarded eggs or chicks. The chicks retain their grey-white juvenile plumage for some months, and then change through brown to a glossy black. Once mobile they form large standing creches, which are watched over by adult birds while others fly off to fish. The UNESCO team found unmistakable signs that the colony had been robbed of eggs by people coming by boat, bringing a wheelbarrow with them to transport the eggs from the nesting ground. The cormorants are severely affected by pollution, especially oil spills. One off the coast of Bahrain some years ago killed an estimated 1,000 birds.

Seeing them on Suwad Al Janubiyah in such numbers, it is hard to realise that they are classed as 'vulnerable' by Birdlife International, but it is

A Socotra cormorant drying its wings.

Breeding ground of Socotra cormorants on the Hawar Islands. The immature birds are pale-coloured.

estimated that the total world population now numbers approximately only 110,000 breeding pairs, a steep decline since recording first began. In the UAE in the 1990s, the Arabian population was estimated to number between 600,000 and 1,000,000 birds, and a flock of 120,000 was observed feeding off Ras Al Khaimah in the northern UAE in 1997.

The breeding population on Suwad Al Janubiyah is down from the 1994-8 estimate of an average 26,000 nests per year, and the population is still affected by a disaster that occurred in November 1997, when heavy rain flooded the whole colony, chilling incubated eggs, drowning chicks by the thousand and leaving thousands more to die from hypothermia. In April 2003, at the end of the breeding season, the population suffered a further catastrophe when a thunderstorm accompanied by strong winds killed large numbers of half-grown chicks and caused the birds to stop breeding. However, a report in 2009 indicated that numbers have picked up and are remaining constant at around 25,000 nesting pairs.

The breeding season begins in September when the first eggs are laid, and lasts until April when the young are strong enough to fly. Once the season is over the Huwar Islands cormorants disperse around the Gulf of Salwa, including the coastal waters of Qatar.

Unlike the more solitary Great cormorants, the Socotra cormorants are comfortable in a crowd, and this is demonstrated by their roosting procedure. They congregate in dense flocks in isolated locations, among them the western shores of off-shore islands lying between Bahrain, Saudi Arabia and the Rubuds, the two most northerly islets of the Hawar archipelago. The birds cram tightly together, shoulder to shoulder, even though plenty of space is available. The reason for this behaviour is not fully understood, but experts theorise that it may be to provide shade for their feet when temperatures can exceed 60° C. In August 2002 a roost of 30,000 birds was recorded on the island of Umm Nassan. Sometimes, during calm weather, the cormorants will form a floating roost out at sea, a 'raft' of birds as tightly packed as on land. They drift for hours along tidal streams or currents.

During the hottest months there is almost total inactivity between dawn and mid-afternoon, when the day's fishing expeditions begin. A common activity pattern is for a group of birds to fly out from the back of an onshore roost and drop into the sea in front of the mass of birds along the water front, triggering them to swim out or fly to join their fellows. More and more birds enter the water, until the entire roost is drifting seawards on the current. The first thing that cormorants do when they leave the land is to bathe, a lengthy and thorough procedure. The feet are used to scratch at the breast feathers to dislodge dirt and parasites. The birds then repeatedly duck their heads underwater and beat their wings against the surface of the sea to throw water over their backs. The wings are then outstretched to dry, followed by preening.

The flock then embarks on a fishing foray, flying along a selected route, each bird watching intently for signs of shoals. As soon as fish are sighted the forward movement comes to a sudden stop, as the birds splash down on the water. Cormorants always dive from a floating position, like ducks.

Birds which have caught a fish often fly a short distance from the flock to avoid being robbed while they swallow their prey. The continuous rolling movement of a flock of Socotra cormorants, as some birds dive while others rise and fly off before returning to the fishing frenzy, was first commented on and recorded by the explorer and naturalist, Robert Cheesman, on his journey down the Gulf of Salwa in 1921.

The formation of a flock of birds in flight varies according to the activity. A departure for fishing involves the simultaneous movement of an entire flock, a dense sheet of birds flying just above the sea surface. The birds move en masse without a leader, and the front of the flock can be hundreds of metres wide. But when fishing comes to an end and groups of birds break off their activities to head for home, they form the familiar long, wavering, V-shaped skeins or undulating strings. A flock will often make a trip of close to 100 km to their fishing grounds and back.

The decline of the population of Socotra cormorants on Suwad Al Janubiyah may in part be due to the natural disasters in 1997 and 2003, although the decline of fish stocks in the Gulf due to over-fishing by

Above: Socotra cormorants share a small foothold above the waves.

Below: Socotra cormorants in flight.

humans will also inevitably affect their numbers. Disturbance of the breeding sites and theft of eggs are another threat to their existence. It remains to be seen whether, given time, the population will remain stable.

Ospreys

One of the most charismatic birds frequenting the coastline of Qatar is the osprey. Although globally widespread, in many parts of the world they are persecuted by hunters, egg collectors and vandals. But in Qatar ospreys are relatively common, and can be observed from the Corniches in Doha and Al Khor and on the coastline all around the peninsula.

On the Huwar Islands archipelago off the north-west coast of Qatar, 20 pairs of ospreys nested in 1998-9, and a total of 47 birds were in residence. Sometimes two pairs will occupy one small island. These birds fish not only in the waters around the islands but also along the coastline of the Qatar peninsula.

The osprey is a bird of prey with a highly-specialised diet, living almost exclusively on fish. However, the ospreys nesting on the Huwar Islands off Qatar's north-west coast are known to include Socotra cormorants as a regular part of their diet. They have also taken to fishing in effluent lagoons where fish have been introduced, such as the pools at Abu Nakhla near the Salwa Road. One was photographed carrying a toad at this site.

Although it closely resembles other fish-eating birds of prey such as eagles, the osprey is a unique species. It belongs to a family of its own, the genus *Pandion* and the species *haliaetus*, the latter meaning 'sea-eagle' in Greek. Worldwide there are four sub-species: the nominate *haliaetus* breeds in Europe, North Africa and the Middle East. The three other sub-species, which vary slightly in size and colouring, breed in North America, the Caribbean and Australasia.

An adult bird is around 60 cm in length, with a wing span of between 145 and 165 cm. The upper parts are dark brown but the flanks and belly are white with a brown band across the breast, so that it is sometimes mistaken for a large gull as it swoops and glides. The head is white, with a distinctive dark brown stripe through the brilliant yellow eye, reaching to the back of the neck. The powerful legs are greenish-grey and equipped with long black talons, with a reversible outer toe, allowing the osprey to grip fish with two talons forward and two back, the rough scaly skin on the feet providing further purchase. When it spots a fish it plunges onto its prey and snatches the fish from the water in its talons. Once in the air, the bird manoeuvres its catch so that the body of the fish is aligned with the direction of flight, to provide minimum wind resistance. The powerful black beak is strongly hooked for tearing up its meal. Ospreys can be distinguished from true fishing eagles by their long, narrow wings which are distinctively angled while gliding.

In Qatar, ospreys are both resident and migrant. Elsewhere they usually build their large, untidy nests of sticks at the top of tall trees, but here, where suitable trees are not available, they have no choice but to nest on the ground, choosing jebel outcrops or small, rocky islands. Usually between two and four eggs are laid, but it is rare for all the chicks to survive - one or two is the norm.

Ospreys almost certainly nested on the mainland of Qatar in the past, but owing to the increased human population they have moved out to the islands around the coast. Many visitors to Khor Al Adaid have seen the huge nest towering atop a rocky pillar

An osprey nest at Khor Al Adaid.

between two islets on the far side of the lagoon, with a spectacular background of barren hills of pink-coloured rock. It offers a golden opportunity for bird watchers to observe the comings and goings of the resident ospreys without disturbing them. We have been watching ospreys at this nest annually for almost three decades, and have often seen the adult male soaring high and then repeatedly swooping over the sea, the pale underside of his wings gleaming, while his mate watches from the nest. From time to time he makes his display call, a distinctive high-pitched 'kee-kee-kee-kee'. In some years immature juveniles from the previous year's hatching will return and occupy the nest without breeding. Another nest about 1.5km away stands on a small, low-lying island in the inner lagoon.

It is surprising that ospreys in that barren environment are able to collect sufficient material to build such a huge nest. The nest itself is many years old, but each breeding pair refurbishes and rearranges it before settling down to egg-laying and incubation. We have seen ospreys flying towards it carrying branches in their talons. In that treeless land they must have covered long distances to collect them. They also make use of dried seaweed, and sometimes human debris such as driftwood, and lengths of polypropylene rope. The nest is lined with seaweed and seagrass, and the construction of such huge nests represents a substantial amount of time and energy.

Ospreys are remarkably tolerant of the presence of man. In Europe they have been known to construct their nests on electricity pylons and coastal navigation beacons. In North America they are even encouraged to build their nests close to human habitation so that people can enjoy watching their movements. In spring 1993, an osprey used a flagpole in the back garden of the Embassy of Japan in the West Bay area of Doha as a perching post for his morning's fishing activities. Only metres away from the windows of the building, he was to be seen each day for several weeks, turning his head this way and that to survey the sea, then launching himself into the air to return to the pole with a fish struggling in his talons.

It is estimated that there are currently around 30,000 breeding pairs of ospreys in the world. So at present the species is not endangered, but this was not always the case. Not so long ago they were ruthlessly hunted in Europe, along with all other birds of prey, and their eggs were either bought by collectors or smashed by vandals. Although this still happens, laws carrying harsh penalties have been passed in many European countries to protect the osprey and these help to deter almost all but the most determined criminals. The fate of ospreys in Europe is closely linked, of course, with that of our own resident birds, as they are a migratory species.

In Europe people travel long distances for the pleasure of watching ospreys at the reserves, and pay for the privilege, so in Qatar we are fortunate in being able to freely observe these magnificent birds both nesting and fishing. When the Qatar Natural History Group was established in 1978 it adopted the osprey as its logo, a fitting representative of the beautiful and varied wild life of this region.

An osprey consuming catch on its fishing perch.

The Mangrove Forests

Mangroves at low tide, with pneumatophores sticking up through the mud.

Around Al Khor and Al Thakhira, on the north-east coast of Qatar, the coast is fringed with forests of mangroves, interspersed with shallow tidal creeks. The thick, grey-green foliage of the trees forms a clear dividing line between the pale yellow salt marshes which fringe the shore and the deep blue of the sea and sky. Home to a host of creatures of all kinds, mangroves are, ecologically, among the most important vegetation in the country.

Qatar has only one species of mangrove, *Avicennia marina*, sometimes called the Grey mangrove to distinguish it from other species with darker leaves. Worldwide there are almost 50 species of mangrove. *Avicennia marina*, called *gurm* in Arabic, is the most widely distributed. Mangroves are tropical trees and generally will not survive where average temperatures fall below 19°C, although one species is known to exist in New Zealand on sites where the temperature occasionally drops below zero.

The mangrove is a very tough plant, capable of tolerating extreme conditions, which is demonstrated by its existence here and in the UAE, where the seawater contains around three times the salt content of seawater elsewhere. However, the energy required for the plant to excrete salt stunts its growth, resulting in the dwarfed appearance of the local trees. The excreted salt crystallises and forms a thick coat on the undersides of the leaves.

Mangrove fruit.

At Al Khor and Al Thakhira, the area immediately inland from the mangroves is often flooded and turns into wet and muddy salt marshes. These are home to other salt-tolerant species of plants known as halophytes, including the widespread succulent *Halocnemum strobilaceum*, and the dense shrubs of *Arthrocnemum glaucum*.

The salt flats are popular recreational areas for bird watchers, kite fliers and for people taking the dog for a run at weekends. To casual visitors the mangroves may appear simply as a group of trees on the seashore, without their importance as key elements in a complex ecological system being realised. Mangroves are extremely beneficial, not only in stabilising the coastline but also in providing the initial link in the food chain of organisms which nourishes the inhabitants of the intertidal zones.

The algae cover of the mud flats between the mangroves assists in binding together the mud particles, but cracks and dries when exposed to the sun by low tide. When high tides wash over, it is rejuvenated. The pale, creamy colour of the mud on the surface is determined by diatoms, minute organisms which release oxygen. The substrate of the mangrove habitat is dark, heavy silty mud, rich with rotting organic material. It is virtually anaerobic, i.e. it contains very little oxygen, and anyone who wades into the waterlogged mud between the trees will notice a strong, sulphur-like smell as their feet disturb the ground. This is hydrogen sulphide, which is produced by bacteria that exist without light or oxygen.

Mangroves have evolved a specialised system to cope with the anaerobic conditions. Aerial roots called pneumatophores poke up above the mud and water surface to allow the plant to breathe and are connected with the main root system which anchors the tree into the ground. From a mature tree long lines of pneumatophores can be seen radiating in all directions.

A further specialised mechanism enables seeds to germinate in the saline and anaerobic conditions. Seeds falling into the mud would suffocate without oxygen, so the mangrove solves the problem by being viviparous: producing seeds that germinate while still attached to the parent plant. The tiny plant receives water and nutrients from its parent and continues to grow until the weight of the seedling causes it to fall into the mud beneath the tree. Even if covered with water, seedlings are able to withstand long periods of inundation. Some continue to grow near the parent tree, trapped in the web of pneumatophores, while others are carried by the tides to new sites. Mangroves have two methods of reproduction: new shoots also grow directly from the spreading lines of pneumatophores.

The complex webs of pneumatophores and root systems surrounding the mangrove stands restrict tidal flow and thus cause a build up of silt. Gradually, a new muddy coastal habitat is established, encouraging the development of other plants. The build up of mud continues, and the coastal area becomes stabilised. Other marine organisms then develop within the habitat.

To have some idea of just how complex and fascinating is the ecology of mangroves, one needs to brave the muddy conditions and wade in among the trees. Only then can one observe at close quarters the small creatures living among the roots and the myriad of insects feeding on the flowers. The thick leaf-cover and stout branches provide ideal cover for nesting birds. Great care is needed to avoid damaging the lines of aerial roots, and stout

footwear is essential: accidentally stepping on a spiky root can be painful!

Small crabs inhabiting the muddy flats and the banks of the channels help to remove rotting organic matter, including the fallen mangrove leaves, and their burrows help to aerate the waterlogged ground. The flowers of the mangroves are a rich source of nectar for insects such as bees, which make their nests among the branches. The shallow waters are a haven for small fish during their juvenile years until they are big enough to survive in the open sea. These include commercial varieties of fish.

Oil pollution is clearly a hazard for mangroves, as even a thin film of oil on the spiky aerial roots can suffocate the trees. Another danger is over-grazing by camels. Camels enjoy munching on the salty leaves, and it used to be believed by the bedouin herders that eating mangrove leaves made camels strong and able to undertake long migrations.

The vital difference an established mangrove ecosystem can make to a coastline was borne home to the world by the effect of the tsunami of December 2004 on the coast of Thailand. Since 1960 over half the mangrove forests of Thailand have been cleared away to make room for intensive fish farming or tourism-related development. Many of these areas were devastated by the tsunami, whereas villages protected by the remaining mangroves escaped major damage and loss of life.

The mangroves of Al Khor and Al Thakhira are home to a wide variety of birds. A good site for bird watching is the causeway leading to the small island in the bay of Khor Shaqiq known as Jazirat bin Ghannam. Here both the White-breasted kingfisher and the Common kingfisher can be seen during the winter months, their brilliant plumage flashing like a streak of brilliant iridescent blue against the green of the mangroves. Greater flamingoes pick their way among the wider stretches of open water, and Western Reef herons and Little egrets stand patiently in the shallows. The haunting cries of Curlew sandpipers

and redshanks echo over the forest, and above the fishing, squabbling and calling waders circle the watchful Marsh harriers.

In days gone by mangrove wood was much in use for a variety of purposes: the poles which support the flat roofs of traditional stone-built houses, parts of furniture, the internal fittings of boats, and above all for the production of charcoal. Large piles of mangrove branches would be gathered and covered with a thick layer of sand and ashes. This was then fired and left to slowly smoulder. The combustion

Mangroves near Al Thakhira.

process lasted as long as a week and the resulting charcoal was used by local people for cooking and traded to other regions where the wood was not available. Excavations in the 1980s and in 2000 on Jazirat bin Ghannam revealed ancient hearths containing traces of charcoal, and carbon dating of the charcoal has proved that the mangrove plantations of the north-eastern coast have been established for at least four thousand years.

Sea Turtles

In the golden light of a late afternoon in May, a turtle lay quietly resting in the shallow waters that surrounded a small, remote island, waiting for nightfall. Her mottled shell with its shades of amber, green and brown blended perfectly with the surrounding coral and anemones, while the network of rippled light cast by the sun on the surface of the sea three metres above lent further camouflage.

Only her head moved, as she turned a dark eye on a pair of divers who lay on the sandy seabed observing her. Still, she made no move to swim away, her mind focused on the task ahead. When darkness came she would wait for high tide and then leave the water for the beach, dig a deep hole and deposit around a hundred soft-shelled, round white eggs the size of ping-pong balls, before covering them and returning swiftly to the safety of the sea.

The island was Sharoua, off the eastern coastline of Qatar, and the turtle we were watching, in the summer of 1996, was a Hawksbill. Of the seven varieties of turtle found in the tropical seas of the world, four occur in Qatari waters. They are the Green turtle (*Chelonia mydas*), the Hawksbill (*Eretmochelys imbricate*), the Leatherback (*Dermochelys coriacea*) and the Olive Ridley (*Lepidochelys olivacea*). Of these, only the Hawksbill breeds in Qatar.

Worldwide, these gentle, harmless inhabitants of the sea are under threat, with some species faced with possible extinction. Turtles have roamed the oceans of the world for around 200,000,000 years, but in the last few decades their numbers have plummeted. For centuries turtles have been hunted for their meat, oil and shells, but now they fall victim to the curses of the modern age: poisoned by pollution, strangled by fishing lines and monofilament nets, mangled by speed-boat propellers, their nest sites disturbed by the building of high-rise hotels and the development of holiday resorts.

In 1993 the *Gulf Times* published a detailed report about the threat to the turtles in Qatari waters which contained photographs of turtles openly displayed for sale at the Salwa Road fish market, along with turtle eggs. A law had been passed in 1985 by the government of Qatar prohibiting 'the gathering and catching of sea birds' eggs and turtles', but the ruling was being ignored and it was not actively enforced. After more publicity in both the Arabic and the English press, turtles stopped appearing on open sale. The law was redrafted in 2002, with penalties for those who continued to flout it.

In 1996 the Environment Protection Committee, now incorporated into the Supreme Council for the Environment and Natural Reserves (SCENR), carried out an investigation into the habitats of sea birds and turtles around the coast. Their report, published in June that year, made exceptionally depressing reading. Turtle nests were being robbed with impunity on the northern offshore sandspits of Umm Tais and Ras Reccan, and on mainland beaches like Fuwairit. It seemed that, despite constant publicity in newspapers and on television about protecting endangered species, some people were either ignorant of the law or indifferent to it.

Even without the problems caused by humans, a turtle's chances of surviving to adulthood are very small. Eggs are destroyed by fungi or fly larvae while still in the ground, and predators like foxes and monitor lizards dig up the eggs before they hatch. The most dangerous moment for a turtle hatchling is the frantic sprint between nest site and sea. Birds, crabs and mammals wait to feast on the defenceless young, and once in the sea many more are eaten by fish. Man has now reduced their natural survival chance from one in a hundred to a ratio of far, far less.

Until recently, remarkably little was known about turtles and their unique way of life. Serious research on turtles only began in 1954 in the United States, when biologists commenced investigations in Costa Rica to find out why Green turtle populations in the Caribbean were declining. Each species of turtle has its own specialised niche in the environment. Some eat crustaceans, others eat jellyfish and others prefer sea grass or sponges.

Female turtles always return to lay their eggs on or near the beach where they themselves hatched. Males may never return to land again once they hatch, nearing shore only to mate. They travel thousands of miles in migratory patterns that are still not fully understood.

After mating, the female turtle takes two to four weeks to emerge onto the beach and lay the first clutch of eggs. A mated turtle carries up to 800 eggs, which develop in batches of between 100 and 200 at a time. Thus, the female is carrying eggs in various stages of development. After laying her first clutch of eggs, she will wait two weeks until the next batch is ready. In the Arabian Gulf turtles usually lay about three clutches. But despite the enormous number of eggs laid by each female, the survival rate of hatchlings has been calculated at < 0.01.

Hawksbill turtles dig their nests on sandy beaches, hollowing out an egg-chamber. The sand has to be well-ventilated for the eggs to develop, as gases are excreted during the period of incubation. Sand that is too fine or too coarse is unsuitable, which may be the reason why in

Qatar turtles nest only north of Al Khor and on some of the offshore islands.

The most common, relatively speaking, of the turtles in local waters is the Green turtle, which feeds on shallow sea grass pastures and so is more likely to be seen in coastal waters. In the past I have occasionally spotted them from the Doha Corniche, but I have not heard of any sightings as close to Doha in recent years.

Green turtles can reach a shell length of 1.2 m and weigh up to 200 kilos. The shell is dark green, with darker markings giving a mottled effect. Unlike the shell of the Hawksbill turtle, the scutes, or plates, on the Green turtle's carapace do not overlap.

Perhaps because it is a herbivore, the meat of the Green turtle was, and still is in some countries, the most valued of any. The fat used to be boiled with the cartilage to make a tasty soup and was much prized in 19th century Europe as a gourmet delicacy.

The Hawksbill turtle is smaller and less common in Qatari waters than the Green. A slow grower, its shell when adult is around 90 cm in length and its weight between 50 and 100 kilos. Hawksbills can live as long as 100 years, reaching sexual maturity at 30. The shell is an amber colour, with markings

A Hawksbill turtle, Eretmochlys imbricate.

The turtle begins laying her eggs.

shading through black and brown to red and dark yellow. It is a reef dweller, often inhabiting a reef near its nesting site, and its preferred food is the sponges which grow on the reefs. It is unique among the turtle species in that it does not migrate long distances between its feeding and nesting grounds.

Because of its beautiful mottled markings, the shell of the Hawksbill was used to make ornamental combs, spectacle frames and other small items. Japan was the chief importer of turtle shell for this industry. Until 1992, when the trade was finally stopped under pressure from the United States, Japan had been importing up to 31,000 shells each year.

Leatherbacks, which are occasionally seen far out in the waters of the Gulf by people in boats or aircraft, are giants among turtles. The largest ever recorded weighed almost 1,000 kilos and measured 3 metres in length. The average weight of a leatherback is probably around 400 kilos. Unlike other turtles, Leatherbacks do not have hard plates but a soft skin covering their shell, on which are seven prominent ridges running the length of the shell. They very rarely come close to shore except to breed, preferring the open ocean, where they feed on jellyfish and plankton. Leatherbacks have been recorded diving to depths of 475 metres, and can tolerate cold better than other turtles, as they have a thick, oil-saturated layer beneath their skin.

In contrast to the gigantic Leatherback is the little Olive Ridley, smallest of all marine turtles and sometimes seen feeding in Qatari waters. World-wide it is probably the most abundant species of all. The largest nesting population is in north-east India, where it was recently estimated that an average of 398,000 females were nesting yearly. It also nests in the eastern Pacific. Olive Ridley females form what are known as 'arribadas' – hundreds crowding together to lay their eggs in what is possibly a predator-inhibiting device.

The Olive Ridley measures between 58 and 78 cm in length and weighs between 35 and 45 kilos. The juveniles are charcoal grey, and the dark grey-green shell of the adults gives the turtles its name.

Until recently, when great efforts have been made to clean up the beaches of Qatar, the beaches which the Hawksbill turtles used for nesting were often so covered with oil, assorted rubbish left by picnickers, pieces of driftwood and flotsam and jetsam from ships that it seemed astonishing the turtles could still find a place to dig. The regular beach-cleaning expeditions organised by the Friends of the Environment Centre and other groups are a most positive move as far as turtles are concerned. The Friends of the Environment and the Qatar

After egg-laying, the Hawksbill spends up to an hour filling in the cavity.

Researchers tagging a turtle at Fuwairit beach.

Scientific Club do invaluable work in helping to educate the young people of Qatar into understanding that our wildlife must be valued and protected.

Any conservation strategy to protect turtles needs to be long-term, with continued public awareness campaigns, so that all citizens are aware of, and accept, the need to protect the turtle as an essential component of marine biodiversity. Within Ras Laffan city, the turtle-nesting beach has been protected for several years and a monitoring programme is now in its fifth year. No vehicles have access to the beach and environmental staff keep it clear of tide-borne refuse.

In 2005 regular monitoring of nesting turtles on other beaches in Qatar began to be carried out with a view to implementing conservation, and in May 2010 a three-year satellite tracking system was launched by the WWF to help identify the overseas migration routes and near-shore habitats favoured by turtles. Five countries participated: Iran, Oman, the UAE, Saudi Arabia and Qatar.

Data collected from the programme will help management and conservation authorities with their decisions. The goal of the programme is to use advanced technology to find out more about the turtles' long journeys and develop effective conservation strategies at a regional and international level. Transmitters fixed to the shells of the turtles, using built-up layers of fibreglass, remain active for about 400 days.

In Qatar five turtles were fitted with transmitters after egg-laying and then released, three from Fuwairit beach and two from Ras Laffan city. Information gained from the transmitters indicated that favourite feeding grounds for local Hawksbills lay in the lower Gulf region between Saudi Arabia, Qatar and the UAE.

Rays, Stonefish, Lionfish & Cone Shells

Rays are flattened, rhombus-shaped fish in which the pectoral fins are completely fused with the body. They have long, thin tails with one or more barbed spines at the base which are covered with a poisonous mucus. Rays prey on shellfish and the mouth on the underside of the body has specially adapted plates for crushing shells.

Around a dozen species of ray are known to inhabit the waters of the Arabian Gulf and one more, a whipray, endemic to the Gulf, *Himantura randalli*, has just been identified. The largest of the rays is the beautiful and graceful Spotted Eagle ray (*Aetobatus ocellatus*), which swims in open water, looking like its namesake the eagle as it glides slowly along, beating its 'wings'. Unlike the smaller Stingrays, which swim rapidly away if approached by divers, Eagle Rays show no particular anxiety and indeed will sometimes approach and inspect divers. Rays are often seen swimming around sunken wrecks, which are covered in all kinds of shellfish and so attract the rays to feed there.

Once when my diving buddy and I were swimming along the seabed examining shellfish on an offshore wreck, we disturbed two very large Eagle rays which had been resting on the sand. They swam away, but then changed their minds and decided to take a closer look at us. As they approached they looked like invading spaceships from a science fiction movie, and the light dimmed as they sailed over our heads. I must admit that we flattened ourselves to avoid any accidents with their tails!

Unlike their bottom-dwelling cousins, Eagle rays have a distinct head with eyes on either side, allowing better all-round vision. Large Eagle rays are unlikely to harm a human, but accidents can and do occur with rays which like to bask on the warm sand in shallow water off gently sloping beaches: just the sort of beaches, in fact, that attract humans! These could be the Arabian Banded tail whipray, which is medium-sized and brown with a long thin stripy tail, the Scaly whipray *Himantura imbricata* (small and plain brown with a stubby

A large Spotted Eagle ray, Aetobatus ocellatus.

tail), the handsome Leopard ray, (*Himantura uarnak* group), which has distinctive leopardskin or honeycomb markings, or the Cowtail ray, *Pastinachus sephen*: dark grey to black with a thick, frilly tail.

A Bowmouth guitarfish, Rhina ancylostoma, *and a Spotted Eagle ray,* Aetobatus ocellatus.

The rays cover themselves with a thin layer of sand, so they are difficult to spot, and the best precaution against stepping on one and being lashed by the tail as it swims away is to enter the sea slowly, splashing and disturbing the sand as you do so. Do not allow the kids to dash straight into the water the second they tumble out of the car when you arrive at the beach. Explain about rays and make sure they have shoes on. However, even shoes are not a complete protection against ray stings as the sting can sometimes penetrate the leg rather than the foot.

Sting ray injuries are excruciatingly painful. Fortunately all fish venom is heat labile: the application of heat to the wound changes the chemical make-up of the venom and brings immediate relief. So first aid treatment for sting ray wounds is to immerse the affected area in water as hot as the patient can tolerate and to continue the treatment until the pain subsides. With luck, someone on the beach will have brought along a flask of hot water for tea or coffee. Very often the sting breaks off in the wound. It is important to try to remove it as soon as possible but if it is deeply embedded it may have to be removed under local anaesthetic by a doctor. The patients may well be suffering from shock as a result of the pain, and should be taken to hospital after first aid treatment has been administered. The wound is likely to have been contaminated by bacteria that are carried by the sting and antibiotic treatment is always advisable.

Electric rays (*Torpedosinuspersicii*) are rarely seen in Qatari waters but are quite common in the Emirates and Oman. They are capable of delivering an unpleasant electric shock of up to 100 volts if disturbed. Unpleasant, but not life-threatening. A couple of years ago a recreational diver from Qatar on a diving expedition to Oman knelt on one and was thrown sideways by the shock. He was not in

danger but his diving buddy was: he laughed so much that he swallowed a mouthful of water and choked. And serve him right too.

Also present in the water off the coast of Qatar are guitarfish, of which the White-spotted guitarfish is the most common. Guitarfish are a species of ray, and like sharks, they have skeletons of cartilage rather than bone. In October 2010 a rare species was seen by some tourists on a cruise boat just off the Doha Corniche. It was identified as a Bowmouth guitarfish, *Rhina ancylostoma*, recognisable from the heavy ridges along the head, covered with spiky thorns, which the animal uses to defend itself in head-butting. Like a Whale shark, the two-metre-long blue-grey body is covered in white spots on the body, fins and tail.

These large, slow-swimming fish are quite harmless to humans, and cruise the sea bed in shallow inshore waters and around coral reefs. They prey on crustaceans, crabs and small fish, which they crush between rows of ridged teeth. Widespread habitat destruction has caused populations to decline, and the Bowmouth guitarfish is listed as 'Vulnerable' on the IUCN Red List.

Stonefish (*Synanceia*) are shallow water dwellers and inhabit both rocky and coral reefs. They are perfectly camouflaged as stones, often complete with 'barnacles' and weed growing on top. While in their natural habitat they are virtually impossible to see. Even in an aquarium at a marine museum, when you know one or more are present in the tank because it says so on the label, you have to look very carefully indeed before you can spot them. Most venomous creatures advertise the fact that they are dangerous, either by eye-catching coloration or by making a warning noise, as in the case of land snakes, but Stonefish do not conform to the rules.

In Qatari waters both Stonefish (*Synanceia*) and False stonefish, also known as Scorpionfish, (*Pseudosynanceia*) are present. False stonefish are marginally more visible than Stonefish, having reddish coloured pectoral fins rather like open fans. In a true stonefish the eyes are almost invisible, whereas in the False stonefish the eyes, although well camouflaged, can be detected. They are said to be less venomous than the true Stonefish.

I have seen stonefish on several occasions in shallow coastal waters around Qatar, and recently several were seen close to the beaches of the Ras Abrouq peninsula on the west coast of Qatar. I am not certain whether they were the true or false variety. One was lurking in a crevice on a rocky reef in Zubara Bay, and shot out suddenly to take up an aggressive stance on an empty patch of sand I was about to kneel on. Fortunately my diving buddy saw it in time and alerted me to the danger. I have also seen them in the water around Saffliyah Island, and on the shallow weed-covered reefs at Fuwairit.

Stonefish carry an array of 13 dorsal spines, which project outwards from venom glands. When the spine is pressed the venom is involuntarily expelled, so that the victim actually injures himself. Because they inhabit shallow coastal waters they present a hazard to snorkellers and swimmers exploring reefs. A stonefish injury is very serious, and can prove fatal. Tony Woodward and Frances Dipper, in their book *The Living Seas* (published by Motivate in 1989) tell the story of a doctor from Hamad Hospital who was out fishing one day with his brother. When pulling in their net he was scratched on the arm by a stonefish which was entangled in the meshes. His brother rushed him at once to the hospital and he spent two weeks in intensive care with massive doses of antibiotics and steroids. It was some time before he fully recovered the use of his arm.

Because of the danger to life involved in a stonefish injury, it is best treated by experts as soon as possible. Although the venom would certainly be rendered less concentrated by the application of hot water, as in the case of sting ray wounds, it would be dangerous to delay getting the injured person to hospital.

Apart from being aware of the danger and taking care not to step on unidentified objects, the best precaution against Stonefish injury is to wear shoes while exploring reefs. Rubber-soled boots such as divers and snorkellers wear with their fins are best, and can be purchased from diving shops or, more cheaply, from fishing suppliers and marine chandlers.

The Lionfish or Butterfly cod (*Pterois radiata*) is one of the most spectacularly beautiful of the inhabitants of coral reefs. It has long dorsal spines resembling feathers,

A Scorpionfish.

which it uses to herd small fish into corners where they can be grabbed. The Butterfly cod has a number of names, all referring to its venom or its plumed appearance: Turkeyfish, Firefish, Scorpionfish (a name also given to the False stonefish) and here in Qatar we have a black, grey and white variety known locally as a Chickenfish! In the UAE and Oman they are usually red, orange and pink.

Although the dorsal spines of the Butterfly cod contain an extremely toxic venom, they are less dangerous than Stonefish to divers and swimmers because they do the decent thing and make themselves highly visible, erecting their spines as a warning if approached. Their dramatic coloration and feathery fins and spines advertise their presence and warn would-be predators to keep away.

A memorable experience for me was a night dive in Oman when the reef was covered with dozens of baby Butterfly cod, each no bigger than a mouse, 'walking' around the reef on their fins. During the day only adults were visible, so presumably the juveniles hide until they are big enough to take on all-comers. Here in Qatar Butterfly cod are not uncommon on reefs and on old wrecks which have coral growing on them. We once rescued a large specimen from an abandoned fish trap near Saffliyah Island. As with the stonefish, the venom

The beautiful Butterfly cod, Pterois radiata, *is also known as the Firefish or Chickenfish. Its feathery dorsal spines are highly venomous.*

of the Butterfly cod is so dangerous that it is better to get the victim to hospital at once, without attempting to administer first aid.

Few people would think that handling a shellfish could carry any danger, but there is one species of cone shell (*Conus textile*) which has a miniature harpoon that it uses to immobilise its prey: small worms or fish, or even other shellfish. If handled the creature will defend itself by releasing its sting. This is extremely venomous and can prove fatal to humans. A number of deaths occur each year on the Australian Barrier Reef which is visited by thousands of tourists, not all of whom are alerted to the possible hazards.

Conus textile is present on reefs off the coast of Qatar. Although most of the cone shells are harmless I, for one, am not confident enough of my ability to tell the species apart ever to pick up a cone shell out at sea. In any case, no one should interfere with live shellfish on reefs. So avoidance of cone shell injuries is simple: leave live shellfish strictly alone and confine your collecting to empty shells washed up on the beach.

Sea Snakes, the Myths and the Facts

Of the 53 species of sea snake worldwide, nine occur in the waters of the Arabian Gulf. Of these, six have been identified in the coastal waters of Qatar. All of them are members of the *Hydrophiidae* family.

Distantly related to cobras, sea snakes are thought to have descended from snakes which live on land. Like their terrestrial cousins, they are all extremely venomous. In fact the venom of some species of sea snake is even more deadly than that of cobras. They inject their venom into the small fish and crustaceans on which they prey, and because a fish's circulation is slow the venom has to be highly toxic to work quickly.

In the waters off Malaysia, fishermen sometimes get bitten when sea snakes get entangled in their nets. There is no pain at first after the bite, then about half an hour later stiffness and muscle ache is followed by increasing pain in the bitten limb. This is followed by blurred vision, drowsiness and finally respiratory paralysis. Without treatment, death may occur after 12 to 24 hours.

This sort of information sounds like bad news, and in Qatar some people are understandably a little nervous about encountering a snake while swimming. However, the good news is that, although in other parts of the world there are species of sea snake which can be aggressive to humans, none of them inhabit the waters off Qatar. Most species of sea snake are not aggressive and would never attack a swimmer or diver unless molested. My own experience of sea snakes, having encountered quite a number during many years of scuba diving and snorkelling in the sea around Qatar, is that they take no notice of humans at all. Unlike land snakes, they exhibit no fear, nor do they demonstrate any curiosity, simply continuing to go about their business.

However, during the breeding season there have been occasions both in Qatar and elsewhere when excited snakes have mistaken the air hoses connected to dive tanks for rivals, or possibly female sea snakes! A few years ago a sports diver surfacing near the beach at Mesaieed was found to have a sea snake entangled in his air hose. There

followed some tense moments for him and his buddy, but the snake was successfully dislodged without incident.

Marine biologist Ibrahim Fuad, who has been on the staff of the National Museum since 1978, says that in all that time he has never heard of a single instance of a sea snake attack. This was confirmed by doctors at the Accident and Emergency Unit at Hamad Hospital who say they have never come across sea snake injury.

If you are snorkelling and see a sea snake approaching you from below, there is no need to worry. It is simply coming to the surface to breathe. The snake spends only a couple of seconds at the surface before descending again. They are said to be capable of staying submerged for up to two hours, and can reach depths of 100 metres, although the ones I have observed surface every three or four minutes to breathe.

As well as by surface breathing, sea snakes can obtain oxygen through the skin from sea water and eliminate carbon dioxide and nitrogen in the same way. Up to 20% of their oxygen requirement is obtained in this way.

All sea snakes have a paddle-shaped tail to help them with swimming, but on shore they are helpless because they lack the ventral scales that all land snakes have to give them purchase on the ground as they slither along. It sometimes happens that sea snakes are cast up on the beach and have to wait for the next tide to take them off. You may sometimes come across an apparently lifeless snake on the beach, but do not touch it. It may well not be lifeless!

Sea snakes cannot breed in water where the temperature is less than 18ºC, so they reproduce during the warmer months. The species which inhabit the Gulf are all viviparous, giving birth to between two and eighteen young. Here in Qatar sea snakes are most commonly seen along the coast south of Dukhan, where there are rocky reefs in around 6 metres of water. One reef is even known as 'Snake Alley' by sports divers because of the numbers of snakes which congregate there in a narrow corridor between two rocky walls. They swim up and down, poking their small heads into crevices in search of prey: crabs, shrimps and small fish. Snakes are also encountered on the artificial diving reefs along the coast south of the Sealine Resort, and around Saffliyah Island. Up north, they can be seen in numbers along the east coast off Fuwairit and Maranwah where there are shallow reefs.

A myth about sea snakes I've often heard repeated is that their mouths are too small to effectively bite a human. This is not true: although the snakes have small heads, to enable them to catch prey that is hiding in crevices or under rocks, like all snakes they can unhinge their lower jaw to extend the reach of their 'bite'. They are able to swallow a fish more than twice the diameter of their neck. A sea snake is quite capable of biting a human leg or arm, but that does not mean that it is likely to do so.

Unlike land snakes, sea snakes can control the amount of venom they release, and are capable of biting without releasing any venom at all. A few years ago a British commercial diver and his Filipino buddy were working on a pipe line near an offshore oil rig when they disturbed a large sea snake which bit both of them on their legs, the fangs puncturing the skin through their wet suits. They surfaced and a doctor from Hamad Hospital arrived at the rig by helicopter, but decided to wait for a while until administering the antivenom, as the side-effects of this can be almost as devastating to the system as the bite itself. Eventually, it became clear that all that was needed was treatment for shock.

Inshore, the sea snake most likely to be encountered is the Arabian Gulf Sea Snake (*Hydrophis lapemoides*) which inhabits mangroves areas along the coast. It measures about 95 cm in length and is a pale yellowy/green, with clearly defined dark bands along the whole length of the body. The Reef Sea Snake (*Hydrophis ornatus*) also reaches a maximum length of about 95 cm. It is an olive green in colour with black blotches on the back, reaching about halfway down the body on each side. The Annulated or Blue-banded Sea Snake (*Hydrophis cyanocinctus*) can reach a length of 188.5 cm. The colour is variable and there are 50 to 75 black bars or rings on a yellow or olive background.

Even longer than the Blue-banded Sea Snake is the Yellow Sea Snake (*Hydrophis spiralis*), also known as the Narrow-Banded Sea Snake, which is occasionally encountered in Qatari waters. It can reach a length of 2.20 metres, and is a conspicuous yellow with black bands along the whole length of its body. Its preferred habitat is shallow water. Some authorities describe this snake as aggressive, while others say that is it as docile as most other sea snakes. The same is true of the Shaw's Sea Snake (*Lapemoides curtus*) which is less common in the Arabian Gulf than some other species.

Snakes encountered far out at sea are likely to be the Yellow-bellied sea snake (*Pelamis platurus*) which feeds on pelagic fish, drifting along in the currents on or near the surface. Unlike other sea snakes, the entire length of the body, which is about 90 cm long, is flattened from side to side. It is a dark brown with a pale underside, and the tail has dark triangular markings. This snake is a surface feeder, and sometimes dozens of snakes will coil together in a floating mass, tempting fish to shelter beneath them and so providing an easy meal.

Sea snakes are among the most beautiful and interesting inhabitants of Qatar's shallow coastal waters. They swim with an elegant rippling movement, like a length of ribbon blowing in the breeze, perfectly adapted to their environment. In a world where almost all wildlife has learned to fear man, there is something strangely appealing about a creature which is indifferent to the presence of humans, seeming to accept us as a natural part of its world.

Yellow-bellied sea snake, Pelamis platurus.

Above: The Annulated or Blue-banded sea snake, Hydrophis cyanocinctus.

Below: The Shaw's sea snake, Lapemis curtus, is found in many parts of Asia and Australasia.

Left: The Arabian Gulf sea snake, Hydrophis lapemoides, stranded at low tide among mangroves.

Dugongs: Shy Denizens of the Ocean

Until the last century the Arabian Gulf had a large population of dugongs. They provided a valuable source of protein for the people who for centuries fished and hunted around the shores of the Gulf. On the island of Umm an Nar, just off Abu Dhabi City, dugong bones and tusks were found in the remains of a village and in tombs dating from 2700 BCE. So numerous were the animals that the few taken by humans for food would have made no difference at all to the population.

It is estimated that the maximum sustainable annual harvest of marine mammals is 2% of the total population. Even as late as the 1970s dugong were still widely being caught and eaten by local people; their skin being turned into leather and their fat rendered down into oil. By daily visits to the fish souq in Abu Dhabi in the late seventies, one researcher estimated that the annual catch delivered was between 50 and 70 animals.

Today, it is a different story. The countries of the region are struggling to keep this species safe from extinction. A slow moving, gentle marine mammal, it is an easy animal to kill and the numbers of dugong (scientific name *Dugong dugon*) in the

Arabian Gulf have dwindled, largely due to the influence of man. Because of their very slow rate of reproduction, they cannot sustain heavy culling.

Slaughtered for centuries for its meat, hide and bones, entangled and drowned in fishing nets, poisoned by oil spills, and starved as a result of the dredging of the seagrass beds on which it depends for survival, the dugong is now listed as an endangered species and is protected under several international treaties. Dugongs are no longer hunted, but many still die from being hit by boat propellers or being caught in monofilament fishing nets. Poisoning from heavy metals and polychlorinated biphenyls (PCBs)

is also a hazard, and noise pollution from shipping and offshore development disturbs the animals.

Although a marine mammal, the dugong is more closely related to elephants and hyraxes than to whales or dolphins. Its closest aquatic relative is the Fresh Water manatee. Dugongs are shy and elusive creatures and avoid contact with man.

In the Arabian Gulf, a typical adult dugong can reach three metres in length and weigh about 500 kilograms. The thick layer of fat beneath their skin gives them a bulky appearance. Seen from a distance in the water,

A dugong with two juvenile Golden Trevally, Gnathanodon speciosus, *which often accompany dugongs to feed on the invertebrates stirred up by the grazing animal, and to gain protection from predators.*

the brown skin appears smooth, but is covered with small pits from which grow short bristles, and more bristles protrude from the fleshy lobes on either side of the mouth. The head is round, with small eyes, and nostrils on a fleshy lip which can be curled upwards to assist breathing at the surface. The males, which are larger than the females, show about 8 cm of tusk, which may perhaps be used during mating rivalry or for digging up seagrasses.

The natural life span of a dugong is similar to that of a human, with some dugongs believed to reach 70 years of age. The world's only herbivorous marine mammals, dugongs feed exclusively on seagrass meadows which, along with their bovine appearance, has earned them the English nickname of 'sea-cow'. In the UAE their local name, *baghr al bahr*, also means 'cow of the sea', but in Qatar and Bahrain they are generally known as *arous al bahr*, 'the bride of the sea'. Beds of seagrass serve as the nursery for juvenile fish and shrimps, as well as a habitat for a wide diversity of marine life, and dugongs actually improve the quality and quantity of seagrass beds through their grazing activities, creating a healthy breeding ground for other marine life.

An adult dugong consumes 20-25% of its body weight each day, and leaves long trails through the seagrass beds as it steadily browses. Four species of seagrasses are present in the Arabian Gulf: *Halodule uninervis, Halophila ovalis, Halopiyla stipulacea* and *Syringodium tsoetifolium.* Seagrasses are essential to the continuing existence of dugongs in the Gulf and form very important marine ecosystems. They provide nursery grounds for fish and shellfish, stabilise sediments and reduce coastal erosion. They also help to oxygenate seawater and supply vital nutrients for a wide variety of marine life. Seagrasses are the only flowering plants which have adapted to living in the sea. Mostly they spread through the growth of their rhizome root system, but some species have actually become prolific seed producers.

Dugongs use their fluked tails for swimming and their front flippers for balance and turning. The animals must surface to breathe, but, unlike dolphins and whales, dugongs can hold their breath for only about eight minutes. This means that when dugongs become entangled in fishing nets, they drown. Since they feed in areas rich in commercially valuable fish and crustaceans, drowning is a main cause of dugong deaths. Efforts aimed at protecting the dugong from such a fate has led to attempts to prohibit fishing in some areas where dugongs are known to breed and feed.

Dugongs are found in shallow tropical and subtropical waters of the Indo-Pacific region. They have been recorded as present in the waters of 43 countries. However, in many of these nations, the dugong population is very small. Australia (approximately 80,000) and the Arabian Gulf (between 5,000 and 7,000) have the largest dugong populations, and in the Gulf they can be found in the territorial waters of Bahrain, Qatar, Saudi Arabia and the UAE. Outside the Gulf, the nearest population of dugongs is in the Gulf of Kutch, northern India, which suggests that the Gulf population is genetically and physically isolated.

Dugongs have extremely low reproductive capacities, as they do not reach sexual maturity until they are aged ten or even older. The gestation period is believed to be 12 months, and when a female has a calf, she nurses it for eighteen months or more. In general, the female dugong will reproduce once every three years, mostly with

A dugong trapped and drowned in a fishing net, Ras Abrouq 2013.

just a single calf. The relationship of dugongs with elephants and hyraxes is shown in the fact that the mammary glands in these species are located between the front legs and not all the way down the sides of the abdomen as in most other mammals. The dugong's habit of clasping the suckling calf with one flipper while vertical in the water may have given rise, centuries ago, to sailors' tales of mermaids. Calves usually start eating seagrasses a few weeks after birth and they stay with their mothers for two years or even longer.

Here in the Gulf, as in the rest of their habitat area, the dugong faces numerous threats to its survival, most of them man-made. The dugong's passive nature, its need to surface often, and its general habitat area all combine to make the animal vulnerable to hunting. Although hunting is not nearly the threat that it once was, the decline of the dugong throughout the world can be attributed, in part, to man's predation of the species. A close relative of the dugong, the Steller's sea cow, was indeed hunted into extinction in the late eighteenth century within a year of its discovery by Europeans.

The seagrass beds surrounding the Hawar Islands, just off Qatar's north-west coast, are home to the world's second largest population of dugongs. Other important foraging areas for dugongs are in the coastal waters of Bahrain, off Saudi Arabia between Qatar and the UAE, and off Abu Dhabi. During a survey in 1986, a herd of more than 600 was sighted and photographed between Bahrain and Qatar.

The massive oil spillage in the northern Gulf as a result of the Iraqi invasion of Kuwait in 1991 had a disastrous effect on the dugongs. Very early on it was reported that more than 30 dead animals had been washed up on the coast of Saudi Arabia. When dugongs surface to breathe, they probably ingest oil at the same time. In addition, when the oil forms globules and drops to the seabed their food plants are damaged. Dredging in shallow waters, such as when the port of Ras Laffan in Qatar was created, also destroys seagrass beds. Due to its exclusive diet of seagrasses, the dugong is extremely vulnerable to habitat loss. Scientific studies have demonstrated that where seagrass beds abound, dugong populations tend to remain stable, whereas, when there is a scarcity of available grazing areas, dugong populations experience significant fluctuation. With the expansion of the human population of the Arabian Gulf since the beginning of the Oil Era seven decades ago, extensive development has taken place along the coastal areas of the region. The discharge of waste and the development of coastal areas by the tourism and aquaculture sectors have tremendous negative effects on the health and viability of the area's sea grass beds, and the consequences for the dugong can be severe. With an enormous amount of the world's oil supplies located in the Arabian Gulf region, the transport of oil through the Gulf is a fact of life. Inevitably, oil spills occur, even in times of peace, adding further destruction to dugong habitat.

Throughout the Arabian Gulf, efforts are now underway to preserve the dugong for future generations. Saudi Arabia, the UAE, Bahrain and Qatar all have laws designed to protect the endangered mammal. However, several factors combine to make dugong conservation difficult. The nations of the Gulf are hampered by a lack of scientific data relating to almost every facet of dugong life. Efforts are now being initiated in order to learn more about dugong patterns of movement, feeding habits, population levels, and other factors of concern for those working to preserve the dugong.

Gentle Giants of the Deep

One day in June 2007 a production supervisor on an oil platform 80 kilometres offshore in Qatar's Al Shaheen oil field was looking down at the surface of the sea when he noticed some large fish. Very large. They were Whale sharks (*Rhincodon typus*), the largest fish on the planet. He counted a hundred of the enormous creatures, took some photos and posted them on the Internet.

Fishermen had for some time been reporting sightings of large fish in the area, but they were not at first followed up by scientists. Gradually the news spread, and the photos were seen by a marine scientist, who contacted the Ministry of the Environment in Qatar. In 2010 a programme to study the biodiversity of the Al Shaheen area was set up by the ministry, and the Qatar Whale Shark Research Project was born.

The oil platforms on the Al Shaheen field have created a rich and varied oasis of life the midst of a desert sea.

Together scientists from universities, the ministry and the oil industry are aiming to find out more about the unique aggregation of Whale sharks in the waters of Qatar. Tracking tags have been attached to the sharks' thick dermal layer, and aerial surveys estimate their numbers. The scientists hope to find out if the local Whale sharks interact with other Whale shark populations outside the Gulf. There are several types of tags: one simply records the location of the individual shark but others record depth and temperature. Previously the size of Whale sharks had been estimated by comparing them with a diver swimming alongside, but now a special camera is used which has lasers 50 cm apart, giving a more accurate measurement.

These gigantic fish are one of three species of large shark that feed on plankton, the others being the basking shark and the megamouth. All three feed by swimming along with their mouths open, but Whale sharks also feed by remaining stationary and suddenly opening their mouths so that the plankton-rich water rushes in. The plankton can

include krill, coral spawn, fish eggs, crab larvae and also small squid and fish.

Whale sharks have dark grey skin covered with a pattern of white star-like spots. The term 'whale' refers only to their size. The largest Whale shark ever recorded was caught in Taiwanese waters, it was 20 metres long and weighed 34 tonnes. The sharks are not mammals like whales and dolphins, but cold-blooded like other fish. They inhabit open water, and feed almost entirely on zooplankton: microscopic animals that are dispersed in the water, scooping them up with their colossal gaping mouths as they swim along, before closing their jaws and 'sieving' out the food by forcing water through their gills. In the Arabian Gulf most Whale sharks are accompanied by a crowd of slim grey sucker fish, which swim beneath them and feed on their faeces.

To identify each individual animal, the scientists record its spot pattern in a database. The spot pattern of each shark is unique and the scientists photograph the area behind the fifth gill slit for identification, using software originally developed by NASA to recognise star clusters. The spot pattern of the photographed area is entered into a global database, and will help to confirm that many of the sharks return to Al Shaheen every year. The striking pattern of white spots on a dark grey background has given rise to nicknames for these sharks such as 'papa shillingi' in Kenya and 'domino' in Latin America. Similar research is going on in other countries, and each shark identified in Qatar is entered into the global database to determine if the shark has previously been sighted elsewhere. Already, returning sharks have been recognised by the Qatar researchers. Tissue samples are taken and genetic analysis will reveal if the Al Shaheen sharks are related to populations of Whale sharks in other regions.

Globally, there are many aggregation sites, and among the largest are the gatherings of Whale sharks in the Gulfs of Mexico and California and off the east coast of Africa and Australia. It is now beginning to be recognised that the Arabian Gulf aggregation may be among the major sites. Whale sharks are normally solitary animals but each year between May and October they congregate to feed. On the occasion that no fewer than 150 animals were sighted one visiting scientist was heard to exclaim that he had seen more Whale sharks that day than in the whole of his career.

Whale sharks accompanied by crowds of suckerfish.

Such huge aggregations of Whale sharks are known in only a few places around the world, and the researchers in Qatar hope to find out why the sharks choose to gather in the Al Shaheen area every year. One reason could be that the oil platforms act as artificial reefs, like a marine oasis of life amidst the desert sea. Some of the platforms are more than thirty years old, and have gradually formed their own little ecosystem. An oasis of colourful and varied life has been created in the midst of a desert sea. The massive underwater structures are richly encrusted with a growth of soft corals and sponges, encouraging thousands of fish to gather. These in turn attract predators such as barracudas and sharks, which patrol the platforms, waiting to pounce. Fishing anywhere near the rigs is banned, so except for the natural predators the fish have no enemies and large shoals thrive in the shelter of the platforms. In the warmer months there is a high concentration of spawning tuna in the region, and this is when the Whale sharks start to aggregate to feed on the tuna eggs. Their graceful streamlined bodies seem to move almost without effort, their tall dark dorsal fins slicing through the surface. After feeding on this rich 'egg soup' they dive deep into the cooler waters to avoid the surface temperature, which can reach more than 30º C. The Gulf is relatively shallow, but in other parts of the world Whale sharks can dive as deep as 1000 metres. Researchers were surprised to discover that Whale sharks can tolerate the high surface temperature of the Arabian Gulf at the height of summer.

There is still much to be discovered. No one has ever seen Whale sharks mating, or giving birth to their young, which hatch from eggs inside the mother, nor do we yet know where it takes place. The life span of these enormous creatures may be as long as sixty or even a hundred years, but studies have begun so recently that such figures can only be guessed at. Now widely protected world-wide and categorised as 'vulnerable', they may be facing a decline in numbers due to human impact, through fishing, pollution, loss of habitat, boat strikes and other causes. At one time they were killed for the oil in their livers, used to waterproof hulls of wooden fishing boats, and Whale sharks are being hunted for their fins as other species of shark decline. In some regions today they face a new threat – from tourism. Whale shark watching has become big business, and, tragically, numbers of sharks are injured every year by the propellers of tourist boats. And in some parts of the world Whale shark dorsal fins have become collectors' items and are displayed as trophies, due to their impressive size.

The Qatar Whale sharks have been filmed not only by BBC Two for its three-part series on Arabian wildlife, *Wild Arabia*, which was first broadcast in 2013, but also for a 26-minute film, again released in 2013, called *A Gathering of Giants: the Qatar Whale Shark* which can be seen on www.qatarwhalesharkproject.com

Compare the shark with the swimmer to get an idea of its size.

Dolphins, Porpoises and Whales

No one ever forgets their first sighting of a dolphin. There is something about the seemingly joyous way in which they speed through the water, leaping and criss-crossing the bow-wave of boats, their mouths curved in a friendly 'grin', that makes them instantly appealing. Their apparent benevolence towards humans is legendary. Everyone knows the tales, dating back to ancient Roman times, of dolphins supporting drowning swimmers. Ancient Arab seafarers believed that they brought good fortune to travellers, and their images occur worldwide, on ancient Greek pottery, in sculptures, on Roman mosaic pavements and even on coins. The word dolphin comes from the classical Greek delphis, meaning 'womb', because for the Greeks the dolphin symbolized birth and renewal of life.

In antiquity, just as now, there were numerous stories of dolphins allowing people to ride on their backs. Yet not many people know much about dolphins themselves, and scientists say that there is much yet to be discovered. In many ways, their lives are a mystery.

Dolphins, porpoises and whales belong to the order of mammals known as *cetacea*. The distinction between whales and dolphins is less clearly defined than that between dolphins and porpoises: the so-called Killer whale, or Orca, is in fact the largest species of dolphin. Porpoises are smaller than dolphins, with a stockier body. They

Bottlenose dolphins, Tursiops truncatus.

Humpback dolphin, Sousa chinensis.

have a low, or sometimes no, dorsal fin and have no 'beak', whereas on most species of dolphin the 'beak' is easily identified. The family of porpoises (*Phocoenidae*), is a small one, numbering only about six species worldwide. All porpoises have uniquely shaped spatulate teeth, quite distinct from the sharply-pointed teeth of dolphins.

Several species of dolphins and one species of porpoise have been seen in the waters around Qatar, plus, possibly, three species of baleen whales. The number of dolphins appear to have declined sharply within the last two decades, but we have observed them in the bay near the Gulf Sheraton Hotel, and from the beaches of Mesaieed and Fuwairit on the east coast, Ras Abrouq in the west, and of course, at Khor Al Adaid, the Inland Sea. Once when we camped there a pod of dolphins came into the shallows beside the beach to investigate the kerosene lamp we had hung on a pole, and woke us with their snorting and blowing. However, pods of dolphins, that formerly numbered 20 or more, all too often now seem to be reduced to half a dozen animals.

Sports divers use boats at the weekends to visit and dive on offshore wrecks, and schools of dolphins are frequently observed. On one occasion a school of 13 Long-beaked Common dolphins surrounded the boat while it was anchored on a wreck. Divers were scrambling into their gear to get into the water and join them, when suddenly someone noticed that the creatures circling the boat were actually eleven dolphins and two large Tiger sharks. This is not the first time that sharks have been observed to accompany dolphins.

Long-beaked Common dolphins (*Delphinus capensis*) are so named to distinguish them from the Short-beaked Common dolphins (*Delphinus delphis*). The distinction between the two species was recognized only quite recently.

Among the dolphins recorded in the waters of Qatar are the universally-familiar Common Bottlenose dolphin (*Tursiops truncatus*) – the one with the pronounced beak and familiar 'grin' – and its slightly smaller relative the Indian Ocean Bottlenose dolphin (*Tursiops aduncus*). The Indo-

Female Bryde's whale, Balaenoptera edeni, *with calf.*

Pacific Humpback dolphin (*Sousa chinensis*) is also seen here. Both Tursiops and Sousa are generally to be found in inshore waters. Tursiops has a shorter, more snubbed beak than Sousa, and generally swims much faster. The bodies of both are dark grey above and lighter beneath.

Further out to sea you are more likely to encounter the Long-beaked Common dolphin. Found throughout the oceans of the world, it is easy to identify with its slender, streamlined silhouette and long beak. The back is black or dark grey, with a white belly, and there is a distinctive hourglass-shaped pattern of grey and cream on the flanks.

Long-beaked Common dolphins travel in larger groups than Bottlenose dolphins in Qatar; but do not reach the really massive group sizes of this species in the Gulf of Oman and Arabian Sea, where thousands of individuals have been seen travelling together. This dolphin enthusiastically rides the bow-waves of ships, and is capable of spectacular leaps, sometimes clearing the surface of the sea by three or four metres.

Pantropical Spotted dolphins (*Stenella attenuata*) have also been recorded in Qatari waters. Researchers can estimate the age of an individual dolphin by the distribution of spots on the body. It is also possible that the Spinner dolphin (*Stenella longirostris*) occurs locally, as it has been observed elsewhere in the Arabian Gulf.

In July 1994 a group of sports divers reported seeing 'a pair of small, light grey dolphins with no dorsal fins' which crossed the bow of their boat at speed as they were heading towards Doha. In fact, what they almost certainly saw was a pair of the rare Finless porpoises (*Neophocaena phocaenoides*). They often travel in pairs and are the only porpoise without a dorsal fin.

People are sometimes surprised to hear that Orca (*Orcinus orca*), also known as Killer whales, are found in the Arabian Gulf. These large, striking-looking black-and-white animals are present in all the oceans of the world. They are high social and always hunt in groups, like smaller cetaceans. Orcas have been filmed recently off the coast of the United Arab Emirates, and recently fishermen reported seeing a group of eight in the northern Gulf circling a Common dolphin. Every time the dolphin tried to escape an Orca moved to cut it off, until finally they closed in for the kill.

No one knows for sure why in some species of *cetacean*, for example the Orca, the dorsal fin is as tall as 180cm whereas other species can apparently get by with a small or even no dorsal fin. They may help with balance, or they may assist different species to recognise each other quickly. The populations of Finless porpoises have been badly affected by pollution in other parts of Asia and this is possibly the only recorded sighting in Qatari waters.

One December morning a few years ago a party of divers camping near the mouth of Khor Al Adaid observed three large whales approaching the shore. There were two adults and a calf which swam close to its mother. They swam parallel with the shore about 50m out, repeatedly surfacing and clearly curious about the on-shore watchers. These were Bryde's whales (*Balaenoptera edeni*), which reach a maximum length of 14m. Other baleen whales found in the Arabian Gulf are the Humpback whale (*Megaptera novaeangliae*) and, very rarely, the Blue whale (*Balaenoptera musculus*). In 2001 a dead Humpback whale was washed up on a beach between Doha and Al Wakra. It is possible that the Bryde's Whale may live all year round in the Arabian Gulf and breed here. If so, they may be genetically isolated from other whale populations.

Recently it was discovered that the Arabian population of Humpback whales is unique and is genetically quite distinct from populations in other parts of the world. There are only about 100 individuals left in this whale population, and they have not bred with Humpback whales elsewhere for around 60,000 years. The song is said to be simpler than that of whales in other Humpback populations. They are unusual in that they do not migrate in search of food – they do not need to, as each year cold, food-rich currents off the coast of Oman carry food to them, rather than the other way around. Humpback whales are not common in the Arabian Gulf, but it is thought that during stormy weather in the Indian Ocean some may pass through the Strait of Hormuz to seek shelter in calmer waters.

Commercial divers here have reported dolphins coming to watch them at work, apparently fascinated by human activity. A favourite story is of a pair of dolphins which arrived daily to keep pairs of divers company as they worked on a pipeline at Mesaieed. The dolphins deliberately imitated the clumsy swimming movements of the divers, waggling their bodies up and down and making eye contact as if inviting their human 'friends' to share the joke. As each pair of divers surfaced after 30 minutes the dolphins raced back to the beginning of the pipeline, ready to join the next pair as they descended. This continued for weeks until the work was completed.

A group of sports divers on one of the two artificial reefs at Mesaieed were joined by several dolphins which caught fish, held them crosswise in their mouths and then brought them to show the divers before swallowing them, seeming to indicate, 'Look what I can do!' It is no wonder that humans have long felt an affinity with dolphins.

What of the future of cetaceans in the Gulf? Experts estimate that, worldwide, about half a million dolphins and porpoises die every year as a result of human activity. Some are accidental victims of fishing nets, but in some parts of Asia fishermen kill dolphins, believing that they threaten the fish stocks.

A far more dangerous long-term threat is pollution. After the Gulf War of 1991 the numbers of dolphins in Qatari waters appeared to increase for a while, and some scientists theorised that many left the northern waters of the Gulf to escape the horrific quantities of oil and other pollutants in the water. Such pollution is added to every time a ship, accidentally or deliberately, allows oil to enter the water. Oil slicks are encountered both inshore and far out to sea, and it is common to see quantities of rubbish floating on the surface. Dolphins tend to move in surface waters and are badly affected by oil spills.

Aerial surveys have provided evidence that dolphin populations in the Gulf have suffered a drastic decline over the last two decades. The cause is unknown, but some believe it may be due not only to over-fishing by humans causing a big decline in fish stocks, but also by a reduction in fish prey species, which may have been impacted by dredging and related activities.

Above: A Killer whale, Orchinus orca.

Right, below and overleaf: A Humpback whale, Megaptera novaeangliae, *diving.*

Acknowledgements

Many people contributed to this book, helping to track down and verify information, freely lending me their photographs, and providing kind encouragement. My greatest debt is to my husband David, who has supported all my endeavours over the years, is the driver and navigator on our weekend desert expeditions, and has taken many of the photographs in this book. Marijcke Jongbloed's many publications on the flora and fauna of the UAE first inspired me with the idea that one day I might attempt something of the sort myself. She encouraged me to go ahead, neither of us realising at the time that her support would eventually extend to her editing and publishing the first edition of the book in 2006!

Mohammed al Bloshi, who in 2006 was the Director of the Department of Museums and Antiquities, The National Council for Culture, Arts and Heritage, kindly assisted me in locating some early photographs of Qatar and arranged for them to be made available. Professor Dionisius Agius of the University of Leeds and now of the University of Exeter, and Shirley Kay, an archaeologist and writer formerly resident in Bahrain and the UAE, kindly allowed me to use photographs of theirs which had appeared in their own publications. Dr Sibba Einarsdottir, Curator of the Ethnographic Collections at Moesgaard Museum in Denmark, spent much time selecting and sending photographs taken by my late friend Dr Klaus Ferdinand and his colleague Jette Bang during the months they spent with the bedouin people of Qatar in 1959.

Dileep Kumar, who has generously allowed me to use his marvellous photographs of birds in my books and articles, took almost all of the bird images which appear in the book. Dr Henning Schwarze, who was with me on a UNESCO expedition to the Hawar Islands in 2003, let me use his pictures of ospreys and cormorants taken on that occasion. Dr Nick Pilcher, an internationally-recognised consultant on the conservation of sea turtles and a regular visitor to Qatar, gave me much information. Dr Robert Baldwin, a marine consultant resident in Oman, and Dr Drew Gardner of Zayed University, Abu Dhabi, both gave me enthusiastic encouragement and supplied me with many of their superb pictures. For this edition both Catrin Hammer, the former curator of mammals at the Al Wabra Wildlife Preservation and Richard Roswell, the present curator, supplied photographs of sand cats. At the Breeding Centre for Endangered Arabian Wildlife in Sharjah, Cyringa Barwise-Joubert took photographs of their honey badgers especially for this edition. Steffen Sanvig Bach of Maersk Oil Qatar, who is involved with the Qatar Whale Shark Project, kept me updated with news of the latest exciting developments, and freelance photographer Simone Caprodossi generously allowed me to use his stunning photos of the gigantic creatures.

To all these, and to all the members of the Qatar Natural History Group who kept asking, 'When are you going to write a book on Qatar?', my thanks. That this book is now in its third edition in eight years shows the widespread interest held by so many in this fast-developing country – not only in its rapid progress and astonishing achievements but in 'the other Qatar', the Qatar that was there all the time.

Picture Credits

Front cover: main image, Gillespie David; *inset left to right,* Shirley Kay, Dileep Kumar, David Gillespie, Mohsin Al-Ansi, Marijcke Jongbloed. *Back cover:* Dileep Kumar. *Title page:* Marijcke Jongbloed.
Map pp6-7, clockwise from top left: University of Wales, Georg Gerster, Qatar Museums, Kanold Inge Boesken, David Gillespie, Georg Gerster, Dileep Kumar, David Gillespie, David Gillespie, Qatar Museums.

Text pages:
Agius, Dionisius 67t, 70, 71 t & b.
Al-Ansi, Mohsin 157
Albert Londres Collection, National Archives, Paris 58 (x2), 62.
Al Wabra Wildlife Preservation 107, 109.
Arabian Leopard Trust 105r
BBC Worldwide 172
Baldwin, Robert 160, 162, 163, 165, 166, 167(x2), 176–177, 178, 181t.
Bari, Hubert 56, 57, 60 (x2).
Beech, Mark, ADIAS 53
Berlin Ethnographic Museum 66
Boesken, Kanold Inge 29.
Breeding Centre for Endangered Arabian Wildlife, Sharjah 101m, 108 (Cyringa Barwise-Joubert)
Caprodossi, Simone 173, 174-175.
Carter, Robert 61.
Centre for Geographic Information Systems, Doha 89.
Donaldson, Bronwyn 15tr, 82-83,152.
Eriksen, Hanne & Jens 86, 102,110m,113t, 123, 133, 135, 179,181.
Farnell, Gavin 104
Gardner, Andrew 105l, 106, 112, 113b,115b, 117l, 119, 120 (x2), 122, 125 (x2), 126, 128br, 132,181m,182–183.
Gerster, Georg 14, 24, 25, 37, 43.
Gillespie, David 4 (x2), 12, 13, 15b,16, 26, 30, 35,40,44, 50-51, 52, 65 (x3), 69, 72, 73 (x2), 74b, 84-85, 90, 91(x2), 92, 96, 97, 98, 99 (x3), 100, 101b,111r, 117r, 124, 153, 155, 158 (x2), 159, 166-7, 171.
Hilden, Joy 77t.
Hornby, Graeme 116.
Hornby, Richard 161
Jongbloed, Marijcke 94, 110b, 111.
Kay, Shirley 64, 68.
Kennedy, Fergus 168–169, 170.
Kumar, Dileep 101t, 115t, 121b, 125b, 136,137, 138, 139(x2), 140(x3), 141, 142(x2), 143(x5),146, 150,151.
Ministry of Culture, Arts and Heritage, Qatar 21t&b, 22, 74t
Moesgard Museum, Denmark 76, 77m&b, 78–79, 80, 81.
Morris, Neil 128t, 149(x2).
Qatar Museums 18 (x3), 19, 31, 32, 34, 36, 38 (x3), 41 (x5), 42, 48, 49t, 67.
Richer, Renee 99l.
Schreiber, Jurgen 17
Schwartz, Henning 148.
Sheraton Doha Resort & Convention Hotel, Doha 27t.
Smith, Anthony 54–55, 103, 110b, 121t, 127,128bl, 129, 130.
Takacs, Zoltan 111l, 118,131.
Trustees of the British Museum 67
University of Wales 46t&b, 47, 49 t&b
Yağiz, Dursun 95
Oryx GTL 27b

Bibliography

Abdel Bary, Eklas (2012) *The Flora of Qatar. Vol 1 The Dicotyledons*, Qatar University, Environmental Studies Centre

Abdel Bary, Eklas (2012) *The Flora of Qatar. Vol 2 The Monocotyledons*, Qatar University, Environmental Studies Centre

Agius, Dionisius (2002) *In the Wake of the Dhow. The Arabian Gulf and Oman*, Ithaca Press

Agius, Dionisius (2005) *Seafaring in the Arabian Gulf and Oman*, Kegan Paul

Agius, Dionisius (2008) *Classic Ships of Islam*, Brill

Ahmed, Ibrahim Fouad *Qatar and the Sea*, Ministry of Information, Doha, Qatar (undated)

Al-Kuwari, Saad I. and Suda, Seiji (1987) *A Report on Mangrove Afforestation in Qatar*, JICA consultant

Al-Othman, Nasser (1984) *With Their Bare Hands: The Story of the Oil Industry in Qatar*, Longman

Anscombe, Frederick (1997) *The Ottoman Gulf: The Creation of Kuwait, Saudi Arabia and Qatar*, Columbia University Press

Baldwin, Robert (1995) 'Abu Dhabi and the Disappearing Dugong', *Tribulus*, Journal of the Emirates Natural History Society Vol. 5.2

Baldwin, Robert (1995) 'Marine Turtles of the UAE', *Tribulus*, journal of the Emirates Natural History Society, Vol. 5.2

Baldwin, Robert (1995) 'Whale and Dolphin research in the UAE', *Tribulus*, Journal of the Emirates Natural History Society, Vol.5.2

Baldwin, Robert (2003) *Whales and Dolphins of Arabia* (privately printed)

Batanouny, K.H. (1981) *Ecology and Flora of Qatar*, University of Qatar

Bari Hubert & Lam, David (2009) *Pearls*, Skira (English and Arabic)

Beardmore, Rebecca and others *The Qatar National Historic Environment Record: a bespoke cultural resource management tool*. Proceedings of the Seminar for Arabian Studies 40 (2010)

Bibby, Geoffrey (1996) *Looking For Dilmun* (Reprinted) Stacey International

Bulloch, John (1984) *The Gulf: A Portrait of Kuwait, Qatar, Bahrain and the U.A.E.*, Century Publishing

Carter, Robert 'The History and Prehistory of Pearling in the Persian Gulf', *Journal of the Economic and Social History of the Orient*, 48.2 1-71

Carter, Robert (2012) *Sea of Pearls, Seven Thousand Years of the Industry that Shaped the Gulf*, Arabian Publishing Ltd

Crystal, Jill (1990) *Oil and politics in the Gulf: rulers and merchants in Kuwait and Qatar*, Cambridge University Press

De Cardi, Beatrice (ed.) (1978) *Qatar Archaeological Report: Excavations 1973*, OUP

Dipper, Frances and Woodward, Tony (1989) *The Living Seas: Marine Life of the Southern Gulf*, Motivate Publishing, Dubai

Edens, Christopher (1994) *Chiefdoms and Early States in the Near East, Monographs in World Archaeology* No.18, Prehistory Press

Edens, Christopher (1999) *Khor Ile-Sud, Qatar: The Archaeology of Late Bronze Age Purple Dye Production in the Arabian Gulf*. Iraq No.61

Egan, Damien (2007) *Snakes of Arabia, A Field Guide*, Motivate Publishing

Eriksen Hanne & Jens, Frances Gillespie (2010) *Common Birds of Qatar* (privately printed, English and Arabic)

Facey, William (1987) 'The Boat Carvings at Jabal Al-Jussasiyah, Northeast Qatar', *Proceedings of the Seminar of Arabian Studies*, No 17

Facey, William (1994) *The Story of the Eastern Province of Saudi Arabia*, Stacey International

Fromherz, Allen (2012) *Qatar, a Modern History*, IB Tauris

Gallagher, Michael (1993) *Snakes of the Arabian Gulf and Oman*, (privately published)

Gross, Christian (1987) *Mammals of the Southern Gulf*, Motivate Publishing, Dubai

Harrison, D.L. (1981) *Mammals of the Arabian Gulf*, Allen and Unwin, London

Hawar Islands Biosphere Reserve Study, Bahrain. (2003) UNESCO Office, Doha

Hawkins, D.F. (1987) *Primitive Rock Carvings in Qatar*, P.S.A.S. No.17

Hoyt, Erich (1991) *Meeting the Whales*, Camden House

Hoyt, Erich (1992) *Riding With The Dolphins*, Camden House

India Office Records

Jennings, Michael (2010) *Fauna of Arabia: Atlas of the Breeding Birds of Arabia*, published in Frankfurt,
    Germany and Riyadh,Kingdom of Saudi Arabia

Jongbloed, Marijcke (1987) *The Living Desert*, Motivate Publishing, Dubai

Jongbloed, Marijcke (1997) 'Observations in a Dhub colony', *Tribulus*, Journal of the Emirates Natural
    History Society, Vol.7.2

Jongbloed, Marijcke (2000) *Wild About Reptiles*, Barkers Trident Communications

Jongbloed, Marijcke; Llewellyn-Smith, Robert; Sawaf, Moaz (2002) *Wild About Mammals. A Field Guide to
    the Terrestrial Mammals of the UAE*, Zodiac Publishing

Kapel , Holger (1967) *Atlas of the Stone-Age Cultures of Qatar*, Jutland Archaeological Society Publication

Kay, Shirley (1992) *Seafarers of the Gulf*, Motivate Publishing, Dubai

Kelly, J.B. (1968) *Britain and the Persian Gulf*, Oxford University Press

King, Howard (1999) *The Breeding Birds of Hawar*, The Ministry of Housing, Bahrain

KUML (1954 –1961) *Arbog For Jysk Arkaeologisk Selskab* (Danish with English summaries), The University
    of Aarhus, Denmark

Kursun, Zekeriya (2002) *The Ottomans in Qatar*, The Isis Press Istanbul

Lorimer, J.G. (1908-15) *Gazetteer of the Persian Gulf, Oman and Central Arabia*, Calcutta

Mission Archeologique Francaise à Qatar, Tome 1 1980, Tome 2 1988. Ed. Jacques Tixier, Ministry of
    Information, Qatar

Moorehead, John (1977) *In Defiance of the Elements: A Personal View of Qatar*, Quartet Books

Morris, Neil, Gillespie Frances (2014) *Irkaya: Celebrating Biodiversity in Qatar*, The Ministry of the
    Environment, Qatar.

Norton, John and others (2009) *An Illustrated Checklist of the Flora of Qatar* (privately printed)

Osborne, Patrick (ed.) (1996) *Desert Ecology of Abu Dhabi*, Pisces Publications, Newbury

Palgrave, W.G. (1877) *Narrative of a Year's Journey through Central and Eastern Arabia*, London

Pilcher, Nicholas J. *Marine Turtle Conservation and Management in the State of Qatar*, Marine Research
    Foundation, Sabah, Malaysia

Porter R F., Christensen S., Schiermacker-Hansen P. (1996) *Field Guide to the Birds of the Middle East*, T and
    A D Poyser, London

Potts, D.T. (1990) *The Arabian Gulf in Antiquity: Vol I*, Clarendon Press Oxford

Proceedings of the Seminar for Arabian Studies 1971-2009

Rahman, Habibur (2005) *The Emergence of Qatar*, Kegan Paul

Rice, Michael (1994) T*he Archaeology of the Arabian Gulf*, Routledge

Robinson, Dave and Chapman, Adrian (1992) *Birds of Southern Arabia*, Motivate Publishing, Dubai

Said Zahlan, Rosemarie (1978) *The Creation of Qatar*, Crookhelm London

Saroufim, Nabil (1987) *Zubara and Murwab: A Report on the Recent Excavations Ministry of Information*,
    Qatar (Arabic only)

The Emirates, A Natural History (2005) ed. Peter Hellyer & Simon Aspinall, Trident Press Ltd

Vine, Peter and Casey, Paula (1992) *The Heritage of Qatar*, Immel Publishing

Wernery, Ulrich (1992) 'Camels, world champions in water conservation', *Tribulus*, Journal of the Emirates
    Natural History Society, Vol.2.2

Williamson, A. (1973) *Hurmuz and the trade of the Gulf in the 14th and 15th centuries AD*, P.S.A.S.

Ziolkowski, Michelle (2000) 'The Shasha – traditional fishing craft of the UAE's East Coast', *Tribulus*, journal
    of the Emirates Natural History Society, Vol. 10.1

Index